TOWARDS A NEW LIBERAL INTERNATIONALISM

LSE MONOGRAPHS IN
INTERNATIONAL STUDIES

Published for The Centre for International Studies,
London School of Economics and Political Science

The Centre for International Studies at the London School of Economics and Political Science was established in 1967. Its aim is to promote research on a multi-disciplinary basis in the general field of international studies.

To this end the Centre offers visiting fellowships, sponsors research projects and seminars and endeavours to secure the publication of manuscripts arising out of them.

Whilst the Editorial Board accepts responsibility for recommending the inclusion of a volume in the series, the author is alone responsible for views and opinions expressed.

LSE MONOGRAPHS IN INTERNATIONAL STUDIES

DAVID LONG
Towards a new liberal internationalism
The international theory of J. A. Hobson

ANDARGACHEW TIRUNEH
The Ethiopian revolution 1974–1987
A transformation from an aristocratic to a totalitarian autocracy

CHRISTOPHER HILL
Cabinet decisions on foreign policy
The British experience October 1938–June 1941

BEATRICE LEUNG
Sino-Vatican relations: Problems in conflicting authority 1976–1986

URI BIALER
Between East and West: Israel's foreign policy orientation 1948–1956

SELIM DERINGIL
Turkish foreign policy during the Second World War
An active neutrality

INGRID DETTER DE LUPIS
The law of war

CHO OON KHONG
The politics of oil in Indonesia: Foreign company–host government relations

JOO-HONG NAM
America's commitment to South Korea
The first decade of the Nixon doctrine

B. J. C. MCKERCHER
The second Baldwin government and the United States, 1924–1929
Attitudes and diplomacy

ROBERT S. LITWAK
Detente and the Nixon doctrine
American foreign policy and the pursuit of stability, 1969–1976

PROCOPIS PAPASTRATIS
British policy towards Greece during the Second World War 1941–1944

PAUL BUTEUX
The politics of nuclear consultation in NATO 1965–1980

ROGER BUCKLEY
Occupation diplomacy
Britain, the United States and Japan 1945–1952

IAN NISH (editor)
Anglo-Japanese alienation 1919–1952
Papers of the Anglo-Japanese conference on the history of the Second World War

JAMES MAYALL and CORNELIA NAVARI (editors)
The end of the post-war era
Documents on Great-Power relations, 1968–1975

MARTIN SELIGER
The Marxist conception of ideology
A critical essay

YITZHAK SHICHOR
The Middle East in China's foreign policy, 1949–1977

KENNETH J. CALDER
Britain and the origins of the New Europe 1914–1918

For a list of titles out of print please see back of book.

TOWARDS A NEW LIBERAL INTERNATIONALISM

The international theory of J. A. Hobson

DAVID LONG

The Norman Paterson School of International Affairs

Carleton University

Ottawa

CAMBRIDGE
UNIVERSITY PRESS

CAMBRIDGE UNIVERSITY PRESS
Cambridge, New York, Melbourne, Madrid, Cape Town, Singapore, São Paulo

Cambridge University Press
The Edinburgh Building, Cambridge CB2 8RU, UK

Published in the United States of America by Cambridge University Press, New York

www.cambridge.org
Information on this title: www.cambridge.org/9780521454971

First published 1996
This digitally printed version 2008

A catalogue record for this publication is available from the British Library

Library of Congress Cataloguing in Publication data

Long, David.
Towards a new liberal internationalism: the international theory of J. A. Hobson /
David Long.
p. cm. – (LSE monographs in international studies)
Includes bibliographical references.
ISBN 0 521 45497 2 (hardback)
1. International relations. 2. Economics. 3. Imperialism. 4. International organization.
I. Title. II. Series.
JX1395.L63 1996
325′.32′01 – dc20 95–7646 CIP

ISBN 978-0-521-45497-1 hardback
ISBN 978-0-521-05804-9 paperback

For my mother and father

Contents

Acknowledgements *page* x

1 Introduction 1

2 Rationality, welfare and the organic analogy 8

3 Co-operation, the surplus and the theory of underconsumption 28

4 An evolutionary framework for international relations 49

5 The domestic determinants of an imperialistic foreign policy 72

6 The international relations of imperialism 97

7 Economic internationalism, free trade and international government 121

8 International government and the maintenance of peace 144

9 J. A. Hobson and liberal internationalism 173

Notes 198

Bibliography 241

Index 267

Acknowledgements

I have incurred many debts while writing this book. As my Ph.D. supervisor, Michael Banks was always a source of encouragement and sensible advice. Michael Freeden, Rebecca Grant, Paul Taylor and Peter Wilson read the manuscript in its entirety. Each made a number of important suggestions and advanced telling criticisms of arguments I had presented. Martin Ceadel, Robert Jackson, Cornelia Navari and Hidemi Suganami provided comments and criticisms on various chapters. I am also grateful to Ronen Palan, Gautam Sen and Rob Walker for giving time to more general discussions of my research. Furthermore, I am grateful to the Economic and Social Research Council for making me a Competition Award that provided three years of funding for my doctoral research.

Presenting my work in a number of different fora provided me with stimulating discussion and also constructive criticism of my arguments. Earlier drafts of chapters were read in the LSE International Relations department at the Concepts and Methods seminars in 1987 and 1988, at the Politics of the World Economy general seminar in 1987 and at the Conflict and Peace Studies seminar in 1989; at the University of British Columbia Political Science departmental seminar in 1990; at the International Studies Association Annual Convention, the Canadian Political Science Association Annual Convention and at the Hobson conference in Malvern, convened by John Pheby, all of which took place in 1990; and at the Norman Paterson School of International Affairs in 1992.

Chapters 3, 7 and 9 include material previously published as, respectively, 'Three Modes of Internationalism in the Work of J. A. Hobson', in John Pheby (ed.), *J. A. Hobson After Fifty Years*, by Macmillan; 'J. A. Hobson and Economic Internationalism', in David Long and Peter Wilson (eds.), *Thinkers of the Twenty Years' Crisis*, by Oxford University Press; and 'J. A. Hobson and Idealism in Interna-

Acknowledgements

I have incurred many debts while writing this book. As my Ph.D. supervisor, Michael Banks was always a source of encouragement and sensible advice. Michael Freeden, Rebecca Grant, Paul Taylor and Peter Wilson read the manuscript in its entirety. Each made a number of important suggestions and advanced telling criticisms of arguments I had presented. Martin Ceadel, Robert Jackson, Cornelia Navari and Hidemi Suganami provided comments and criticisms on various chapters. I am also grateful to Ronen Palan, Gautam Sen and Rob Walker for giving time to more general discussions of my research. Furthermore, I am grateful to the Economic and Social Research Council for making me a Competition Award that provided three years of funding for my doctoral research.

Presenting my work in a number of different fora provided me with stimulating discussion and also constructive criticism of my arguments. Earlier drafts of chapters were read in the LSE International Relations department at the Concepts and Methods seminars in 1987 and 1988, at the Politics of the World Economy general seminar in 1987 and at the Conflict and Peace Studies seminar in 1989; at the University of British Columbia Political Science departmental seminar in 1990; at the International Studies Association Annual Convention, the Canadian Political Science Association Annual Convention and at the Hobson conference in Malvern, convened by John Pheby, all of which took place in 1990; and at the Norman Paterson School of International Affairs in 1992.

Chapters 3, 7 and 9 include material previously published as, respectively, 'Three Modes of Internationalism in the Work of J. A. Hobson', in John Pheby (ed.), *J. A. Hobson After Fifty Years*, by Macmillan; 'J. A. Hobson and Economic Internationalism', in David Long and Peter Wilson (eds.), *Thinkers of the Twenty Years' Crisis*, by Oxford University Press; and 'J. A. Hobson and Idealism in Interna-

Contents

Acknowledgements *page* x

1 Introduction 1

2 Rationality, welfare and the organic analogy 8

3 Co-operation, the surplus and the theory of underconsumption 28

4 An evolutionary framework for international relations 49

5 The domestic determinants of an imperialistic foreign policy 72

6 The international relations of imperialism 97

7 Economic internationalism, free trade and international government 121

8 International government and the maintenance of peace 144

9 J. A. Hobson and liberal internationalism 173

Notes 198

Bibliography 241

Index 267

tional Relations', in *Review of International Studies*. I thank the publishers of each for allowing me to use this material here.

All researchers rely on a variety of librarians and administrative staff as they go about their work. The staff of the British Library of Political and Economic Science (BLPES) and the libraries of University College, London, the University of British Columbia and Carleton University helped make my research a pleasant occupation rather than a chore. My special thanks go to the officers of the South Place Ethical Society who permitted me to consult materials in the congenial surroundings of the library in Conway Hall and also to the archivists at the BLPES and the Brynmor Jones Library at Hull University who patiently helped me find obscure pamphlets and unpublished papers in their collections.

Most of all, though, I thank Fran for her patience, her acute criticisms and her unstinting support.

CHAPTER I

Introduction

J. A. Hobson was a writer, journalist, lecturer, political activist, and propagandist for a group of left liberals in the late nineteenth and early twentieth century. While he is justly famous in the discipline of international relations for originating the theory of imperialism subsequently adopted by Lenin, his contribution to thinking on international relations is much wider and more profound than this single aspect suggests.[1] Hobson's writing on international affairs in fact constitutes a significant modification of the tenets of earlier liberal international theory. He developed a new liberal internationalist framework that laid the bases for much of the subsequent liberal thinking on international relations and organisation since the Second World War. Concentrating in the main on Hobson's writings on international relations, this study explores the theoretical structure of, and tensions in, Hobson's international theory; his critical analysis of, and concrete proposals for, contemporary international relations; and the social, political and economic theory that underlies his approach to international relations.

Hobson created a framework for analysing international relations that is a modification of traditional nineteenth-century liberal internationalism. His development of a new liberal internationalism, as I shall call it, entails the application of his theory of co-operative surplus beyond the boundaries of national societies and of his idea of an organic unity to international relations and the world economy. Hobson's new liberal internationalism suggests that international relations and the world society as a whole is, like the several national societies, shifting away from isolated individualism and *laissez-faire* towards increased social organisation and collectivism.

The coherence of Hobson's international thought, and some of its problems too, results from the logical extension of the central tenets of his analysis of social, political and economic life to international relations. For instance, the all-encompassing dichotomy of internationalism and imperialism in Hobson's writings reflects the dual aspect of his theory of the social surplus. While internationalism is associated with peace and democracy, through rational conscious collective control of social life by the people (or international life by nations), imperialism connotes militarism and dictatorship, through the imposition of rule by a powerful sectional interest within the national (or international) social organism.

The study assesses the important contributions Hobson made to international theory, in the theory of imperialism and beyond. Along the way, a prevalent opinion of Hobson's imperialism theory as 'second image reductionism' and 'economic determinism' will be refuted. Instead, Hobson emerges as an important figure in the transformation of liberal internationalism, as he was for liberalism as a political ideology, and a forerunner of the functionalist approach to international organisation. His work represents a stage between classical and 'embedded' liberalisms in what is now called the liberal approach in international political economy, although current trends in liberal international relations theory have tended to marginalise the concerns which were central to Hobson.

A word of warning to the reader is in order. This study examines theoretical issues in Hobson's writings on international relations primarily through textual analysis. It is, thus, none of the following things: a chronology of Hobson's thought on international relations; a study of Hobson's international relations in terms of the great events of his lifetime, e.g., the Boer War, the Great War and the Great Depression; a consideration of the specifics or the policy implications of Hobson's proposals on international economic issues, like tariffs; or a discussion of the theory of imperialism beyond Hobson's contribution to it. Some of these would be reasonable ways of approaching Hobson's work on international relations, with different strengths and weaknesses to each. However, they are beyond the scope of this study.

A NOTE ON METHOD

My analysis draws on recent work on Hobson in political theory and the history of political ideas to develop a framework for his discussion of international relations. Despite the fact that he did not for the most part expressly state his position this way, this is Hobson's framework because the arguments are based on an articulation of what Michael Freeden has called a new liberal approach, which was applied by

Hobson to international relations. One of the problems in researching Hobson's ideas on international relations is that his writings on the subject are scattered through his work over a period of fifty years, only occasionally appearing in the sustained form that is found in *Imperialism* or *Towards International Government.* When he does discuss international relations, it is usually tightly knit in with a series of domestic issues, such as civil liberties or economic recession. While he wrote on many other subjects, a number of which have a stronger claim to being his core concern, Hobson had an abiding interest in international affairs and wrote consistently about them. Yet, while the creation of a framework may in some respects 'improve' on Hobson's sometimes flawed arguments, it does highlight an overall coherence that underlies his work on international relations. This does not mean that this study eschews criticism; on the contrary, throughout, the study brings to the fore fundamental theoretical tensions in Hobson's new liberal internationalism which underpins his writing on international relations.[2]

Hobson's evolutionary framework for international relations is described in this study as a new liberal internationalism. This is a useful term, I believe, despite my qualms about adding another term to a field already overburdened with labels, categories and neologisms. Other terms have been suggested for the general approach to international relations that Hobson takes, such as welfare internationalism, embedded liberalism or compensatory liberalism.[3] While none of these terms was current in Hobson's time, new liberal internationalism is preferred because it reflects more closely the historical and ideological development of Hobson's thought. Hobson's internationalism was liberal in its assumptions of rationality, the harmony of interests, and the possibility (or inevitability) of progress in human affairs.[4] Hobson's approach was new in a couple of respects. It was, at the time, a novel approach to international relations, using the organic and surplus concepts to highlight the importance of international organisation. It was also a new liberal approach. The new liberals, of whom Hobson was an important figure, turned away from *laissez-faire* and towards intervention in social and economic affairs through the instrument of the state as representative of the whole of society. His was a new liberal approach to international relations because his modifications of liberal international theory were consonant with the changes in liberalism at the turn of the century.

Hobson's new liberal internationalism did not appear complete all at once; rather it developed over time as Hobson wrote on international issues. Beginning with the Boer War, his writing on international relations became more concrete, explicit and sophisticated. He was led as were many writers during the first decades of the twentieth century, initially to consider international affairs as a perspective or dimension of a domestic issue, such as unemployment, poverty, or social reform; especially notable in this regard is the impact on domestic affairs of the Boer and Great Wars. The sophistication of Hobson's writings on international relations varies; many would say that he never bettered the analysis, both economic and political, provided in *Imperialism*. The tone also varies, mostly according to the state of international relations at the time: Hobson was pessimistic at the turn of the century, largely optimistic in the decade before the First World War, was horrified by the War and pessimistic immediately after it, recovered somewhat during the twenties, only to become very disillusioned in the thirties. Yet he increasingly devoted more of his writing specifically to international relations as a problem in itself rather than merely an aspect of a domestic issue.

This study is organised into nine chapters. The philosophical outlook and political economy that are the theoretical underpinning of Hobson's new liberal internationalism are set out in the next two chapters. The framework of four types of international system that form the basis of Hobson's analysis of international relations is presented in chapter 4. Chapters 5 and 6 challenge the orthodox interpretation of Hobson's theory of imperialism in international relations. Chapter 7 examines the tension in Hobson's economic internationalism between his defence of free trade and his interventionist constructive internationalism. Chapter 8 sets out the conflicting logics behind Hobson's proposals for international government. Chapter 9 concludes by locating Hobson's new liberal internationalism within the liberal tradition of international thought. The rest of the present chapter is devoted to a sketch of the man behind the writings.

BIOGRAPHICAL SKETCH

John Atkinson Hobson was born in Derby on 6 July 1858, the second son of newspaper proprietor and local Liberal luminary, William Hobson. The young Hobson was sent to the local grammar school before obtaining an open scholarship to Lincoln College, Oxford in 1876. Graduating from Oxford in 1880, Hobson was a school-teacher in Faversham, until 1882, and Exeter, from 1882 until he left for a life of journalism in London in 1887. In Exeter, Hobson met his future wife, Florence Edgar, an American, and A. F. Mummery, a businessman and mountaineer, with whom Hobson co-wrote his first book, *The Physiology of Industry*.[5]

Hobson's move to London brought him into contact with a variety of radical intellectuals and groups. He was a member of the London Ethical Society from 1890 to 1895, when he left to join the more reformist South Place Ethical Society. In 1894, he was a founder-member of a meeting club of radical intellectuals and politicians called the Rainbow Circle. For most of the rest of his life, the Rainbow Circle and the South Place Ethical Society provided congenial fora in which Hobson could develop his ideas and have them subjected to sympathetic criticism.[6]

Imperial and international affairs constituted major influences on the development of Hobson's liberal thought. An early significant turning-point in his career, for instance, was an invitation in 1899 from C. P. Scott, editor of the *Manchester Guardian*, to go to South Africa to report for the paper on the turbulent political situation in that country.[7] In South Africa, Hobson became convinced of the mine-owners' conspiracy and manipulation of politics. He returned to England to, among other things, a 'Welcome Home' dinner at the National Liberal Club, co-chaired by David Lloyd George. However, the anti-war, anti-imperialist lecture tour on which Hobson subsequently embarked had its meetings frequently disrupted or broken up by jingoistic mobs. In the next couple of years, as part of his anti-war campaigning, Hobson published a collection of his reports for the *Manchester Guardian* in book-form as *The War in South Africa* in 1900; spelled out his response to the hostile reception of his anti-war views in *The Psychology of Jingoism* in 1901; and analysed the phenomenon of imperialism at greater length in *Imperialism: A Study* in 1902.

Hobson's main occupation, besides writing books, was journalism. He published much of his work and tested many of his ideas in the various liberal periodicals of his time. While the high point of his journalistic career was his contribution to the *Nation* from 1907 to 1923 under the editorship of H. W. Massingham, he also contributed to numerous other journals.[8]

When he first arrived in London, Hobson was a university extension lecturer for Oxford and London Universities. Though he taught two courses at the London School of Economics, his university lecturing was to play a lesser role after his inheritance from his father's estate gave him sufficient income to allow him to concentrate on his books and journalism. The poor reception of the economic heresies of his first book had contributed to his exclusion from academic life, a source of rancour for Hobson and his supporters. He was not offered a university position until late in his life, when he turned down an offer from the University of Manchester because of ill health.[9] However, he continued to lecture outside the strictly academic context at South Place and was a frequent speaker to a wide variety of groups.[10] He also travelled abroad a number of times, for example to Denmark, Switzerland, the United States and Canada, on lecture tours and to conduct research for his articles and books.

Hobson was a political activist until the last decade of his life in the 1930s. Many of the groups in which he was involved were concerned, at least indirectly, with international issues. Prior to the First World War, besides his political activity during the Boer War, Hobson was a member of the Free Trade Union and the International Arbitration League. In the summer of 1914, Hobson and others set up the British Neutrality Committee to campaign against British intervention in a European war, just in time to hear Grey make the speech that committed Britain to defend Belgium militarily.[11] During the First World War he campaigned for an early, negotiated peace settlement, and against a number of the restrictions of civil liberties imposed by the National Government in the name of the war effort.[12] Hobson was a member of the Bryce Committee, set up to investigate possible arrangements for a post-war international order, and a member of the League of Nations Society. *Towards International Government* was Hobson's dissenting opinion from the Bryce Committee's deliberations. He was also a member of a number of peace groups, by far the most significant of which was the Union of Democratic Control (UDC). He wrote the UDC's Fifth Cardinal Point as well as a number of UDC pamphlets, such as *A League of Nations*, *Labour and the Costs of War* and *The New Holy Alliance*, sat on its executive committee for over a quarter of a century, and was a regular contributor to the UDC journal, *Foreign Affairs*.[13]

Once again, international affairs, in this case membership of the UDC, was to influence Hobson's politics, though more his affiliations than his ideas. Having become increasingly disillusioned with the Liberal Party, Hobson resigned from the party in 1916 over the proposed abandonment of free trade by the Government at the allied negotiations in Paris. In the UDC, he had made the acquaintance of Labour politicians and intellectuals. Hobson himself joined the Labour

Party in 1924, though, by his own admission, he never really felt 'at home' there.[14]

Hobson wrote increasingly on international affairs after the Great War. Like Keynes and other Liberals, he opposed the Versailles Treaty, especially the economic provisions such as reparation payments.[15] In addition to the activities noted earlier, Hobson attended meetings at Chatham House.[16] He was an important figure in the 1917 Club. By this time, Hobson was establishing quite a following for his economic ideas. He was also a regular witness to, and participant on, expert committees, both for the Government and for the Official and Independent Labour Parties, dealing with practical economic matters such as industrial relations. He contributed to the ILP policy statement, *The Living Wage*. He was also a member of the ILP Advisory Committee on International Relations.[17]

By the 1930s Hobson was into his seventies. Though he was by now attracting disciples both in politics and academe, he had outlived many of his closest friends and associates, such as William Clarke and L. T. Hobhouse. Nevertheless, though his political activism tapered off, his writing continued apace. He opposed the rise of dictatorship in the thirties, and was a critic of appeasement.[18] He called for the greater involvement of the USA in world affairs and his last paper pleaded for the early intervention of the United States in the Second World War.[19] J. A. Hobson died at his home on 1 April 1940 at the age of 81.[20]

CHAPTER 2

Rationality, welfare and the organic analogy

This chapter and the next examine the theoretical system that underpins Hobson's analysis of social, political and economic issues. It studies the philosophical outlook that supports his views of human rationality, welfare and society. Hobson's 'almost mystical attachment' to the 'alarming' organic analogy is much more than rationalising rhetoric.[1] Though today references to society as a 'social organism' seem dated, quaint or a little alarming, Hobson built his progressive, new liberal approach to society and social reform on the basis of the analogy. The terminology is now often associated with the ruthless theories of social Darwinism or with Parsonian structural functionalism in sociology. Darwin's evolutionary doctrine did indeed have an immense impact on social, political and economic thought in the nineteenth century.[2] As Freeden has shown, however, the use of a biological analogy and ideas of evolution were by no means limited to social Darwinists. Hobson, for instance, lifted the conception of the social organism from Herbert Spencer, but turned it to the cause of liberal social reform.[3]

Three aspects of Hobson's deployment of organic terminology are considered. First, when his ideas on human rationality and development are considered, we find that 'organic' refers to the nature of human beings as biological organisms. Hobson not only emphasised the physiological aspect of humanity but also used the analogy to attack the Cartesian dualism of mind and body, and other forms of separatism in the social sciences. Organic was also a device for Hobson to organise and give the impression of unity to his own work, and a way of indicating his approval (or disapproval) of concepts, ideas and approaches. Second, in his conception of welfare, he used the idea of organism to stress the physical basis of needs. He also deployed the analogy of society with an organism to suggest that human welfare could only make sense when understood as social welfare, not just aggregated individual welfare. Third, the organic analogy played a part in his political project of transforming liberalism. He justified the increased role of the state and the supersession of *laissez-faire* by means of the analogy. The organic analogy's substantive emphasis on the interdependence of modern society and its methodological holism suggested that society must be studied as the organic whole that it is. It also suggested that the state should be seen as a representative of the social whole and not just a container for society.

RATIONALITY

Underlying Hobson's study of political, social and economic questions is an instrumental, evolutionary notion of human rationality. He emphasised the unity of individual human personality and of society, and urged the need for a social science to reflect this unity and guide social improvement.

Hobson's central hypothesis is that man can be understood and judged as a rational animal. While this view was shaken by the experience of war, Hobson clung to the presumption of at least partial rationality as the hope for civilisation and progress. For Hobson, human reason was part of the urge towards a fuller, better life, pursued through an increasing control over the physical environment. He conceived reason instrumentally as a 'scientific instrument ... applied to furnish means to the satisfaction of the particular instincts, interests, and desires of man'.[4] At the same time, rationality was the 'passion of Wholeness'.[5] The fuller life would therefore satisfy the whole of the human being, not only conscious intelligence associated with rationality but also the instincts and passions. While Hobson tried to reconcile his instrumental view of rationality with a broader emotional sense, it is nonetheless clear that it is reason that guides the passions and not vice versa.[6]

For Hobson, the emergence and growth of consciousness and reason were part of human evolution. They were initially a survival strategy.

> In all organic life there is a limited amount of transmitted energy, or urge, capacity to strive, directed to secure the survival and growth of the individual and the species. It belongs to the economy of this struggle that some direction of the several instinctive urges and desires in the interest of the organic whole should be exercised. This directive control, so far as it is conscious, is some thin form of 'reason', and it involves some conscious or intuitive valuation of the claims of the several instincts upon the organic resources.[7]

The development in humanity of conscious purpose, and the ability thereby to reason, transformed the nature of human social evolution. The blind fumbling of nature was replaced by the conscious application of reason. Consciousness and, particularly, rationality permit purposeful action and, specifically, the pursuit of an ideal of human progress towards the further growth of reason and civilisation. In short, according to Hobson, consciousness and rationality also themselves evolved.

The development of reason permitted humanity, as a higher organism, to interfere with the processes of reproduction and adaptation to the environment, and even drastically change the environment itself. However, the teleology of civilisation and the inexorable growth of human reason that seemed exogenous to the process of evolutionary selection appeared because humans were reasoning animals.[8] While certain evolutionary dictates such as the basic drive for survival were superseded, a new conscious evolution towards greater civilisation emerged.

Hobson maintained his belief in man's rationality despite the setbacks of the Boer War and the First World War.[9] While developments in philosophy and in science threw some doubt on the certainty of the claims of nineteenth-century determinists, Hobson stoutly defended the rationalist tradition. 'The wide significance of rationalism surely demands a reasonable explanation of every course of human thought and conduct, especially in that great area, or arena, of political, social, and economic reconstruction which confronts every reasonable man or woman as essential to the salvation of a civilised world.'[10]

Science and social science

For Hobson, 'the chief organising process of Reason' was science.[11] Consonant with his idea of reason, his notion of science was instrumental. Hobson described the origin and ultimate purpose of science in the ordering and control of the human and physical environment.[12] Science is thus set in the context of human development and social life. While shaped by practice, or social 'art' as Hobson called it, science in its turn limited social development by determining the methods and attainability of social improvements.[13] However, Hobson's instrumentalist approach to science brought with it relativism: he denied the possibility of pure disinterestedness and value-freedom in scientific investigations.

While Hobson followed Comte and Spencer in his belief in the applicability of the term science to studies of human action and society, the social context and instrumental nature of science led him to make a distinction between the natural and social (or, as he occasionally called them, mental) sciences. In *Wealth and Life*, for example, Hobson delimited four realms of science: the inorganic, the organic, the psychic (by which he meant psychological, particularly its physiological aspects) and the self-conscious.[14] He distinguished the exactitude of the physical sciences from the relative vagueness of the human sciences.[15] What marked off the human sciences from natural sciences was, in the first place, the intractability of the subject matter, its complexity and the impossibility of constructing any historically generalisable 'laws'. This cast doubt on the idea that it was possible to have a social science: 'It is not merely that ethics, politics, economics, sociology, are backward in the discovery and formulation of their laws: the laws are not 'there' to be discovered, in the sense in which they are 'there' in physics and chemistry.'[16]

Hobson believed that 'natural laws' did not apply to individuals and society because the moving force was human will rather than physical causes. However, he equivocated on this point, not wishing to jettison a scientific approach to society altogether. He claimed that 'human nature is after all only a branch of nature, and is amenable to laws as regular in their normal operation over the human field of enquiry as is the case in other fields'.[17] His main concern was the unreflective application of the scientific method to studies of human activities and society; his qualifications can be grouped together in two major tendencies in the social sciences, academic specialisation and quantification. Successes with specialised and quantitative methods in the natural sciences could not hide the fact that their application to social studies reflected, according to Hobson, the mentality of industrialism, a mode of thought that saw all progress in terms of the technological advances of the Industrial Revolution.

Specialisation and division of the social sciences into economics, politics, sociology, psychology and so on broke up examination of human experience into separate parts, thus denying its essential unity. Hobson argued that the implicit mechanistic metaphor underlying specialisation 'den[ied] the existence and operation of the creative power of the human will, by presenting human nature itself as a static being, responding to laws that are immutable in the same sense and degree as those which govern the operations of stars and plants'.[18] For

Hobson, this method was fallacious: 'This is no doubt the way to simplify science. But it is also the way to falsify it.'[19] Scientific specialisation resulted in what Hobson called 'overwrought theory', that is, increased abstraction as a consequence of the scientist's distance from the subject of his study.[20] Quantification also artificially separated elements of complex objects of study, such as an individual or society, because in order to measure them, social facts had first to be reduced to their constituent elements.[21] The reductive analytical methodology of quantitative social science was merely 'intellectual gymnastics'. It was useless as a guide for human conduct, Hobson's instrumentalist touchstone.[22]

Hobson denied the validity of inductively based empiricism as a basis for scientific knowledge: facts could not be understood without some prior ordering. He claimed that all scientific studies relied on ideas to order the 'facts' being studied.[23] However, this created another obstacle to objectivity in the social sciences because measurement, selection and interpretation of the facts would be influenced by the values of the observer. Beneath these methodological concerns, Hobson was making a significant ontological claim that in society, and thus for the social sciences, values and beliefs were facts.[24] It followed that the separation of 'ought' and 'is' was artificial. All scientific work involved a prescriptive element.

> The 'ought' is not something separable or distinct from the 'is;' on the contrary, an 'ought' is everywhere the highest aspect and relation of an 'is.' If a 'fact' has moral import . . ., that moral import is a part of the nature of the fact, and the fact cannot be fully known without taking it into consideration.[25]

These facts included illusions and superstitions. Thus Hobson concluded that there was no objective fact in the human sciences as there was in the physical sciences.[26] Values did not just interfere with scientific method, they imbued the very subject matter being studied.

Sociology as a science of social reform

Hobson's attack on the objectivity of social science might seem to lean towards relativism. His relativism is tempered, though, by his evolutionary understanding of the development of human reason. There were no fixed social facts, because humanity and human society were evolving. But this negative reflection regarding the impossibility of objectivity in social science also implied that social science entailed the identification, examination and enhancement of human values, following from the insight that science was the tool of human reason whose purpose was progress. Social science would be unable to establish any fixed facts or have any fully objective standards for methods because of the possibility of human improvement. Science, nevertheless, retained its ultimate purpose, the normative injunction to guide human conduct. The practical influence of social science would be as the guide for social reform.[27] Hobson's other refutation of relativism relied on an argument that the 'reign of law' could be extended to all spheres of human conduct because of the fundamental uniformity of human nature: people were more alike than unlike each other. For Hobson, this was 'a valid assumption for the possibility of any social science'.[28]

Hobson suggested that a science of society, or what he called sociology, at once analysed and prescribed appropriate social reforms and institutions, which 'by the distinctively intellectual operation of enabling individuals to realise society as an elaborate organic interaction of social forms and forces, and so to understand the worth of social conduct, will alter the scale of human values and desires'.[29] This sociology would analyse society as a whole, because '[t]he study of social value of individual men no more constitutes sociology than the study of cell life constitutes human physiology. A recognition of the independent value of the good life of a society is essential to any science or art of Society.'[30] Thus sociology was based on a unified conception of the social whole and, according to Hobson, was the most important of the social sciences, co-ordinating as it did the separate sciences of ethics, politics and economics.[31]

In summary, Hobson's vision of sociology was of a holistic or synthetic science (as opposed to an analytical or reductive one) correlating the separate studies of human value (ethics), material value (economics) and government (politics). This science was unlike physical sciences because in human society facts were neither easily accessible nor forever fixed. As Hobson concluded, this made his sociology a difficult and ambitious enterprise, but '[b]ecause a "unified social science" is so much more difficult, that is no reason for neglecting it, but is rather a reason for putting more intellectual energy into its pursuit'.[32] Hobson attempted to implement this view of social scientific method in his own work and this is one reason that his writings range across the spectrum of academic social sciences.

The immediate context of Hobson's sociology was that it was the intellectual underpinning and justification for his political project, the transformation of liberalism, as we will see below, and, specifically, the source of his arguments for radical social reform. His vision of a unified and unifying sociology was to provide a basis for a comprehensive social, economic and political reform as a result of an examination of the society as a whole, rather than the piecemeal practical measures that would result from fragmentary, specialised analysis.[33] Should his sociology be ignored, Hobson believed that reformers would,

> pay the price which short-sighted empiricism always pays; with slow, hesitant, and staggering steps, with innumerable false starts and backslidings, they will move in the dark along an unseen track towards an unseen goal. Social development may be conscious or unconscious. It has been mostly unconscious in the past, and therefore slow, wasteful, and dangerous. If we desire to be swifter, safer, and more effective in the future, it must become the conscious expression of the trained and organised will of a people not despising theory as unpractical, but using it to furnish economy in action.[34]

The ideals of social reform should be flexible, according to Hobson. They would shift, he said, with the changing needs of individuals and society.[35] The need for practical measures and the constantly changing facets of society meant that social reformers should not seek grand theories or universal laws, but rather 'middle principles' that demonstrated the interconnectedness of different arenas of human society and could be comprehended and acted upon by significant numbers of ordinary people.[36] Most importantly, the practical experience of the common people should fill out any ideals or principles. There was a need for 'sound information and sound modes of thinking ... [which must] percolate into the general mind. Thus alone can progress of a people become conscious and rational, and, therefore, take at once a faster and surer pace.'[37] The principles for social reform could not, then, be what Hobson decried as the vapid theorising of ivory-tower academic professors.

Hobson believed that through social reform, progress was possible, despite his criticisms of nineteenth-century liberalism's complacency in this regard.[38] The First World War and the rise of Fascism was certainly a setback to the progress of democracy, civilisation and justice, but he expected this to be temporary. Indeed, Hobson believed that some notion of progress was a fundamental element and prime motivator of human action: 'If we really disbelieved in any process of betterment of ourselves and for humanity, every human activity would be sapped at the source ...'.[39]

An organic unity in Hobson's writing

Hobson's discussion of human rationality and development is co-ordinated by his use of organic terminology. As has been pointed out by Michael Freeden, among others, the use of the word organic is crucial to Hobson's work. First, Hobson saw individual human beings and human society in terms of their biological basis, that is, they are literally organic. Hence, the instrumental nature of reason in evolution, the role and significance of consciousness, and the interpretation of social activities and society itself in biological terms. Second, Hobson used organic as a metaphor for a unity, or being unified, and organised. For Hobson, the organic analogy had its basis in the fact of the literally organic nature of human beings in the first place. Furthermore, Hobson used organic to highlight the unity of social facts, of human reason and knowledge, and of measures for social reform.

The word organic serves one final purpose for Hobson. It operates as an organisational device for his work and a rhetorical device providing at least superficial coherence to his diverse studies and writings, from poor relief to internationalism, from taxation to eugenics, and thereby creating a coherent campaign for social reform. It linked together and brought a common theme to his political and economic principles, such as the differentiation of functions (division of labour), the theory of surplus value, the human law of distribution, and the principle of federalism, as we shall see in the following two chapters. Though his use of organic terminology waned, the emphasis on the unity of politics, economics and ethics in a single social science remained.[40]

Hobson's understanding of rationality, science, and the relationship of social science and social reform has a number of weaknesses and has not gone unchallenged. To begin with, the organisational use of organic slips sometimes into mere rhetoric, as organic becomes a gesture of approval, a way to apportion praise and blame. This point is not trivial because, on occasion, Hobson's arguments might be made without recourse to organic terminology and yet remain substantively unchanged. The phrases 'organic interconnection' and 'organic unity' are good examples. For instance, Hobson states that '[t]he organic unity of man as producer and consumer renders invalid the statistical separatism which our neo-classical economics seeks to impose'.[41] The use of organic here tells us little more than that Hobson approved of connection and unity, and disapproved of separatism. Beyond this there is little substantive distinction, for instance, between mechanical and organic systems, other than that Hobson approved of the latter over the former.[42] Again, to read *Imperialism* is to read Hobson complaining about the parasitical nature of capitalism. 'Parasitical' conveys some explanatory meaning but is also highly effective as a derogatory slight against capitalists.[43]

The use of organic masks a deeper problem with Hobson's ideas. According to the *South Place Monthly Record*, Hobson was 'strangely unworldly' and 'an unrepentant idealist'.[44] Hobson's idealism is, as R. N. Berki has stated more generally, 'born of the endeavour to comprehend political reality in *unitary* terms, in a series of straightforward and precise propositions'. However, this means that Hobson's world is, again quoting Berki in a more general context, 'the bifurcated, abstract world of good and evil, black and white, desirable and undesirable, something to be advocated and justified, something to be relentlessly opposed, rejected'.[45] Hobson's work is full of dichotomies between good and evil. His organic analogy confronts the general interest in organic harmony and unity with sectional egoistic irrational interest. This leads (as we will see in the next chapter) to the contrast of co-operative surplus with the sectional appropriation of 'unproductive surplus'. Upon this dichotomy, Hobson produced a series of oppositions, such as wealth and 'illth', socialism and capitalism, combination and competition, and justice and force. These dichotomies were given their most stark presentation in *Democracy After the War*, where Hobson lines up the forces of reaction on one side against the forces of peace, democracy and internationalism on the other.[46] In each opposition, we find that Hobson idealistically condemned present arrangements for failing to come up to the standards of his rational ideal.

Yet, the organic analogy remains a useful start for a holistic analysis of society and Hobson's use of the analogy was certainly progressive for his time. In terms of contemporary sociological analysis, it is also worthwhile remembering that Emile Durkheim deployed a similar analogy between mechanical and organic solidarity in feudal and industrial social organisation.[47] As we saw, science consists, initially at least, of metaphor and analogy. It might be valuable, as Manning points out, to multiply analogies, if only to avoid being under the commanding influence of one, probably misleading analogy.[48]

HUMAN WELFARE

According to Hobson, human progress meant enhanced well-being. Human welfare rather than freedom or liberty, order or justice was Hobson's ideal. Hobson's understanding of welfare is central to his social science; welfare is a social good, and in his analysis, it marries his evolutionary, organic ideas with political economy. His study of welfare is the focal point of his work, joining economics and ethics as complementary studies of individual and social, material and spiritual value. Human welfare was a standard; it was the ideal that focused social reform and also the measure of social progress.[49] Hobson's notion of organic welfare entailed the satisfaction of social as well as individual and spiritual as well as material needs. Hobson's ideas for a humanistic political economy based on his organic welfare thus extended scientific study beyond economic measures to a valuation of overall well-being.

When discussing welfare, Hobson invoked the nineteenth-century romantic John Ruskin but with a utilitarian twist: the ideal of human welfare was '[t]he largest number of happy and healthy human beings'.[50] Though he eschewed the narrow hedonistic calculus of the utilitarians Jeremy Bentham and James Mill, his conception of welfare was still utilitarian and he admitted as much, arguing for an ethics based on 'a New Utilitarianism in which physical, intellectual, and moral satisfactions will rank in their due places'.[51] His approach was to modify the utilitarian calculus of classical political economy as a measure of welfare, rather than reject it altogether.

Hobson understood welfare in organic terms as the well-being and health of the entire human organism. He advised that we should 'seek our standard [of welfare] in the conception of man as a psycho-physical organism with various related satisfactions of its functions'.[52] According to Hobson, the satisfaction of human needs was achieved through work. The production of what he saw as human value, that is, well-being, was central to Hobson's writing; thus, the titles of a number of his books involve the words 'work', 'wealth' and 'life'. The relationship of welfare to work, and more specifically to consumption and production was a major element of his work towards a humanistic economics.

While his use of organic terminology highlighted the physical nature of humanity, it also pointed to the fact that each individual human personality was an integrated whole that could not simply be analysed into its separate parts – physical, emotional and intellectual. Such separatism entailed a loss of scientific accuracy (though not exactitude) and fundamentally misconstrued the organic unity of humanity. 'Welfare consists of ordered, organised values', Hobson argued, and thus 'value and purpose [are], if anywhere[,] in the total harmony of nature as a whole'.[53]

As we have seen, Hobson saw human civilisation in organic terms. In the context of welfare, the organic analogy suggested that human society could be seen as a spiritual or even physical organism. From the physical point of view, humanity could be considered at least as a collectivity of human organisms or perhaps an organism itself, Hobson believed. Furthermore, the social function of industrial production and consumption could be interpreted directly in the biological terms of nutrition and development.[54] For instance, utilising the fictional case of Robinson Crusoe as an example, Hobson claimed that at the primitive stage of development, each person or group produced what they needed for more or less immediate consumption, and consumption itself provided the physical energy needed for subsequent production.[55] A natural, biological balance of production and consumption was created. From the more spiritual perspective, Hobson was profoundly influenced in his study of human welfare by John Ruskin's critique of political economy. He adopted a number of Ruskin's maxims, most notably, 'There is no wealth but life.' Following Ruskin, he defined wealth not in money terms, but as 'vital' value, 'the power to sustain life'.

Human society also could be understood in terms of the analogy to an organism. Despite its complexity and the introduction of psychological and spiritual needs as well as the strictly physiological in modern industrial societies and economies, the balance of production and consumption still had to be struck at the level of the human society. In modern society, Hobson wrote, production and consumption still had various costs and satisfactions. Production involved costs in terms of the expenditure of life, i.e., work or labour, to produce the necessaries of life, but it was also a fulfilment of a natural human function and thus a way of satisfying certain needs. Consumption promoted life and/or happiness, contributing to the potential productivity of the individual, but it could also be bad for the individual if it was what Hobson called (following Ruskin once more) 'illth', that is, it harmed the individual in some way.[56] According to Hobson, the standard of human welfare should include '[h]onest production, just distribution, [and] wise consumption'.[57]

Because humanity at large and human societies were in a sense organic entities, an examination of human welfare had to take into account the social aspects of humanity. Thus '[h]uman welfare will be not merely the welfare of human beings taken as an aggregate, but of society regarded as an organic unity', Hobson argued.[58] Furthermore, from a methodological point of view, an objective social standard of welfare was possible not only as a result of this unity but because '[i]n so far as the members of a society own the same nature, habits, education, institutions, and range of vision, they possess a common grasp of what is good for the society'.[59] Hobson assumed, as we saw, that people were in large part similar, the precondition for a meaningful social standard.[60] This standard would shift with the change in level of civilisation of a people, for sure. However, at any one time, in any one place, there would be a standard which would address the question: 'Given a number of human beings, with a certain development of physical and mental faculties and of social institutions, in command of given natural resources, how can they best utilize these powers for the attainment of the most complete satisfaction?'[61] The goal of this standard would be 'objective social good' rather than individual self-interest; 'our standard must be conceived in terms of a life that is [socially] good or desirable'.[62]

Hobson's humanist political economy: from economic to human valuation

Hobson's writings on welfare were concerned not only with what welfare was, but also with how it could be measured. His more philosophical writings thus impinge here on his work in political economy. Hobson's adopted approach to measuring human welfare was to start with classical economics and modify it. He broadened the economic valuation of wealth to include non-market and other than monetary values. In many respects, Hobson's welfare economics was little more than a systematisation of Ruskin's humanist critique of 'commercial science' into an alternative political economy.[63]

His procedure for transforming the monetary valuation of welfare in orthodox economics to a human valuation involved four steps, reflecting the physical, spiritual and social aspects of human welfare.[64] First, money values of goods were to be translated into the concrete wealth that they engendered, what they were in terms of goods or services. So, each five dollars, say, was translated into what that money figure represented in terms of food, clothing, shelter and so on.

Second, these concrete goods were to be translated into the subjective satisfactions and dissatisfactions of the people who produced and consumed them. For example, the food or clothing was valued according to what each person who either consumed or produced the commodity derived from them in terms of satisfaction or exertion. Different persons had different needs and capacities. Thus, the same good would result in different valuations of welfare. Third, this second step had to be qualified by the recognition that each person was an 'organic unity', and therefore both a producer and consumer of goods and services. Furthermore, the overall distribution of work and income affected the potential satisfaction of individual and social needs, i.e., if some in society got more than they deserved and others less, the valuation of certain goods would be skewed from their true welfare value. For example, the creation of a wealthy elite would create the appetite for luxury items that might not otherwise exist. Fourth and finally, all these satisfactions had to be translated from their measure as they were actually desired to the standard of the objectively desirable. In each person's individual standard of consumption and conditions relating to production, there would inevitably be 'illth' as well as wealth, for the individual and for society as a whole. That is, items such as cigarettes would be 'illth' for an individual and certain luxury items were 'illths' for society, having negative consequences in terms of welfare.[65]

This humanistic political economy reflects Hobson's ideas of welfare, which saw both the individual and society as organic unities. Though not as precise as the money standard of economics, the human standard would be more accurate. Hobson accepted that there might be theoretical difficulties, some of which might prove to be strictly insuperable. For instance, he admitted that '[t]he general conception of human well-being is itself vague and insubstantial, until it has acquired and assimilated the very sorts of knowledge the collection of which it is here assumed to be able to direct'.[66] That is, how can we know what the standard of welfare is to consist of until we have got detailed empirical knowledge about the specifics of human welfare? On the other hand, how can empirical data be gathered without some overarching conception of welfare in the first place? For all practical purposes, however, Hobson believed, reasonably reliable physical indices of welfare would be attainable.[67]

In summary, Hobson attempted to create a science of human welfare, bridging the gap between economics and ethics in a renewed, widened utilitarianism. Despite his attempt to humanise his standard of welfare, it remains utilitarian. This leaves Hobson's analysis open to the criticisms levelled at utilitarianism generally, such as the problems of consequentialism, the difficulties of measurement and the contradiction with human integrity.[68] Furthermore, just as far as Hobson mixed humanism with utilitarianism, he is led into the contradiction of the ultimate sanctity of human life as against the overall welfare of individuals and society.[69] What if the happiness and health of the greatest number involved the slavery of some? In what amounts to a very large leap of faith, Hobson was content to rely on his organic analogy to reassure himself that a natural social harmony existed that meant, essentially, that such difficult questions were not of practical relevance.

THE TRANSFORMATION OF LIBERALISM

In the political arena, the analogy of society to an organism was the basis for Hobson's transformation of liberalism away from *laissez-faire* to the new liberalism.[70] Hobson's new liberalism, inspired by the organic analogy, brought the state into the liberal conception of the common good and placed social reform on a firm theoretical footing.[71] Yet Hobson's socialised liberalism was still recognisably liberal because it affirmed the importance of the individual in the interdependence of organic co-operation, and denied the authoritarianism and bureaucracy of Fabian (and other scientific versions of) socialism as well as Oxford Idealism. His perspective was forged in political debate and its aim was political. Nevertheless, Hobson's justification is couched in theoretical terms and it is the theoretical status of the organic analogy with which this study will largely be concerned as we see how Hobson applied the analogy to international relations.

The key issue for Hobson was certainly methodological as well as ideological. The organic analogy shifted the methodology underpinning liberalism away from individualism and atomism (or monadism) towards a methodological holism. For Hobson, the organic view of society demonstrated the fallacy of the individualism in nineteenth-century liberalism. Such monadism 'look[ed] upon society as embodied in the separate action of individual wills, without allowance for any organic relation among those wills, constituting spiritual solidarity'.[72] Thus, 'such separatism and atomism is the repudiation of creative action and the organic unity which it expresses'.[73] It was not possible to construct a theory of individual, let alone social, value on an individualistic basis because of the changes wrought by social interaction and co-operation.[74] Society was more than the mere aggregation of individual personalities; it was an entity in its own right:

We are told indeed that 'Society only exists in individuals.' This, however, is only true in the same restricted sense in which it is true that an animal organism only exists in the life of its cells. There is nothing but the cells *plus* their organic cooperation. But I should rather say that the organism exists in the cooperation of the cells. So I should say that Society exists in the cooperation of individuals.[75]

Furthermore, only from an individualistic perspective would co-operation seem to involve the sacrifice of individual development:

Not only industrial but social life in general requires a certain sacrifice of free individual development, represented by a specialisation of certain powers and a comparative neglect of others. This, of course, is only a sacrifice, so long as we regard individuals as self-sufficient units, which they are not: the so-called sacrifice becomes a gain as soon as we recognise the social character of man, which requires that he be formed not merely with regard to his individual perfection, but with regard to the perfection of the social organism of which he is part.[76]

According to Hobson, developments in society and the economy had undermined the viability of *laissez-faire* liberalism. The new liberalism with which he was so closely associated had to recognise the social nature of production and social determination of value.[77] These changes spurred the need for a change of policy, 'a coherence of purpose, an organic plan of social progress, which implies a new consciousness of Liberal statecraft'.[78] Hobson's new liberalism entailed a changed, beneficent view of the state. There were philosophical and practical rationales for this extended role for the state. From a philosophical perspective, Hobson's conception of the development of conscious control as a superior form of human rationality suggested that, in so far as society was an organic unity, there was reason to believe that rational control would be beneficial. Conscious, i.e., deliberate, central planning, most likely through the instrument of the state, was a prerequisite of social progress. By contrast, the idea of *laissez-faire*, that the economy should be left alone, denied and would obstruct rational progress, wrote Hobson. Markets and market economies were anarchic, or at best diffuse systems, that would perform better with a measure of central social, i.e., state, control.

In economic theory and in liberal ideology, Hobson rejected *laissez-*

faire, and claimed that while '[t]he idea that man is really a social being and that his reason can be applied so as to make his social cooperation effective for the common good is still regarded as the supreme economic heresy',[79] in fact '*laissez-faire* ... is not only impracticable in view of the actual forces which move politics, but it is ethically indefensible in the last resort'.[80] For practical politics and economics, the state could be seen, through the organic analogy, as the central social direction needed to control the powerful sectional interests of industrial combination, both of business and labour, that had emerged as political forces in modern society. This vision of the role of the state in the economy and in social policy contrasts sharply with the night-watchman state of *laissez-faire*. Hobson proposed the state as a bulwark against separate interests. He claimed that *laissez-faire*, individualism and the autonomy of politics and economics envisaged in classical political economy could no longer be sustained owing to the growth of combination and monopoly in industry. Yet the doctrine of *laissez-faire* remained prevalent nonetheless as an ideological support to the interests of the ruling class. Whereas *laissez-faire* had originally been a liberative ideology envisaging the freedom of individuals from the prohibitions of an oppressive, aristocratic-dominated state, it now defended wealth, power and privilege. Under the guise of individual liberty it sanctioned the right of individuals to take what they could for themselves. Because some people were more powerful or wealthier than others, this effectively blessed the predominance of stronger groups or classes.[81] Hobson's vision of a new liberalism was an attempt to reinvigorate liberalism with reforming zeal, and to move it away from the influence of the wealthy classes, particularly the powerful industrial magnates and financiers. Substantively, its aims included more state intervention in socio-economic affairs and a reformation of democracy.[82]

The organic metaphor was deployed not only against the individualism and separatism of *laissez-faire* liberalism, however. Hobson also used it to distance his new liberalism from the authoritarian visions of certain socialists and also the Idealists. Here, his political point is made by contrasting organism with mechanism and holism. Hobson claimed that a mechanistic conception of society underlay arguments for a 'rational' control of society by an elite of experts, be they the captains of industry envisaged by some economists or the administrators of Fabian or Soviet-style bureaucratic socialism. He pointed out that the mechanistic analogy is drawn from the natural sciences, and so stressed a version of cause, process and system, which divorced them from human will and intervention. Society was instead seen as a giant manipulable mechanism: 'Great national issues really turn, according to this judgement, upon the arts of political management, the play of the adroit tactician and the complete canvasser.'[83] In attempting to reduce individual and social life to quantifiable, malleable categories, however, mechanism 'can neither handle an organism as structure, nor as the system of activities in which the organism expresses itself', that is, it fails to understand the nature and relations of society.[84] This failure to acknowledge society as an organic system resulted in an anti-democratic, authoritarian view of society, favouring the views of political conservatives and the bureaucratic establishment.[85]

Hobson adopted a different tack in his critique of the Idealists, such as Bernard Bosanquet. They emphasised the whole over the parts and the spiritual over the material factors in human existence, and thus failed to see the integrated nature of human beings as organic unities. As Peter Clarke has pointed out, the organic analogy can also have conservative implications. The emphasis on the importance of social welfare and order in an organic harmony as the basis for individual well-being verges on being a conservative tautology and ultimately a defence of the status quo.[86] This was the case with the Oxford Idealists' neo-Hegelian conception of society, which Hobson attacked for its abstractness, its failure to address the concrete practical issues of society, and for its authoritarianism.[87] He criticised the Idealists' prescriptions for ameliorating the conditions of the poor because they stressed individual spiritual salvation to the exclusion of physiological and material factors in the social maladies of unemployment and poverty. Most of all, he objected to the authoritarian tone of the Idealist prognosis on social problems: 'The organic conception of society ... demands a self-government in which the whole of the self, the organic experience and judgment of the whole rational system, shall find direct conscious expression.'[88] The use of organic terminology entailed for Hobson the acknowledgement that individuals could not be sacrificed for the good of the social whole.

Society exists, not, as is sometimes maintained, in order consciously to secure the separate welfare of its individual members, but to secure the health and progress of society always realised as a social organism; but this end, interpreted at any given time in terms of 'social utility,' has been seen to involve the care and promotion of individual health and progress. It can never be the interest of society to attempt to dominate or enslave the individual, sucking his energies for the supposed nutriment of a State; any such endeavour would be futile, for ... an attempt to exploit those energies, or to take away that 'property' which nature has set aside for individual support and progress, would defeat its end by drying up the sources of such energy and 'property.'[89]

Any conservative implications of Hobson's own use of the organic analogy were tempered by the superimposition on it of an evolutionary socialism, produced by his theory of surplus value, which is considered in the next chapter. Hobson's vision of the social good would do away with the status quo as society evolved towards greater democracy and enhanced individual and social welfare.

CONCLUSION

Hobson's new liberalism, like his ideas on human rationality, social science, and welfare, was inspired by organic terminology. It was an attempt at a democratic compromise between the *laissez-faire* of nineteenth-century liberalism and the authoritarian tones of contemporary socialistic doctrines of both the Idealists and groups of the radical Left. Hobson's formulation of social organisation and the need for state intervention is also influenced by his theory of surplus value. Through his analogy of society to an organism, Hobson ably demonstrated the failures of methodological individualism and supported his holistic perspective on society. He successfully undermined the atomistic presuppositions of the Manchester School of *laissez-faire*, the hedonistic utilitarianism of the Philosophic Radicals, and the individualistic prejudices of classical political economy.

There are, nonetheless, certain weaknesses of the organic analogy that should be noted. Among its methodological shortcomings are the intrinsic weaknesses of analogy as an explanation of human actions or institutions. The organic analogy suffers from the same problems as other analogies, that it does not have the validity of logical reasoning and that there are disanalogies as well as analogies.[90] However, this criticism can be overdone. Language, even science, relies on analogies and metaphors.[91] Hobson's overt use of the organic analogy might be a useful antidote to the use of mechanical metaphors in international relations, where we consistently hear talk of the *balance* of *power*, the use of *force*, trade *flows* and so on. These physical and mechanical analogies and metaphors are so prevalent that we hardly realise that they are there. While biological analogies are also common in the social sciences, it is only recently that scientists and social scientists have become interested in the biases and the rhetorical power of these linguistic forms.[92] In any case Hobson was aware of the effects and defects of metaphor generally and while he was particularly critical of the use of mechanical metaphors, he was also reflective on his own use of the organic analogy.[93]

It can be argued that Hobson's use of organic contributes little to our understanding of society because it is such a broad generalisation. Indeed, all the organic analogy tells us is that society can be understood as a whole made up of related parts. But both system and mechanism convey this meaning. While Hobson made a significant turn to methodological holism, he was not in practice greatly aided by the biological terminology. Hobson's use of organic terminology may, indeed, just give a pseudo-scientific gloss to common liberal presumptions about the nature of people and society.[94]

The analogy was, Hobson admitted, an 'unphilosophic compromise'.[95] The resolution of the competing claims of the social and the individual or the whole versus the parts is problematic. Hobson, for instance, assumed that this antagonism cannot take place in an organic system, except as a result of the influence of sectional interests. Here, Hobson has assumed a version of the harmony of interests between individuals or groups in society that he claimed to have refuted elsewhere. This was not the natural harmony of the *laissez-faire* liberals, to be sure, but rather a harmony emergent in conscious collective human control of the physical and social environment.[96] Yet, a consciously willed harmony of interests is more difficult to realise in practice than *laissez-faire*'s simple appeal to a natural order when the diversity of individual interests have to be reconciled.

Hobson's discussion of separatism and separate interests is also problematical. Inasmuch as each individual or group should realise its fullest potential within the whole, this can be dealt with through education as to true interests. Hobson, however, admits the possibility that separate interests might gain, at least in the short run.[97] But this puts any harmony, natural or 'conscious', into question. How long is the short run? On what grounds should an individual prefer these short-run gains to long-term common interests? Hobson did not resolve the issue of the possible conflict of individual and social rationality, though he acknowledged as much in his discussion of the continued requirement for individual incentives to work.[98] What is missing from Hobson's discussion is an acknowledgement that organic harmony is not itself immanent but is a project of his new liberalism, to be realised in the future.

Finally, Hobson's organic analogy emphasises the similarity between societies and between the various levels of social co-operation. Yet not all social forms are similar; it is far from clear whether, for instance, it is helpful to call a family a society. Furthermore, the differences between a local community based on affective ties and a multinational society under a single state are huge. In short, the use of organic terminology commits Hobson to an isomorphism of social forms that is illegitimate. Different social forms have different structures, different dynamics and different modes of operation and maintenance.

Hobson is not without a defence against these charges. Despite doubts as to whether organism was an overstretched term in discussing what he called the spiritual dimension of human life and what might more properly be described today as the cultural aspects of human existence, Hobson maintained his use of the organic terminology because he believed that a spiritualised interpretation of organism was more appropriate than any other description of the essential unity of humanity.[99]

The isomorphism charge is not compelling because it is important to draw attention to the similarity between forms of co-operation and community as much as the contrasts. The assumption of an implicit harmony of interests is an issue that cannot finally be settled one way or the other. Whether social relations are essentially harmonious or conflictual is perhaps not the right way of looking at it. The most that can be said is that Hobson's assumption of a harmony is no less unjustified than the assumption that there must be a conflict of interest.

Thus, as long as the organic analogy is not pushed too far, or used too specifically, e.g., in the search for a social sensorium equivalent to the brain, the use of the term, organic, may be helpful. We should not expect too much from the analogy, but rather look, as Hobson did, for the broad vision of society implied by it.

CHAPTER 3

Co-operation, the surplus and the theory of underconsumption

While welfare needs were satisfied through the production of value in work, this might only have resulted in a social system in stasis were it not for the possibility of producing surplus value beyond immediate needs or efforts. Hobson believed that human welfare was enhanced through co-operation and, especially, co-operative labour. This chapter considers Hobson's two theories of surplus value and his theory of underconsumption. It begins with a consideration of Hobson's theory of co-operative surplus. He stated boldly that '[o]rganized co-operation is a productive power'.[1] The possibility of surplus value propelled Hobson's evolutionary view of human society and his theory of the co-operative surplus gave dynamism to his arguments for increasing social organisation.

Hobson used the term 'surplus' more often to mean unproductive surplus, a product of an inequitable system of income distribution. Analysis of the unproductive surplus underlies much of his critical commentary of the contemporary arrangement of international relations as well as one aspect of his theory of underconsumption. The theory of underconsumption has for some time been considered Hobson's major contribution to heterodox political economy. In the context of his ideas on surplus value, underconsumption appears as an economic manifestation of a social and ethical malady. Furthermore, there are three distinct aspects, almost three different theories, of underconsumption that need to be considered.

THE CO-OPERATIVE SURPLUS

Hobson used a parable involving three men building a boat to explain the co-operative surplus, in a way that closely resembles Adam Smith's telling of the story of a pin factory to demonstrate the importance of the division of labour.[2] Though his account of the production of co-operative surplus was straightforward classical political economy, his conclusions were less orthodox. Hobson asked, if three people build a boat, could one of them have built the same boat taking three times as long or could one have built a third of the boat in the same time? Hobson answered no. Co-operating, the three people can produce something together that they could not have produced alone. The boat is a group product, only possible as a result of co-operation as a group. For instance, a designer, a carpenter and a painter could follow their respective trades. Additionally, there might be extremely heavy loads to lift, requiring the effort of all three. The co-operative surplus was the difference between the sum of the values of the individual contributions and the total social value produced.

The social aspect of the endeavour could be widened beyond the narrow confines of the group itself. Each person's skills and the provision of materials for their project depended on the co-operation or assistance of the wider society of which they were a part. If the group planned to sell the boat, the social institution of the market would also contribute to the boat's value. Where exchange in markets determined the value of an item, this was what Hobson called social determination of value.[3] Social co-operation modified individual welfare and value; social determination of the total value of a good or service was beyond any individual or group's control. Even markets were forms of social co-operation, according to Hobson, despite their disorganised nature.

From his theory of surplus value, society or any co-operative activity is seen to be irreducible to its component parts. Furthermore, a social feeling was engendered: 'organised co-operation, voluntary participation of individuals in some common activity, can produce a valuable effect, spiritual or even material, different both in quantity and in character from that which the unorganised activities of the individual participants could compass'.[4] Though classical economists had demonstrated the value of co-operation, they had marginalized the importance of the social aspect when compared to the emphasis on individual contributions and capacities.[5]

Hobson's theory of surplus value was, nevertheless, closer to classical political economy than it was to Marxism. Hobson followed the premises of liberal economics but highlighted the social and co-operative aspects over the individual and competitive. From a Marxist perspective, Hobson's humanist conception of political economy (discussed in the previous chapter) and his notion of co-operative surplus were irredeemably bourgeois, as was quite apparent to Lenin, who correctly identified Hobson's debts in political economy to John Stuart Mill rather than to Marx. Hobson admired the scope and ambition of Marx's political economy but found it deficient analytically. For instance, he criticised socialist economics' reliance upon a crude labour theory of value, its failure to show how the capitalists expropriated the surplus from labour, and its neglect of the pressures of competition on capitalists. The difference between Marx's and Hobson's theories of surplus value was that for Marx labour was the creator of value, whereas for Hobson co-operation was the producer of surplus value rather than wage labour. Hobson's bourgeois approach was exposed by his practical suggestions that the payment of profits and interest could be justified as maintenance costs and that wages could include elements of unproductive surplus.[6]

Evolution and organisation

Hobson's theory of surplus value might seem rather economics-oriented and materialistic in a way that compromised his concern for a broader standard of human welfare.[7] Such a view is mistaken. Co-operation produced surplus in all forms and at all levels of social interaction.[8] The possibility of co-operative surplus was a critical element of Hobson's ideas on social progress. The development of human personality depended on the ability to devote time and energy to diverse 'higher' pursuits. This was only possible if there was more than sufficient time and energy to satisfy immediate needs. The production of economic, material value is the prerequisite for the development of higher values of human personality and society. The surplus permitted more than enough material value to be created so that time and energy could be devoted to spiritual or cultural pursuits. Surplus value thus produced the evolutionary dynamic that permitted, indeed, drove the development of human consciousness and rationality. Influenced by Spencer, Hobson used evolutionary ideas to explain social change.[9] Human culture and society evolved just as physical organisms did. This view of society added a dynamism and a responsiveness to external change that was lacking in the static models and mechanical approaches of other sociologists and classical economists.[10]

When he explained the importance of surplus value produced through social co-operation, Hobson occasionally used the example of an isolated family or village or a version of the Crusoe story as his 'original position'. While he acknowledged the importance of social interaction even in the early stages of the development of the human species, initially he speculated value was in the main produced through control of the material environment alone.[11] Yet, the centrality of the co-operative surplus to human development, as Hobson saw it, is clear in a passage that deserves to be quoted at length:

Taking the life of an individual in society, and regarding that life as constituted as an organic complex of functions – physical, intellectual, moral, etc. – we find a continuous evolution of wants and satisfactions. In a general historical review of this development, there will arise first the want of foods, clothing, shelter, absolutely necessary to support the continuance of physical life. Certain improvements in quality, character, and variety of these prime satisfactions will follow. Complementary food appealing to taste, ornamental elements in clothing, commodiousness and dignity of dwelling, may come next. Gradually, higher or more delicate sensations are educated, craving satisfaction; crude arts grow, providing utilities which were 'unnecessary' to primeval man. The beginnings of aesthetic, intellectual, and moral needs are manifested; a general widening of life, bringing a conscious and continuous process of developing new wants whose satisfaction gives increased value to life, ensues.

In tracing the historical process of development of wants and satisfactions, each earlier element seems more important than each succeeding one, the need of food and physical protection being more pressing and essential than the needs of 'the higher nature.' Logically, however – or in the order of nature, considered as a complete system, not as a process – each subsequent need or satisfaction is more important and more valuable than the preceding one in time, because it represents a higher type of life.[12]

This evolutionary perspective on social interaction underpins the whole of Hobson's work though he rarely stated it as explicitly as this. Lower values were historically prior, that is, they should come first. In practical terms, Hobson's evolutionary perspective imposed the temporal priority of physical needs over spiritual; it put economic reform before moral reform. People needed to be free from physical restraints before they could have access to higher values, as in culture and so on.[13] However, in terms of valuation at any one particular time in history, higher values were prior to lower. A comparison of the worth of spiritual and material values showed that the former were of higher value than the latter.[14]

Surplus value produced through co-operation raised life to a higher level of civilization. At this higher level, further co-operation was possible and further progress in civilization could be achieved. Hobson stressed the efficiency and economy of organisation; it was *organised* co-operation that was a productive factor. Utilising his organic analogy Hobson suggested that co-operation is most efficient and productive when centrally planned and organised. Consciousness and reason gave human beings the ability to organise and plan rationally, thus reducing waste.[15] Hobson applied this insight directly and by analogy to society. Directly: the development of rationality made possible more comprehensive and complex social organisation. By analogy: central, i.e., state, direction maximized society-wide welfare, as did the development of individual personality, rationality and social feeling.[16] 'Civilisation has its chief meaning in the extension and growing realisation of this unity of Society', he asserted, 'by utilising these secret threads of social feeling for the weaving of the fabric of social institutions.'[17]

Following Hobson's evolutionary theory of surplus value an 'expanding circle' of co-operation and organisation was completed.[18] Co-operation created a social surplus that could be maximized by organisation; the existence of surplus permitted the pursuit of higher activities; co-operation in these activities resulted in the creation of further surplus as well as the possibility of organisation, the latter maximising the benefits from the former.

The theory as it has been set out here is rather abstract. Hobson was ever practical, using his ideas of a co-operative surplus to illuminate the development and growth of industrial combinations and social institutions of many forms, not only, as the logic seems to suggest, social control expressed in state direction of the economy. Hobson found the evolutionary development of society and economy in his examination of the development of modern industry. At the time he was writing, industrial and financial combination were already established and were increasingly salient facts, and social control of industry was also advancing apace. Hobson argued social control of industries would increase. With some qualifications, society should be expected to organise its resources to reduce or eliminate waste, and Hobson believed that this was what was in fact occurring in industrial combination and increasing state involvement in the economy.[19] Small firms were being merged into joint-stock companies which themselves were being transformed into trusts and private monopolies. Subsequently these would be 'nationalised', so that some form of social control would give the benefits of combination to the whole of society rather than only one portion of it. The development of routinised mass-production techniques reaping economies of scale within firms and trades, and the ability of industry to provide for the growing set of routine needs in society such as food, clothing, etc., came together to provide both the necessity and possibility of social control of those private commercial and industrial monopolies in the public interest because: 'The natural evolution of modern industry is bringing many large routine businesses into a position of dangerous power, to which State organisation will be found to be the only effective remedy.' The state's economic role would thus grow naturally to cope with the problems of the capitalist system: 'There are certain wastes of economic power involved in all competition; there are certain dangers of monopoly attaching to all private conduct of industry. Collective control deals with these wastes and dangers, adjusting itself to their extent and character.'[20] Hobson's critique of the liberal policy of *laissez-faire* is founded on the recognition that the era of many small firms competing in a free market had ended; his theory of surplus value led him further to propose the state control of industries that had, to all intents and purposes, already been largely socialised.

Hobson's position on combination in industry might seem at first sight somewhat ambivalent. He applauded the replacement of wasteful competition, yet he condemned the combinations themselves.[21] In fact, combinations were good for their eradication of blind competition; they were, he said, the 'highest reach of capitalist evolution'. However, they were a problem because, following the organic analogy discussed in the previous chapter, they were a strong sectional interest which might wield power over society.[22]

As portrayed so far, Hobson's theory might seem rather authoritarian: the process of organisation being inexorable, human life would come increasingly under centralised control. However, this was not the case, because the social surplus was not applied just to social activities and institutions such as the state, but also went to individual development. Socialism, as Hobson described the socialisation of the economy and the increased role of the state, was balanced by individualism, the freedom of individuals to pursue their own goals.

Hobson argued that collectivist organisation was limited so far as individual tastes differed.[23] According to Hobson, state organisation of industry would not eliminate private industry because, though public industries could provide for routine common needs, private enterprise could devote itself to providing those higher differentiated needs, which were in their nature less regular or standardized and which had been cultivated by the satisfaction of 'lower' routine requirements such as the fundamentals of nutrition and shelter.

Hobson also claimed that in so far as the 'economy' of organisation allowed individuals to satisfy their lower needs easily, they could turn more time and energy to higher-valued pursuits.[24] Thus individual personality development came with the growth of social organisation, the latter freeing the former from less productive or valuable work. Hobson's evolutionary framework is beautiful in its simplicity and symmetry: following the theory of surplus value, the involvement of the state in the economy and increased standardization would release energy and time for the pursuit of higher ends. Thus, while the absolute level of standardized industry would continually rise, its proportion of society's industrial energy would fall.[25] Hobson called this shift to the higher private needs the qualitative conception of social progress (as compared to the quantitative conception of progress found in the counting of material benefits from standardized production and so on).

Finally, Hobson once again deployed his organic analogy in defence against a charge of authoritarianism or centralism. Complete control from the centre was mitigated by the fact that information was supplied by individuals to planning agencies and those agencies had to cater to the needs of individuals to be viable.

COSTS, SURPLUSES AND THE HUMAN LAW OF DISTRIBUTION

While the co-operative surplus was the foundation of Hobson's explanation of social progress, most of his references to surplus have less benign connotations. This is because he identified another form of surplus, the unproductive surplus, which he saw as the source of social and also international problems. Unfortunately, classical political economy neglected this malign factor in social and economic life and thus Hobson expended much time and energy examining it.

In classical political economy the rewards from production, including the surplus produced through co-operation, were assumed to be distributed fairly among the various contributors to production, that is, the four factors, land, labour, capital and ability.[26] Eschewing this categorisation, Hobson outlined an innovative and critical theory of distribution in which income is distributed to costs and surpluses. This theory was first rigorously outlined in *The Industrial System*, but dates back to his extension of the concept of rent from land to the other factors of production earlier in the century.[27]

In Hobson's scheme, there are three categories: costs of maintenance (or subsistence); costs of growth (productive surplus); and unproductive surplus (or waste).[28] Costs of maintenance are subsistence wages and salaries for labour and ability and wear-and-tear funds for capital and land. If these are denied production is halted, for instance in the case of subsistence wages, because the workforce is starved.[29] Costs of progress, or growth, 'consist of the minimum payments needed to call into industrial use the various sorts and quantities of labour, land, capital and ability needed for effective co-operation in the enlarged structure of industry', i.e., beyond current levels of production or into new areas.[30]

Costs are 'payments necessary for the maintenance and efficient functioning of the factors of production', says Hobson.[31] Because they are necessary, they are rationally distributed and there is a harmony of individual and social interests in regard to their apportionment. That is, without costs of maintenance, production would be impaired or halted.[32] However, as we have seen, the co-operative surplus belongs to no single co-operant and thus will not necessarily be rationally distributed. Hobson argued:

> Contrasted with the 'costs' it may be regarded as an irrational element in the system. [The surplus] belongs nowhere by necessary law ... There is a sense in which the economic surplus is entirely rational ... [It] is the sole source and substance of economic progress. Its irrationality lies in the defective provision for its serviceable distribution.[33]

In capitalism, the unproductive surplus resulting from the flawed system of distribution, was that income that was appropriated through scarcity, whether natural, artificial (e.g., monopoly power) or purely fortuitous, rather than earned through work. Because the co-operative surplus has no necessary place and because of the absence of a rational mechanism or scheme for distribution, any surplus is distributed according to bargaining power or force. The owner of a scarce factor, be that land, labour, capital or ability, made forced gains.[34] The main gainers from such a system were, then, the economically or physically strong. Under capitalism, it was the capitalists. Classical political economy, according to Hobson, was an ideological defence of privilege since *laissez-faire* permitted the appropriation of the surplus by sectional interests to the detriment of others and of society as a whole under the guise of individual right to private property.

Hobson argued that unproductive surplus is a harmful element in industry and society in a number of respects. It diverted resources from a possibly productive use. Specifically, because of the appropriation of the co-operative surplus, an important claimant on this surplus, the state, was deprived of funds. It resulted in no stimulus or incentive to production, as was the case with the costs of maintenance and growth. Indeed, it acted as 'a demand for idleness' and so depressed production further.[35] Finally, because its appropriation was a matter of struggle rather than rational distribution, the unproductive surplus was the source of discord in industry and society.[36]

How should the surplus be distributed? Hobson's answer was that it should go to benefit all, according to needs, in order to maximize social welfare as Hobson saw it. The solution to this problem of strife resulting from the struggle over the surplus was to apply what Hobson called the human (or on occasion, organic) law of distribution. This law was a modified rendering of the Saint-Simonian doctrine: 'from each according to his powers [or capabilities], to each according to his needs'.[37] According to Hobson, the human law of distribution allocated work and wealth according to needs and capacities and so maximized social welfare. Refuting the claims of those who emphasized effort or productivity, Hobson suggested that it was best to allocate according to needs, and interpreted needs as the costs involved in producing for society and the need for personal growth. The co-operative surplus, if rationally distributed, would be absorbed into individual and social costs of growth.

From the economic point of view, just as '[e]very failure to put the right man or woman in the right place, with the best faculty of filling that place, involves social waste', so does any system of distribution that deprives some and produces 'illth' for others. The balanced application of income to individual needs as incurred costs and revealed values would obtain the maximum level of production. While orthodox economic theory considered individuals as specialized producers or isolated consumers, the human law of distribution saw them as whole persons whose consumption affected their production and vice versa. Distributing work and wealth according to each individual's needs and capacity to use the wealth would 'secure the minimum of Human Costs and the maximum of Human Utility'. It would thus be the 'true principle of "economy"'[38] inasmuch as it obtained the greatest welfare possible out of current production, and led to the development of production and consumption in the future so as to maximize welfare, even if this were to mean the reduction of current material well-being. The law would economize industrial resources and 'liberate more and more time, energy and conscious interest of its members for occupations, both individual and social, that lie outside the distinctively economic field'.[39]

The application of the human law of distribution entailed the concerted action of the whole society through the instrument of the state. In any event, implementation of the human law in capitalist societies would mean significant redistribution of income. This would clearly, Hobson observed, mean an extended role in the economy for the state:

> an enlightened community, recognizing the growing social needs, will continually use its enlarging income from State monopolies and taxation to raise the standard of public consumption, by providing a fuller, richer, and more complex social life, as well as by furnishing such support and aid to the weaker members of society as is held to be consistent with a true interpretation of social utility.[40]

Taxation of the unproductive surplus was Hobson's basis for state finance, but it was based on a morality of state involvement in the economy and society.[41] The state was not only a device through which to implement taxation and other measures to effect redistribution. As the representative of society, the state was owed a portion of the co-operative surplus of members of the society; taxation of individual incomes was its rightful due as one of the co-operants in individual, group and social activities.

Critical commentary

In the science of economics, Hobson's concept of surplus and his theory of distribution contradicted neo-classical marginal analysis. According to marginalism, Hobson noted, value was determined, not by a rational decision from the centre, but by what he viewed as peripheral expenditures. Hobson understood marginalism well enough to realise that it was a methodological substitute for the dogma of *laissez-faire*, where there was no unproductive surplus because wealth was distributed according to worth under a perfectly competitive economy. However, Hobson's lack of understanding of mathematical analysis and of the idea of margins in the new marginal economics, as well as his misconstruction of the notion of opportunity cost, weakened his criticisms of mainstream economics.[42]

There are certain difficulties and lacunae in his theories of surplus value, both co-operative and unproductive. It has been argued that it is impossible to operationalize the concept of surplus. Lacking the precision of neo-classical economics, it is too vague to inform tax policy, unless it is supplemented with an *ad hoc* assumption, for example, that the unearned element in income rises proportionately with increases in income, without which the level of surplus in any level of income is unspecified.[43]

According to Hobson, an income is co-operation's due, and he admitted that this made distribution problematic because no single individual or group was clearly its rightful owner. But he assumed that the state had a clear claim on the value produced in social co-operation. Not all forms of co-operation are appropriately regarded as the state's responsibility, surely. Hobson's suggestion that the state is the representative of the interests of society as a whole is a tendentious statement resting on an over-extension of his organic analogy, apparently hinting that the state could be considered the social analogue of the brain of an individual.[44]

Hobson suggested distribution according to needs would remove the unproductive surplus. But he defined needs as costs of production and the need for personal growth mediated by the value of that individual to society. This idea is either circular, because individual needs are determined by their social value, or reduces to Hobson's despised individualism, because needs are a matter to be individually determined. By *Wealth and Life*, Hobson had collapsed needs into 'the capacity to use', thus rendering the human law of distribution redundant; it becomes 'from each according to his capacities, to each according to his capacities', not far from neo-classical economics.[45] Furthermore, empirical estimates of capacities, needs and/or costs would require a fantastic amount of work to complete, collate and compile. The theoretical and practical difficulties associated with assigning whom in society needs what and determining the social utility of one course of action as against another appear insurmountable.[46]

The difference between Hobson and his critics in the economics profession lies in his claim that the social surplus is beyond the 'rational' distribution of the market and in his emphasis on the social dimension of co-operation. Hobson's was a repoliticised and socialised view of economic distribution. This is not insignificant even today in the face of the depoliticising discourse of rational (or social) choice theorists in economics and philosophy alike, where bargaining power is the be-all and end-all, and game-theoretic constructs are used to explain the division of spoils in different social, economic and political contexts. Nonetheless, Hobson's theory of the co-operative surplus is weakened by his failure to take into account genuine conflicts of interest between individuals and groups. His analysis thus stops where philosophers such as Rawls, Nozick and Barry now begin.[47]

Despite these criticisms, Hobson made a significant contribution with his theories of surplus value. The criticism that the surplus concept is difficult, if not impossible, to operationalise does not mean that surplus does not exist.[48] As Hobson was keen to stress, because something was difficult was an injunction to try harder, rather than give up the effort. Hobson's discussion of human needs was certainly incomplete; his ideas on wider notions of welfare all but disappear in his discourse about the surplus, which is discussed, perhaps for practical reasons, in quantitative terms. Subsequent developments in modern societies have made Hobson's surplus analysis and its focus on imperfect competition and monopoly even more plausible. The social emphasis of his theories of surplus value underlies his essentially ethical vision of economics and his moral critique of the contemporary state of economic analysis from which considerations of a common good had been all but banished. Such an ethical perspective still has resonance today.[49]

THE THEORY OF UNDERCONSUMPTION

The relationship between the theory of underconsumption, one of the most famous aspects of Hobson's work, and his theories of surplus value has been examined by a few Hobson scholars, such as John Allett. Here, I will present the three arguments underpinning his explanation of underconsumption, only the last of which is closely connected to his idea of unproductive surplus. The three arguments are overproduction resulting from technological progress, oversaving caused by the 'any/every' paradox, and maldistribution of income. Only Hobson's account of the origins and bases of underconsumption in a modern economy is dealt with. The various stages through which trade depression passes and the relationship of underconsumption, oversaving and overproduction to depression, are not discussed.[50]

What was underconsumption according to Hobson? It was a situation in which there was a general excess of production over consumption, that is, a condition of general oversupply in an economy. The result was a surplus of consumption goods and also of capital. Orthodox political economy and modern neo-classical economics had denied the possibility of underconsumption on the grounds that a capacity to purchase was created with each good produced, following Say's Law that all markets must clear, and also because it was argued that the interest rate would correct the level of saving relative to spending, making underconsumption impossible by definition. Hobson demurred from this view arguing that desire to purchase was not the same as the capacity to do so and that the market mechanism and interest rates failed to deal with the critical problem, a deficiency of aggregate demand.

Underconsumption through overproduction

Hobson's first explanation for underconsumption was overproduction resulting from technological progress. As we have seen, Hobson argued that organisation, concentration and planning increased productivity. The technology of machine production, improved transportation facilities and increasing returns to scale immensely enhanced production possibilities. A huge quantity of goods could be produced, Hobson claimed, but there was no proportionate increase in consumption because habits of consumption were conservative.[51]

> [T]he improved technique of every branch of industry, in manufacture, mining, agriculture, commerce, transport and finance, in every part of the civilised world, has developed a power of production which is wildly excessive in the sense that goods it could put on the market cannot be sold at a price that would cover costs and yield a profit.[52]

This technological explanation tends to accompany the next two elements, but is relegated by Hobson to background status.[53] This is because Hobson realised that it ignored the fact that each act of production was rewarded by an income which, theoretically at least, was sufficient to purchase the good. That is, Hobson accepted Say's Law in theory, that what is produced will be consumed, and that therefore markets will clear:

> Whatever is, or can be, produced, can be consumed, for a claim upon it, as rent, profit, or wages, forms part of the real income of some member of the community, and he can consume it, or else exchange it for some other consumable with someone else who will consume it. With everything that is produced a consuming power is born.[54]

Underconsumption through oversaving

If Say's Law were in actual fact true, there would be no fixed limit to demand and no overproduction or underconsumption. Yet this was clearly not the case during times of economic recession such as occurred in the later decades of the nineteenth century and again in the 1930s. Hobson reasoned:

If ... there are goods which cannot get consumed, and if there is a quantity of capital and labour which cannot get full employment because its products cannot get consumed, the only possible explanation of this paradox is the refusal of owners of consuming power to apply that power in effective demand for commodities.[55]

Underconsumption was a result of too much saving and too little spending in the economy; in aggregate, the result was too little demand for commodities. Hobson's qualification of Say's Law was rooted in his belief in the possibility of oversaving, that is, levels of saving in excess of the future requirements of society and levels that compromise the levels of consumption presently. In *The Physiology of Industry*, Hobson and his co-author Mummery attempted to demonstrate, against the classical political economy orthodoxy, that general oversaving was both theoretically possible and actually the cause of industrial depression. According to their analysis, Say's Law did not operate because there was no rational mechanism to equate social saving and spending.

Mummery and Hobson argued that any individual in society could save as much of their income as they wished. This was possible because others committed to consume the saver's income now and remunerate them later. Individual consumption could be postponed to the limit of starvation if necessary, Hobson noted, somewhat scathingly.

There was, however, a limit to saving by society as a whole. Mummery and Hobson argued that there was an appropriate saving–spending ratio for the provision of a level of consumption presently and in the future. Social levels of saving could exceed requirements, thus depressing consumption currently and over-providing for capital supply in the future. The problem was, wrote Mummery and Hobson, that

the thrift of the community is composed of the thrift of individuals. It is clear, then, that if the united thrift of individuals passes the limit imposed by the interests of the community, thrift ceases to be as effectual as before, even from the individual's point of view; that is to say, though any individual may anticipate all future labour, every individual cannot.[56]

This is Hobson's 'any/every' paradox, a variant of his critique of the separatist fallacy, that parts can be considered in isolation from the organic whole that they make up. In contrast to the orthodox classical economic view, according to Mummery and Hobson, individual interests did not harmonise with or add up to the social interest:

> If the interests of each individual in the community were always identical with the interests of the community there could be no such thing as over-supply. It is impossible to suppose that a company of men, producing in common for the common good, would at any time produce more than required for consumption in the present or near future. It is, in fact, the clash of interests between the community as a whole and the individual members in respect to Saving, that is the cause of Over-supply.[57]

Scandalising other late-Victorian political economists, Mummery and Hobson exposed the fallacy of the virtue of individual thrift. Individual thrift, they claimed, could lead to socially detrimental effects.[58] Though they blamed the wealthier sections of society in particular, the logic of their argument merely suggested that individually rational saving did not accord with socially rational decisions.

Rebutting the classical political economists, Mummery and Hobson claimed that a cut in wages or employment to reduce costs or a drop in the rate of interest would not solve the problem. Instead, falling wages and interest rates were manifestations of and further contributors to economic depression because they acted to reduce consumption.[59] Mummery and Hobson's alternative solution was that the state should intervene to balance saving and spending at the appropriate societal level; specifically, expanding consumption relative to saving in periods of oversaving. Fighting a war as a large stimulus to consumption was one way of alleviating the problem, but there were other less destructive alternatives:

> [I]f the community, instead of expending its surplus accumulations in the endeavour to cut its members' throats, consented to increase its consumption of luxuries, or applied the surplus funds to the improvement of the condition of the working classes or the sanitation of its great towns, all the contingent economic advantage of a war would be reaped, and the direct advantage of increased consumption of luxuries, of an improved condition of labourers, or of sanitary towns would be obtained.[60]

It was this version of underconsumption that attracted the attention of John Maynard Keynes. Though it was overtaken in Hobson's work by the third explanation of underconsumption, the 'any/every' paradox reappeared in later work, in his account of the international aspects of the Great Depression. The oversaving explanation only appeared in its pure form in Hobson's collaboration with Mummery, which suggests that Mummery made the greater contribution, but the argument greatly influenced Hobson's economic thought and the any/every paradox was integral to his thinking.[61]

Underconsumption through maldistribution

Hobson argued that 'our main economic troubles are of a distinctively moral origin'.[62] Underconsumption was actually a social malady with an economic manifestation, depression of trade. The 'fundamental logic' of Hobson's third argument about underconsumption was 'that rents, excessive interest and profits constitute an irrational surplus income, the irrationality of which must be represented in an attempt to save and invest a larger proportion of the total income than can be utilised as capital'.[63] Say's Law did not work in practice because of the maldistribution of income in capitalist society.

In an early version of the argument, without a discussion of the influence of unproductive surplus, Hobson argued that distribution was the root cause of underconsumption:

> In a well-ordered society, where distribution of wealth as consuming power was proportioned either to the efforts or the needs of the producers, every increase in the powers of production of the community would automatically be attended by a corresponding rise in the general standard of consumption, effective demand rising to correspond with every increased power of supply.
>
> If, on the other hand, inequality of economic opportunities is such as to impose a grave inequality in the distribution of wealth, some classes getting a power of purchase greater than is required to supply legitimate and pressing needs, we have an economic condition which explains the paradox of over-production, under-consumption, and unemployment.[64]

Later, Hobson identified the source of the irrational surplus of income for certain classes by arguing, as we have seen, that under capitalism income and profits were distributed according to bargaining power, predominantly in favour of the capitalists themselves. Some sections of the community, i.e., the capitalists, got more than they deserved and some, i.e., the working class, less according to Hobson's criterion of needs in his human law of distribution. Maldistribution of income disrupted the 'economically sound ratio between saving and spending'.[65]

Where property is acquired by labour, involving personal cost, it is naturally and proportionately related to some personal utility of consumption. If all property and all purchasing power were apportioned in accordance with this natural law, no disequilibrium could arise between the rate of production and the rate of consumption.[66]

But if in any society you get considerable groups of men whose incomes come to them by others' toil instead of their own, and if these incomes are so large as to afford them little or no additional satisfaction by any considerable increase of their expenditure, [the] natural balancing of present against future enjoyment is upset.[67]

For the wealthy, the unproductive surplus that they had appropriated stimulated little or no desire to consume. Therefore, 'a large part of the surplus unearned income of the rich is found to be excessive, even for purposes of luxurious and wasteful consumption, and accumulates to form an investment fund of capital which is larger than is required'.[68] They saved too much and consumed too little. Furthermore, too little purchasing power was allocated to the working classes who would have consumed the extra income to improve their standard of living, reducing underconsumption.[69]

Thus, the workers had the desire but not the ability to consume, and the capitalists the ability but not the desire. The result was a failure of aggregate effective demand. However, the wealthy would attempt to invest their surplus income anyway. Maldistribution caused a disjunction of production and consumption, thus undoing Say's Law, because productive capacity increases despite insufficiency of demand. The ultimate outcome was trade depression with declines in prices, profits, and production. Unfortunately, these falls did not themselves solve the problem, as economists had claimed, because a decline in production reduced wages, but a reduction in wages in turn reduced effective demand.

Hobson's solution for underconsumption resulting from maldistribution was straightforward: tax unearned income from the wealthy and apply the funds raised either to public works, state-run industries or income redistribution. This would be both just and economically sound. He claimed that:

The application of this surplus ... to enlarge the spending power and consumption of the workers and the community, will remedy [the] chronic maladjustments [of saving and spending] by raising the aggregate power of consumption to keep pace with every increase of productive power.[70]

Critical commentary

The theory of underconsumption has been the focus of much critical attention but mainly outside the context of the rest of Hobson's work. The first criticisms of Hobson's theory of underconsumption came from those economists who had succeeded in excluding him from the economics profession. For these economists, the theory was the economic equivalent of claiming the earth was flat. A fall in the interest rate or in costs would restore equilibrium and prosperity, according to this argument.[71] However, as we have seen, Hobson had a reply to this charge and his emphasis on maldistribution further countered a proposed interest rate solution to underconsumption by suggesting that saving is more closely related to income than to the interest rate.

E. E. Nemmers has suggested that Hobson's account of underconsumption was 'realist', that is, it discounted the role of money as an active factor in the determination of economic activity. Hobson played down the influence of monetary factors and the role of credit in the trade cycle in his depreciation of other explanations of cyclical depressions and unemployment, from the classical arguments to the 'social credit' proposal of Major Douglas.[72] Nemmers also points out that Hobson understood investment as the extension of current productive potential, i.e., 'capital widening'. As Nemmers suggests, investment can also go towards 'capital deepening', the improvement of productive technique and the change of processes of production. Such use of capital might be much larger than Hobson anticipated, using up the surplus he identified.[73]

However, the 'root of Hobson's mistake' as identified by J. M. Keynes was his equation of saving and investment. This means that Hobson shared the classical economists' ideas that savings and investment are in equilibrium. The possibility of disequilibrium between saving and investment was one of the central tenets of the so-called Keynesian revolution in economics. Where Hobson believed that saving and investment were basically the same process, Keynes distinguished saving of funds from investment in plant and showed not only that they were separate processes but that they were carried out by different sections of the community, i.e., individual savers and institutional investors, such as banks. This distinction leads to the difference between Hobson and Keynes on the cause of deficient aggregate demand that both identified as the root of trade depression. For Hobson, oversaving was over-investment and meant underconsumption, through both too little aggregate demand and an excessive stimulus to production. For Keynes, oversaving meant underinvestment, that is, savings were not being translated into investment in capital goods understood as a form of consumption. Hobson's problem was too much capital investment; Keynes's was too little. Thus their proposals for recovery also differed: Hobson proposed redistribution in an attempt to increase aggregate demand for consumption goods; Keynes preferred government spending and direction of investment to make up the gap in investment and to restore aggregate demand through a stimulus to aggregate income. The implication follows that while Keynes called for deficit finance by the state, Hobson did not.[74]

In today's terminology, Hobson's maldistribution argument explains underconsumption as a result of a falling marginal propensity to consume with rising income. However, Hobson only hinted at this formulation of the problem, preferring instead to emphasise the surplus income of the wealthy as a cause of oversaving. This use of the surplus concept, often couched in organic terms, led Hobson astray, and could be the reason why Keynes felt the earlier Mummery-Hobson discussion to be more valuable.

It is easy to be unfair to Hobson, however; particularly, it is easy to fall into the anachronism of wondering why Hobson was not Keynes, as Clarke has put it.[75] For instance, the criticism that Hobson failed to distinguish savings and investment can be anachronistic. When Hobson was writing, economists had not distinguished the two functions, and it was only with Keynes that the distinction was drawn. Indeed, Hobson's and Keynes's theories may not be as irreconcilable as has been portrayed, and there have been attempts to systematise Hobson's theory into modern economic terms.[76]

Hobson's theory of underconsumption still has some value. The theory of underconsumption is a persuasive defence of the economy of high wages. But it is probably best understood as part of his theory of unproductive surplus and his moral and social critique of political economy and capitalist society. Generally, Hobson's explanation suggested that social equity would lead to efficiency, whereas, for Keynes, the requirement of efficiency could only be reached with some measure of equity. This might seem a fine distinction, but in terms of liberalism in the early part of this century it was significant.[77] Hobson's theory of underconsumption did, as Keynes pointed out, mark an epoch in economic thought. Hobson broadened the concerns of economics by highlighting important economic problems neglected or rationalised by classical and neo-classical economists, such as welfare, unemployment, poverty, depression, trade cycles, deficient demand, and the possibility of social and state remedies to economic problems.

CONCLUSION

This chapter has examined the role of the second of Hobson's two central concepts, the surplus. Hobson emphasised the importance of co-operation in all organic life, from the simplest organism to the most complex society. His theories of co-operative and unproductive surplus value provide the bases for a framework for economic, political and social life, nationally and internationally. The international aspect of the framework is the subject of the next chapter.

To sum up, the origin of social surplus was co-operative activity. The surplus is the fount of human progress providing the basis for improvements in welfare. Hobson believed that there was an evolutionary process towards increased organisation, and that welfare would be enhanced by social organisation and his human law of distribution. His theory of distribution accounts for the strife in capitalist society through the appropriation of the surplus by powerful sectional (usually business) interests, in violation of his law of distribution. Hobson called for state intervention and taxation policy to redistribute wealth according to his analysis.

Hobson's theory of underconsumption was not always a prominent part of his writing. Indeed, it is all but submerged in much of the first decade or so of the twentieth century; the theory of underconsumption was merged into his ideas on distribution and the unproductive surplus after *The Industrial System* in 1909. This period was also Hobson's more idealist phase in many respects, which might account for the playing down of his highly critical theory. It has also been suggested that Hobson was stung by the hostile reception of the *Physiology* and sought to diffuse the controversy in his later work. Underconsumption was resurrected during and after the First World War as an alternative explanation, first, for the economic dislocations in Europe immediately following the war and, later, as an alternative to monetary explanations of the Great Depression of the thirties, as well as other radical and left-wing diagnoses.[78]

While he was usually concerned with the domestic social and economic policy implications of underconsumption, the theory had wider significance in, for example, the theory of imperialism. In trying to avoid the losses associated with a depression in trade, those with surplus income were prompted to look for investment opportunities abroad, Hobson argued. Another tactic was the dumping of consumption goods on foreign markets in order to maintain prices at home.[79] According to Hobson, both these pressures, but especially capital export, contributed to the drive to modern imperialism considered in chapter 5.

CHAPTER 4

An evolutionary framework for international relations

The organic analogy and theories of surplus value discussed in the previous chapters were the basis of Hobson's holistic and evolutionary framework for his analysis of international relations. Utilising the organic and surplus concepts, Hobson created a novel approach to international relations, the pinnacle of which was a new liberal internationalism, his conception of an emergent world society being forged by international co-operation and organisation.

The holistic aspect of the framework, the application of the organic analogy to all humanity and international relations, is investigated first. Hobson's world was not made up of interacting states but was rather a network of individuals, groups and communities within a single world society. He also considered nations from an organic perspective, both nationally and globally. The second section delimits four types of international system in Hobson's writings on international relations. They constitute the evolutionary framework, linked together by the logic of co-operative and unproductive surpluses.

AN ORGANIC PERSPECTIVE ON INTERNATIONAL RELATIONS

Hobson viewed international relations as one facet of a society of all mankind. This perspective was clearly internationalist, reflecting 'the idea that we both are and should be part of a broader community than that of the nation or the state'.[1] For Hobson:

> Internationalism, as a policy of peace and progress, demands that the individual feelings of goodwill which give substance to the smaller groupings, from family to nation, shall be so extended that the single citizen of England, America, Germany, France, Russia, shall supersede the governments of these countries as units of internationalism.[2]

Internationalism, in Hobson's writings, is marked both by the peaceful relations of states regularised in intergovernmental organisations and by transnational relations of groups and individuals, though Hobson generally characterised progress in internationalism in terms of improvements in the latter.[3] He was hoping for

> the displacement of national by human sentiment, involving a willingness to sacrifice the interest of one's own nation for the general good of humanity, ... the spirit needed to make the mind of modern man conform to the moral and economic fabric of the world in which we live.[4]

The organic analogy applied to international relations rejects a state-centric approach. If humanity is conceived as a social organism, interstate relations appear as just one part of a global society of all humanity. Hobson suggested that the international realm is an integral part of social life and cannot be understood apart from it. International relations is conceived as one of the outer set of concentric circles of social life. The organic analogy applied to humanity did not lead Hobson to cosmopolitanism, that is, to conceive of humanity as a global mass society of isolated individuals. Instead, Hobson argued that '[e]veryone lives in a series of concentric circles of association which affect him in general as a human being. Such are the home, the neighbourhood (village or town), his class, his country, the world.'[5] This is a vision of a world society of overlapping groups and affiliations, in which nations and international relations are only one facet. Nevertheless, as the widest political expression of solidarity, nations (and by implication, therefore, states also) have an important place in his conception of international relations.

According to Hobson, at the level of human development achieved by the early twentieth century, social problems could only be solved rationally by starting with 'the hypothesis of humanity as itself a collective organism'.[6] Rational solutions to international problems would be international. However, while communications were widening and deepening the international interdependence of social relations, Hobson was not prompted to propose a unified world state. He argued along similar lines to his rebuttal of the Idealist conception of the state, that national and international interests should be balanced.

Nevertheless, contemporary international relations was disorganised. The political division of the world into a system of states did not express humanity's organic unity. The appropriate organic principle for the government of human affairs globally was federalism, according to Hobson. He argued that a federation of nations as a world organisation provided

> an economy of government, each area, from the family through the widening areas of local and national government to internationalism, practising free self-government in such matters as fall predominantly within the compass of its own knowledge, interest and capacity ... Its moral root lies in the basic concept of fraternity, interpreted in various phases and areas of the common life, the humanity which binds man to man ever more closely as civilisation furnishes closer and more numerous modes of communication, material, intellectual and moral.[7]

This conception of federalism permitted international control, while at the same time acknowledging the separate features of individual nations.

Nations, nationalism and internationalism

Nations were central to Hobson's conception of internationalism. During his long writing career, Hobson held a number of different and sometimes conflicting opinions on nations and nationalism. Hobson considered nations as organic unities.[8] Unlike many writers of his time, he clearly distinguished nation, state and government and in his internationalism emphasised the importance of nations as collectivities of people, over the latter, abstract forms of administration.[9]

In his earlier writings, as exemplified by *Imperialism*, Hobson maintains an orthodox nineteenth-century liberal perspective on nations, nationality and nationalism that owes a lot to John Stuart Mill. Nations were the foundations of internationalism, a key feature of civilisation, and a beneficial social form resulting from and in turn encouraging the healthy co-operation that had ended local particularism in the nineteenth century. Nationalism was also a force for the good because it was the political expression of the desire of nations for self-government.[10] In Hobson's view '[n]ationalism is a plain highway to internationalism'. Not only was national self-government the first step to internationalism, but internationalism would not merit its name without self-respecting nations. In *Imperialism* and in later work, Hobson contrasted internationalism with cosmopolitanism:

> A true strong internationalism in form or spirit would ... imply the existence of powerful self-respecting nationalities which seek union on the basis of common national needs. Such a historical development would be far more

conformable to laws of social growth than the rise of anarchic cosmopolitanism from individual units amid the decadence of national life.[11]

Cosmopolitanism disregarded the importance of nations and nationality, and of other groups or cultures, in the creation of world order. It was the global manifestation of the social atomism Hobson so despised. He rejected the cosmopolitan view that considered each person an isolated individual apart from their allegiances and background.

Though he rejected what might be called cultural cosmopolitanism, in his later work Hobson supported the cosmopolitanism of global capitalism and the world market. He often approvingly called this economic internationalism and failed to acknowledge that, contrary to his humanistic conception of welfare, it rendered everyone an 'economic man', and in addition reduced the significance of nations or nationalism, also contrary to his organic perspective.[12]

In line with his growing approval of economic internationalism, Hobson modified his opinion of nations and nationalism. Applauding global financial integration and attacking economic nationalism, Hobson became a strident critic of nationalism and of the sovereign state. With the exception of his most extreme writings on economic internationalism, Hobson maintained his belief in the importance of nations to internationalism. On the other hand, nationalism, which began as a beneficent force, became for Hobson a separatist, exclusive and aggressive ideology, to be strongly opposed in the cause of advancing civilisation. After the First World War, he argued that capitalism and nationalism, as joined in imperialism in particular, were the twin threats to civilisation.[13] With the defeats for democracy, peace and internationalism in the 1930s, Hobson retreated to an idea of internationalism which was a halfway house between a world policy and nationalism.[14] Later still, he began to stress the requirement of a reformed sense of nationhood that would have to come before, rather than in conjunction with, internationalism. At the end of his life he was urging that each nation should put its own social, political and economic house in order before internationalism could succeed.[15]

In advancing his vision of internationalism, Hobson had to counter a number of prevalent arguments that the nation was the outer limit of social co-operation and that systematic international co-operation in the general interest was impossible. The first of these was a sociological argument that the state was the limit of people's 'consciousness of kind'. People only had a limited ability to feel community with others and a national society was its greatest extent. Hobson conceded that a problem with the conception of humanity as a social organism was that there was little feeling for its existence among people at large. He agreed that people were more concerned with, and possessed more knowledge of, their own situation, their family and their friendship ties. He denied, however, that this could be made the basis of a permanent obstruction to international understanding or that such sympathy as was needed for a global social organism, in fact, halted at state boundaries.[16] Hobson re-emphasised 'social instincts, and the loyalties and ideals which flow with them, [that] work through a series of concentric circles of widening area and weaker feeling, from the close circle of the home to the wide limits of humanity'.[17] While such feeling for humanity might be weak, it did exist and indeed was growing. In any case this feeling for others was not held in perpetuity within the national state. Growing international intercourse, especially in commerce, increased nations' reliance on each other and also their mutual sympathy, as '[c]ivilisation has expanded areas and weakened narrower loyalties'.[18] Hobson also claimed that education would overcome national separatism and extend the range of human sympathy. Education would lead people to make welfare valuations based on criteria wider than the nation. Finally, he suggested that experience of international co-operation and organisation would itself inculcate a broader sense of the meaning of internationalism.[19]

State sovereignty and international federation

A second set of arguments positing the impossibility of Hobson's internationalism rested on the importance of state sovereignty. Sovereign states would be unlikely to give up their central role in deciding international policy. One variant of this argument suggested that the historical record showed that states had not given up their sovereign powers in the past and were not likely to in the near future. Another variant argued that on legal and philosophical grounds there was no reason why sovereign states should give up their powers.

Hobson, on the other hand, was a fervent critic of sovereignty. He argued that state sovereignty was the corollary in international relations of individualism or separatism. It was a failure to acknowledge the increasing connectedness and interdependence of the society of nations. Following a conventional liberal argument, he opposed sovereignty as an absolutist doctrine and described it as empirically inaccurate. Hobson objected to the state drawing under one authority the right to decide policy on social, political and economic issues without recourse to reason or even to reasonable discussion. Actions taken purely according to sovereign right were likely to be irrational from the point of view of human welfare, he argued.[20]

Hobson criticised sovereignty as an outdated doctrine no longer reflecting the true interests of the several national elements of humankind. It was, indeed, an obstruction to civilisation as it educated habits of thought opposed to the developing co-operation of humanity. Hobson claimed that sovereignty encouraged a power-oriented view of the world and that this view reinforced the anarchy of international relations.[21] The dogmas of absolute sovereignty fed by the doctrines of nationalism were fomenting international conflict and preventing rational international intercourse. Finally, sovereignty was an obstruction to the ultimate construction of an international government and co-operation between nations because of its emphasis on separate national interests; 'being the judge in your own cause' was the root problem of sovereignty, as it privileged national interests over the global common good.[22] Hobson's new liberal version of internationalism based on an organic world society rejected the claims of priority of separate national interests over the general international interest. For Hobson, national separatism was harmful to the whole of humanity and also to the members of that nation. He argued that:

> History is rife with instances where fear, hubris, or hate, rushes nations into wasteful or destructive wars. So likewise the narrow selfishness of small group-life everywhere cramps the progress of humanity, the preference of our city to our country, our empire to the world, in matters where the wider is the truer economy.[23]

Following his organic analogy, the way forward was to organise international relations along the lines of the principle of federalism. Arguing against the absolute right of national sovereign independence, Hobson claimed that:

> The principle of federalism must qualify the principle of self-determination. This is the harmony of unity and diversity as it shows itself in every field of conduct. Autonomy so far as aims are separate, union so far as they are identical. Federation connotes the political harmony of the opposing principles. Upon every scale of social co-operation, from family to humanity, the problem is continually before us.[24]

He suggested therefore that the international government should be organised according to the twin concepts of federalism and autonomy. Reflecting the concentric circles of community, autonomy did not require, Hobson argued, full sovereign rights in the form of a nation-state. Autonomy could be achieved within the current states, once they had been reformed and democratised, he argued.[25]

Luckily, he observed, sovereignty was increasingly being tempered by obligations under international law and by the growth of international interdependence brought on by trade, travel and so on, despite governments' attempts to control national economies.[26] Attempts at economic planning and control were hindered and often nullified by the cross-national links of the world economy.[27]

An organic world society or a simplistic domestic analogy?

It might be argued that Hobson's organic perspective on international relations was premised on a faulty domestic analogy, the analogy between domestic society and international relations in institutions, theories or units of analysis. Classically, the domestic analogy has entailed the advocacy of the creation of institutions for international relations along the lines of successful domestic institutions or arrangements.[28] His analogy of society to an organism usually refers to domestic society, and applying it beyond the context of the national state to interstate relations or to global society rests on domestic rather than international experience or at most on guesswork about tendencies in international relations. Indeed, Hobson wrote that his proposals for an international government involved 'the introduction of no new political principle, but only an extension of that moving force of the mutuality of interests which has everywhere and always been operative upon smaller areas'.[29]

There are two variants of the domestic analogy in Hobson's writings on international relations. The first is a straightforward application of an analogy between nations in international society and persons in domestic society. For instance, Hobson argues that 'just as an individual can only fully realise his personality in a society of other individuals, that is, a nation, so nations cannot rise to the full stature of nationalism save in a society of nations'.[30] However, this is underlain by a more pervasive, yet more subtle use of the analogy. Hobson's international (or world) society is merely a domestic society writ large. He applies his concepts to international relations with little reflection that they might be specific to domestic, frequently Western, or even just British society.

There are three types of criticisms of the domestic analogy that might apply to Hobson's international thought. First, even if an international society can be said to exist, it is not similar enough to the domestic realm for the unreflective import of domestic institutions and theory into the international realm. Second, it is simply illegitimate to draw an analogy between a domestic society populated by individual human beings and an international society populated by states. There are too many disanalogies: states do not sleep, for instance! Third, and related to the second point, the domestic analogy is flawed because international politics has to deal with the contrasting obligations of people as citizens and as humans.[31]

While superficially a serious problem for Hobson's international thought, the charge of domestic analogy is in fact rather weak. Hobson was as likely to reverse the analogy and import international analogies to discuss, for example, domestic industrial strife, as in *The Conditions of Industrial Peace.* Here, industrial conflict is compared to international war, and the lessons from the international arena are re-imported to domestic affairs. Thus, industries' 'present condition, regarded from the standpoint of human security, appears analogous to the wider political groupings within the various countries, which, by repressing internal conflicts and establishing strong States, enlarged the areas of hostility and made warfare more destructive than before'.[32] Much the same can be said of Hobson's use of the term 'balance of power' in the context of domestic politics. Thus, there is an exchange of metaphors between international and domestic affairs in Hobson's writings rather than a mere application of domestic examples to international relations.

Hobson did refer to international changes permitting the extension of domestic principles to international relations. Such recourse to evidence or principles from the world of international affairs refutes the charge of the domestic analogy relying solely on evidence drawn from the domestic sphere.[33] Hobson argued that communications and facilities for travel had improved, and that institutions such as the Permanent Court of Arbitration and other international arrangements were the basis of the change in international relations.[34] Such reference to changes in the conduct of international relations suggests that Hobson's proposals for international institutional reform are based on an understanding of the changing nature of the international system, not merely an analogy to domestic arrangements. Thus, Hobson's references to the increasing institutionalisation of the Concert of Europe and the developments in the Hague somewhat mitigate the claims that his internationalism was a case of straightforward domestic analogy.[35]

One of the criticisms of Hobson's organic analogy cited in chapter 2 was that it committed him to an isomorphism of all social forms. But this criticism and the domestic analogy critique cannot both be right, and the former holds more water. For instance, Hobson believed that federalism could appropriately be applied to all organic systems including the international system.[36] Hobson's organic analogy blurs the hard and fast division of the social world into domestic society and international relations which is at the core of the domestic analogy. For Hobson, social life is, as we saw, constituted of a series of organic systems overlaid on each other in concentric circles.

THE THEORIES OF SURPLUS VALUE AND FOUR TYPES OF INTERNATIONAL SYSTEM

The two sides of Hobson's theory of surplus value, the co-operative entailing the evolution of social life towards increasing organisation, and the unproductive causing political and economic conflict, generate the two major aspects of Hobson's analysis of international relations: his optimistic, reformist writings on internationalism on the one hand, and his gloomy prognosis of current international relations, especially his writings on imperialism, on the other. The world was becoming increasingly organised, according to Hobson. Struggles over the surplus are superimposed on this secular progress of organisation in international relations to define four types of international system in Hobson's writings: the balance of power, Cobdenism, imperialism, and new liberal internationalism.[37]

Balance of power

Hobson used the term Hobbes–Machiavellianism, and occasionally Prussianism, to refer to this international system in which there was little co-operation between states and precious little organisation.[38] The balance-of-power system was made up of morally self-contained states interacting through the official contacts of traditional diplomacy or through the physical force of war or armed intervention. But essentially the international balance of power was a war-system. Its operation rested on military force, both in terms of maintenance and change. It lacked moral community and instead emphasised the 'splendid isolation' of states. Its economic corollary was autarky or mercantilism.

Hobson savagely criticised this type of international system and its proponents. He labelled moral isolationism in international relations, the 'fundamental vice' of traditional foreign policy:

> this false, immoral doctrine, inimical to humanity, that a State is an absolute morally self-contained being, living in a world with other similar beings, but owing no duties to them and bound by no obligations that it may not break on the plea of necessity . . . [39]

Following Cobden and Bright, Hobson saw the balance of power as the doctrine of a self-aggrandising foreign office keen to interfere in other peoples' affairs and a government which distracted its electors from domestic social reform with foreign quarrels.[40] It was also a 'vile idol', sought by states competing for security through arms races and psychological warfare, and as such was the root cause of international discord. For instance, according to Hobson, the First World War was a result of the secret treaties, covert diplomacy and competitive foreign policies in the pre-war balance among the Great Powers, especially outside Europe.[41]

While his views owed something to Cobden's critique of Palmerstonian foreign policy, and were also influenced by the impact of the First World War, Hobson generalised his criticisms and synthesised them with his new liberal approach. The balance of power was a disorganised and decentralised system that was irrational from the organic point of view. The international balance of power 'present[ed] no true harmony of interest and no organic policy'.[42] He rejected all balances of power, whether domestic or international, because they failed to provide justice: 'the term Balance of Power resolves itself into a policy of Pulls, distribution alike of effort and of product being determined by the relative strength of the parties or groups'. Furthermore, the balance of power was an international equivalent of *laissez-faire*, where states controlled their own territory exclusively, including the economy if they wished. On the other hand, it denied the propriety of interference by other states or international organisations in their so-called internal affairs. As with his theory of distribution, where there was no central mechanism for allocating benefits or settling disputes in capitalism, force became the *ultima ratio*; the powerful won in the resolution of conflicts and the distribution of resources. The inequitable distribution of income he so fiercely attacked in the domestic context was also the result of the logic of a balance of power. In any case, the international balance-of-power system was in principle flawed because balance did not mean equilibrium or justice. It was therefore fraught with the potential for future conflict because of its manifest injustice.[43]

Hobson called the balance of power the 'core of diplomatic falsehood'.[44] Balance of power was the traditional view and operating premise of traditional statecraft and political conservatives. It was promulgated in the academic context by a *Realpolitik* school of political theorists.[45] The realist view of international relations persisted despite growing international interdependence through trade and cultural exchange in part because of the seductive use of mechanical metaphors. Descriptions of nation-states as Powers, great or small, Hobson claimed, were naive records of what politics actually meant.[46] What it actually meant in this international system was the divorce of politics from ethics in the dictum, 'might is right'. 'The fact that peoples are related to one another in the world not as groups of human beings, with the common quality and interests of humanity, but as Powers,' he said, 'is a stark negation of all morality in international relations.'[47] It was also, following his organic analogy, a reduction of organic relations to mechanically related components. Despite international law and treaties, states arrogated to themselves the right to breach commitments according to their own national interests. For Hobson,

> the actual history of treaty obligations indicates that a nation, as a moral personality, is on a lower level of development than an individual ... A nation, in its political aspect as a State, using as an instrument a Government, is not fully realised as a moral being, a personality at all.[48]

Hobson claimed that the different ethics of individuals in society on the one hand and nations in a society of nations on the other implied 'a feebler development of moral personality in the Nation, and a feebler structure of international society'.[49]

Hobson, however, expected this to change. Indeed, it was already changing: moral isolation and mercantilism were increasingly outmoded and obsolete.

> [T]hat political and moral isolation and self-sufficiency, only qualified by agreements or conventions of no final validity, has, under conditions of modern intercourse, given place to an ever closer and more intricate

internationalism ... Under the old philosophy there was no 'society of nations'. States moved 'like dragons of the prime' or like stars in their courses. Now the facts of intercourse have brought into being a rudimentary Society of Nations ...[50]

With growing interaction, states sought more commitments through treaties, international conferences and alliances, and thus increasingly found themselves bound by international law.[51] Hobson was convinced that the advances in communications between nations had rendered the teachings of the *Realpolitik* school unrealistic. For Hobson, interaction between peoples was both inevitable and beneficial; anything that opposed international intercourse, such as realist rhetoric in the study of international relations and the imperialist rhetoric of certain politicians and businessmen, was hindering the progress of civilisation.[52]

Cobdenism

The second type of international system operated according to Richard Cobden's maxim: 'As little intercourse as possible between *Governments*; as much connection as possible between the nations of the world.'[53] This international system consisted of self-governing political communities trading separately and travelling freely, interacting as much as possible, but not interfering in each other's political affairs. Government, both national and international, was reduced to a minimum, its goals limited to the maintenance of law and order, to liberate the intercourse between people and peoples. This was an international society of peoples or nations, not of governments or states. It was premised on the extension of democratic national self-government that also contributed to a pacific international environment.[54] While the balance-of-power system rested on the acts of politicians and diplomats, Hobson interpreted Cobden's doctrine as suggesting that '[i]f the peoples are to get into sane, amicable and profitable relations with one another, that intercourse is best promoted by leaving it to them, with as little interference as possible either in the way of help or hindrance by their respective Governments'.[55] Cobdenism was thus an improvement on the balance of power, because while it was based on *laissez-faire*, this was now applied also to governments' dealings with their own and other peoples. The *laissez-faire* of the balance of power was exercised internationally as part of domestic political power, whereas in Cobdenism it was associated with the economic welfare of ordinary citizens.

There were two sides to Cobdenism: the negative political principle of non-intervention and the positive economic doctrine of free trade. Non-intervention was 'the negative condition' of free human co-operation:

> Remove the fetters and obstructions which governments, laws, and customs have placed upon the free play of the harmonious forces which bind man to man, let their real community of interest have full sway to express itself in economic, intellectual and moral intercourse, the false antagonisms which now divide nations, classes and individuals, will disappear and a positive harmony of mankind be established.[56]

Hobson argued that non-intervention was an antidote to the interference from feudal aristocracies and their influence: 'by removing the active obstacles of diplomacy, war, and protective tariffs it enabled the mutual interests and good feelings of the peoples to operate freely'.[57]

In Cobdenism, while all relations between nations were important, trade was the most important of all, particularly in the encouragement of pacific and civilised relations. Free trade was the positive doctrine of Cobdenism. Cobden himself claimed that 'commerce is the great panacea, which, like a beneficent medical discovery, will serve to inoculate with the healthy and saving taste for civilisation all the nations of the world'.[58] For Hobson, 'commerce has always been the greatest civiliser of mankind. All other fruits of civilisation have travelled along trade routes ... Cut off commerce, and you destroy every mode of higher intercourse.'[59] 'The more numerous and higher tariff barriers by which each nation seeks to minimise its co-operation with its neighbour ...', Hobson continued, was 'a continuous source of friction and ill-will.'[60] And he followed Norman Angell in extending Cobdenite principles to the growth of international finance: 'Modern finance is the great sympathetic system in an economic organism in which political divisions are of constantly diminishing importance'.[61]

Cobdenism as an international system implied the autonomy of politics and economics. It also entailed an international corollary of *laissez-faire*, rejecting any extensive role of states (either severally or in concert) in the running of their economies or remedying social inequity, or of the construction of any international organisation for such a purpose. Free trade was the corollary of *laissez-faire* in international economic relations, non-intervention its corollary in international politics. Therefore, while a certain degree of political separateness between national groups was maintained, this was within the general conception of a world that encouraged international commercial and cultural exchange and co-operation. Both the moralistic tone of non-intervention and the economic verities of free trade were challenges to the *Realpolitik* vision of the international system. Non-intervention brought morality into interstate relations; free trade suggested that international interaction was beneficial and that there was a harmony of interests between peoples.

The First World War, in particular, exposed the frailties of the international system of Cobdenism. After the War, with the rise of economic and political instability, Hobson acknowledged the limits of free trade and called for more state and international intervention to remedy economic ills and limit the private right of states to go to war. The experience of the War taught Hobson that international law and the sense of justice would be insufficient to maintain international peace.[62]

Imperialism

The dramatic experiences of the Boer War and the First World War stimulated Hobson to apply his theories of the co-operative surplus and, particularly, of the unproductive surplus to international relations. Hobson's theory of imperialism, though it has been reduced on innumerable occasions to a set of simplistic propositions, was in fact multifaceted and complex. Indeed, there were at least four dimensions to Hobson's analysis of imperialism. The details and relationship of these various understandings of imperialism are taken up in the next chapter. For now it is useful to note that he meant a modern phenomenon that he often, though not always, described as the new imperialism. In Hobson's writings this imperialism is the domination and dictatorial rule of a foreign people; an aggressive and acquisitive foreign policy; an international system of competing empires; and a phase in world politics. The latter two are pertinent in terms of Hobson's framework for international relations. Imperialism as an international phenomenon resulted from the expropriation of the unproductive surplus by sectional interests, both nationally and internationally, according to Hobson. Writing at the turn of the century, the new imperialism constituted 'the most powerful movement in the current politics of the Western world'.[63]

Hobson usually dated the phase of modern imperialism as beginning in the mid-1880s. He sometimes gives the more precise date, 1884, the year that the Great Powers discussed the division of Africa into spheres of influence at the Congo Conference. This conference and the subsequent treaty highlighted the attempt to settle the rival claims of the imperial powers. Though a superficial contribution to peace for Europe and possibly the world, Hobson thought the collusion in territorial division unlikely to hold because of underlying factors leading to international competition, such as growing concentration of economic monopoly and the aggrandising rivalry of the imperial Powers. Another date for the beginning of the new imperialist phase of modern politics was 1870–1, the unification of Germany and the Franco-Prussian War. This marked the beginning of Germany's challenge to Britain's ascendancy in international relations.[64] The exact date is less important than Hobson's explanation of what had transpired to change national and international politics.

According to Hobson, the new imperialism was a pathological social form in international relations. In terms of ideology, it was a return to *Realpolitik* with a vengeance.

> The exclusive interest of an expanding nation, interpreted by its rulers at some given moment, and not the good of the whole world, is seen to be the dominant motive in each new assumption of control over the tropics and lower peoples; that national interest itself commonly signifies the direct material self-interest of some small class of traders, mine-owners, farmers, or investors who wish to dispose of the land and labour of the lower peoples for their private gain.[65]

Yet Hobson had doubted the viability and equity of Cobdenism as an international system since his analysis of international finance in his *Imperialism* in the first decade of the twentieth century. For Hobson, the significant development in world economics and politics was the growth of combination and the decline of competition, in industrial and financial cartels and monopolies and in political empires. Combination rendered the autonomy of politics and economics, central to both the balance-of-power system and Cobdenism, an untenable premise. Hobson's theory of the co-operative surplus showed that co-operation and organisation were replacing competition. In the context of a modern industrial society, this meant that *laissez-faire* was giving way to the control of the economy by combines, trusts and monopolies. In world politics, it meant that the system of relatively independent nations interacting was no longer possible, and also that the simple harmony of self-interest did not work in international relations either.

The modern world was being divided into spheres by competing empires, the political equivalent of monopolies, vying for supremacy.[66]

Hobson noted that the most significant modern development in international relations resulting from the growth in size and numbers of industrial combination was the development of a truly global world economy, whose indicators were the rise of foreign investment and the internationalisation of capital that had overtaken the importance of international trade. In the theory of co-operative surplus, international finance can be read as the 'highest' level of international economic co-operation. Imperialism, the increasing contact between 'advanced' nations and 'backward' peoples, the end of *laissez-faire* and free trade, were all inevitable by-products of developments from the co-operative surplus. 'Hands off' relations between firms, corporations, peoples and governments were no longer possible in the emerging global economy and world society.

On the other hand, the way in which imperialism transcended Cobdenism as an international system and its conflictual nature was determined by its basis in the expropriation of unproductive surplus by capitalists and imperialists. Hobson argued that in the capitalist system economic surpluses appropriated by the powerful or wealthy for their own ends issue internationally in a drive for imperial ascendancy in the world.[67] The rise of industrial and political combination, and the merging of these political and economic sectional interests, turned on its head the Cobdenite equation of economic relations with peace. In the modern phase of world politics marked by imperialism, economic relations between nations, or especially empires, were now the source of war.[68]

From Hobson's organic perspective of a world society, imperialism was a form of separatism – a denial of the global benefits of international co-operation and organisation – produced in part by separatism within the national societies. Imperialism modified the logic of the division of labour of Cobdenism, that the wider area reaps greater benefits, by applying the logic only to areas under the political control of the state and resorting to protection of those areas. Hobson rejected this, asserting that national or imperial boundaries were not limits to economic intercourse or benefits therefrom. Hobson also objected to the political and moral aspects of imperialism, based as they were, in part on a throwback to the moral isolation of *Realpolitik* and in part on the social-Darwinist theories of the 'survival of the fittest'.[69]

Imperialism was also sectionalism in the sense that a group of international financiers were identified by Hobson as predominant in this stage of world politics. Financiers, who had a significant and beneficial role to play in the growing world economy, were exploiting political division and nationalist ideologies in their own interests.[70] Sectionalism in international relations was also manifested in nationalistic and racialistic ideologies, such as the idea of Manifest Destiny, the provision of 'good government', the pressure of population and the Christian civilising mission.[71] Hobson described the wealthy nations' exploitation of the backward peoples as parasitism. The wealthy few lived off the majority of workers, not only in their own country but in the empire.[72] Concentration, far from being the rational control from the centre, became for Hobson not only a description of modern industry, but the quality that allows finance to dominate other interests: 'the financial interest has those qualities of concentration and clear-sighted calculation which are needed to set Imperialism to work'.[73]

New liberal internationalism

In contrast to imperialism, new liberal internationalism returned to the freedom of international intercourse and the possibility of co-operation for the international good in Cobdenism. However, emphasising growing combination, interdependence and co-operation in international relations, Hobson argued that philosophically it was time to move beyond Cobden's formulation of liberal internationalism:

> Modern internationalists are no longer mere non-interventionalists, for the same reason that modern Radicals are no longer philosophic individualists. Experience has forced upon them the truth that governments are not essentially and of necessity the enemies of personal or national liberty, but that upon certain conditions they may become its creators, either by removing fetters or by furnishing the instruments of active co-operation by which both individuals and nations better realise themselves.[74]

Following his ideas on rationality, co-operation and organisation, Hobson believed that 'conscious collective self-control ... [would] enlarg[e] the orderly political government of the single city or the nation state to that society of nations which comprises mankind'.[75] International co-operation was based in 'rational idealism'.

> [T]he co-operation of one personality with others in membership of a society [was] continually widening so as to comprise in closer contacts the entire body

of contemporaneous mankind, while continually extending its outlook, so as to pay regard to the more distant welfare of humanity.[76]

New liberal internationalism was Hobson's ideal for international relations.[77] But it was based not in sentiments and beliefs. The organisation of international relations now merited it:

There is in the modern widening of human intercourse a large and various growth of common interests and activities among men of different nations which for certain purposes requires and evokes the friendly co-operation of States and calls into being genuinely international institutions.[78]

Hobson argued that the rise of industrialism and the use of machine technology had transformed modern societies and brought them into closer contacts with each other, through improved communication and the growth of mass-production techniques. Increased financial integration of the world was making for a truly world economy, merging together the separate national economies.[79] With the advent of a world economy, co-operation was already international, and Hobson believed that it was time for international control and organisation to regulate and mitigate the excesses of the world market as had been done with capitalism in the domestic context because '[t]he chief desiderata of economic welfare, productivity, and economic justice, are impractical without international government'. 'Real internationalism', he argued, 'means that nations and their governments shall consciously realise and co-operate in achieving common forms of welfare, positive in their nature and consciously conducive to the prosperity of the world.'[80]

Hobson proposed the governance of international relations through increased governmental intervention, both at the national level and in concert at the international level. International organisations, both inter-governmental and non-governmental, and perhaps a central international government to manage human welfare, were also required. The institutional form of his new liberal internationalist ideal was a loose international federation with associated functional organisations.[81]

Hobson expected political internationalism to be shaped by, yet facilitate and further encourage, the growing international cultural and economic intercourse. At first, arrangements would be *ad hoc* and private, but increasingly governments would become involved in dealing with common interests and issues largely (though not exclusively) concerning technical matters, specifically regarding communications, as seen in the emergence of the functional international bodies such as the Inter-Telegraphic Union and the Universal Postal Union. There were also the Hague conferences, establishing general treaties and codifying international law. Hobson regarded the greater institutionalisation of the relations of the Great Powers in the Concert of Europe as a precursor to an international government that he hoped would be found in the League of Nations.[82]

Hobson also proposed international organisation to co-ordinate intergovernmental co-operation for reconstruction in Europe after the First World War. For Hobson, the inter-war period was a time when humanity had to face the task of reconstructing domestic and international, social, political and economic arrangements after the dislocations and destruction of the Great War and the mistakes of the Bad Peace.[83]

Hobson's proposals for an international government varied. Before the First World War they were for the most part rather vague. In *Imperialism*, Hobson proposed international government as one of the necessary elements of a just solution to the problem of the development of backward countries, as an institution to oversee the control of world population growth and as a guardian of free trade.[84] The ideal of internationalism conveyed in his books on human welfare, and even more so in his books on the economic maladies of the Depression period, was an international government supervising a global redistribution of wealth to avoid the world-wide underconsumption. For example:

> Closer and more effective international movements for such improvements in the distribution of income as will enable world consumption to keep pace with and stimulate improvements in production, form the foundation of the progressive economy and the humaner civilisation of the future.[85]

However, it was the First World War that prompted Hobson to formulate a scheme for an international government. Though even this was, he admitted, only an outline, the emphasis on peace and security in *Towards International Government* contrasted markedly with his earlier emphasis on modifying the relations of powerful and weak states and his later expansive ideas on global human welfare.

THE EVOLUTION OF INTERNATIONAL RELATIONS

The four types of international system that make up Hobson's framework for understanding international relations are a product of his organic analogy and the two sides of his theory of surplus value when they are applied to international relations. The evolutionary scale that underlies the framework is created specifically by Hobson's understanding of co-operative surplus; he implicitly suggested a progression from the balance of power, the least co-operative and organised international system, through Cobdenism to his new liberal internationalism, the most organised and co-operative system, with imperialism a dangerous deviant pathology in contemporary international relations. According to the logic of Hobson's theory of co-operative surplus, international relations is in principle both the highest and last social system. In the view of the world as an expanding circle of order and rationality, rational ordering of global relations will constitute the achievement of the highest global welfare for all of humanity, through the co-ordination and organisation of the co-operative surplus of the nations of the world.[86] Having the widest scope of co-operation, it was, however, also to be the last to be organised. Yet, Hobson found evidence of growing international economic, cultural and other links demonstrating that civilised nations were by their nature interdependent, and that the more civilised nations became, the more interdependent they had to become.[87]

While Hobson had high hopes for new liberal internationalism, his evolutionary approach made him bluntly realistic in his assessment of morality in the conduct of contemporary international relations. For Hobson, the contemporary society of nations was a primitive, emergent community rather than a fully established and organised society. Because international relations was a relatively undeveloped realm of co-operation, Hobson did not expect morality to be well developed either. In the current state of international relations, Hobson noted, economic actors, institutions and processes were more likely to be international than political actors, and distribution according to needs was absent. Moreover, *laissez-faire* predominated politically in the form of the balance of power, imperialism and the primacy of national interest, and economically in free trade and the 'open door' for Western economic exploitation of 'backward' peoples. Hobson accounted for international conflict through his theory of unproductive surplus. Because of the pervasive struggle over, and appropriation of, unproductive surplus and the lack of any global authority or morality to prevent this struggle, contemporary international relations, despite its increasing organisation, was dominated by imperialism, a retrogressive stage of separatism, conflict and the use of force.

In addition to the evolution towards increasing interdependence, co-operation and organisation incorporated in the framework of the four international systems, the relationship of politics and economics also changed. In the balance of power and Cobdenism, economics and politics were autonomous spheres. In imperialism, combination in industry (monopolies) and in politics (empires and federations) was merged political and economic power, extended beyond national boundaries.

The framework of international systems also provided Hobson with a version of international history and a typology of ideologies in international relations. The international systems represented periods in recent and future history. They also represented for Hobson the dominant ideology of each phase of history and the contending ideologies of the time Hobson was writing. Balance of power was the predominant vision of the international system in the pre-Industrial Revolution era. It reflected a world before the rise of machine production and communications had undermined national isolation.[88] Cobdenism was ascendant in the mid-nineteenth century, coinciding with the *Pax Britannica* (of which Cobdenism was an important ideology). This period had closed with the rise of imperial activity in the late nineteenth century.[89] Hobson hoped that the end of the First World War would see the establishment of new liberal internationalism. However, with the apparent betrayal and failure of this vision in the League of Nations, his analysis of international relations after the Great War oscillated between the apocalyptic vision of a Great Power condominium of inter-imperialism or the gloom of a reassertion of the competition of the imperial and protective systems in the Great Depression.[90] In terms of contemporary politics, balance of power was the vision of the traditional diplomatist and foreign office minister; Cobdenism was increasingly the view of the moneyed commercial and financial interests; imperialism was the vision of a particular group of financiers, businessmen and ambitious politicians; and new liberal internationalism reflected the hopes of the radical liberals and social democrats, according to Hobson.[91]

An economistic framework?

Though it is implicit rather than expressly stated in his work, the evolutionary framework of international systems was an integral part of the theoretical system Hobson developed to analyse domestic social, political and economic life. While it is open to many of the criticisms discussed previously, Hobson can also be accused of self-contradiction in the economistic bias of his framework. According to Richard Ashley, economism is 'an exaggeration of the economic sphere's importance in the determination of social and political relations, and as a result, an underestimation of the autonomy and integrity of the political sphere'.[92] For example, national income may be seen as the prime indicator of development or of Great Power status, and as the goal of national policy; outflows of capital to foreign countries may be thought to cause imperialism, and free trade to lead to the peaceful relations of states. This criticism suggests that Hobson's extension of the theories of surplus value to international relations leads him to overemphasise the importance of economic relations and factors as the vanguard of his internationalism at the expense of other political, social and cultural elements. Most important, Hobson somehow forgets the centrality of a wider notion of human welfare in his framework and ethics are made subordinate to economics.

Economism in Hobson's internationalism is most evident in his defence of free trade and his hopes for the financial integration of the world. He believed at one point that 'economic peace would lead to military peace'.[93] He has of course also been accused of economic determinism in his theory of imperialism because, it is said, an economic condition, underconsumption, is used to explain a political phenomenon, imperial expansion.[94] In his writings on international relations generally, it might be argued, surplus was an economic variable and economic interests predominated over political or cultural ties in both imperialism and internationalism.

While there are elements of truth to these critiques, as we will see in chapters 5 and 7, the charge of economism is unfair because it artificially divorces Hobson's framework of international systems and his theory of surplus value from his organic perspective, where ethics is accorded priority over economics. In the application of the theory of co-operative surplus to international relations, however, while economic relations were to come first, there was, nonetheless, a dialectic between the improvement of physical welfare brought on by economic exchange and the enhanced satisfaction of more spiritual, cultural or intellectual needs.

Yet, the bias towards economic factors in Hobson's writings on international relations is evident in the volume of his writing on economic internationalism and no amount of apology about the relative backwardness of international relations as a realm of social co-operation helps. Indeed, arguments about backwardness and the fundamental and developmentally prior nature of economic variables only reinforce the sense of economism in the framework.

CONCLUSION

In summary, Hobson's analysis of international relations is founded upon his organic analogy and his theories of surplus value. The framework of four international systems that underlies his writings on international affairs grounded his critique of contemporary international relations and highlighted the increasing level and widening range of global co-operation and organisation. Interstate relations were only one part of a global network of interaction, co-operation, and organisation, encompassing all levels of human relations, personal, professional, social and international.[95] Hobson's framework for international relations can hardly be described as a state-centric approach. It was a holistic approach that considered humanity as a society, although in the contemporary world the most important elements were nations, politically organised as states. The theory of co-operative surplus and the notion of humanity as a social organism both prompt Hobson's ideal of a new liberal internationalism where the world is organised in an international federation with functional agencies.

With the use of the organic analogy and the theories of surplus value, Hobson's framework constitutes the basis of a novel liberal approach to international relations that mirrors the development of the new liberalism. This general framework is the setting for Hobson's analysis of contemporary international relations, notably his theory of imperialism, and his specific prescriptions for a better world, that is, his ideas for economic internationalism and an international government.

CHAPTER 5

The domestic determinants of an imperialistic foreign policy

Imperialism is the most famous part of Hobson's work, a classic in the field of international relations and the basis of his reputation as a social theorist. His theory of imperialism influenced Marxist and neo-Marxist theories of imperialism from Lenin onwards. This chapter examines Hobson's analysis of the forces behind imperialism as a foreign policy of developed states. It counters a prevalent misreading of Hobson that he attempted to provide a scientific theory of imperialism and that he viewed the forces behind imperialism as solely economic. Hobson's critique of imperialism was a political statement, not the statement of scientific theory. Hobson intended to unmask the ideology of imperial necessity and, in doing so, transform the liberal discussion of international relations. In the next chapter I turn to the international aspects of Hobson's theory of imperialism and counter the proposition prevalent among scholars of international relations that these are reducible to his account of its domestic causes.

This chapter demonstrates that Hobson's theory of imperialism is more sophisticated, ambiguous and contradictory than is frequently given credit in the international relations literature. It first deals with Hobson's understanding of the meaning of the word 'imperialism'. He used one basic meaning of imperialism and elaborated upon it in his discussion of the 'new imperialism'. Hobson's theory of the economic determinants of imperialism as an aggressive foreign policy is then presented. Hobson drew on his theories of underconsumption and unproductive surplus as an explanation of the drive to imperialism. Combination created powerful organised financial and industrial interests that possessed both economic and political power and had an interest in an imperialist foreign policy. The third section details Hobson's account of the politics, psychology and ideology that masked the true nature of the imperial enterprise and provided motivations for the broad base of support that imperialism obtained. Hobson's proposed reforms of imperial societies based on his diagnosis of imperialism are examined next. And last, the caricature of Hobson's theory of imperialism in the international relations literature is dissected, concentrating first on Kenneth Waltz's elegant and powerful summary exposition before proceeding to a consideration of further extensive criticisms.

THE MEANING OF IMPERIALISM

Imperialism has been a term with a wide variety of uses, so wide in fact that some have suggested that the concept is too broad to have any meaning and should be dropped from academic discourse. Hobson was well aware of the shifting meaning of political 'isms', imperialism included.[1] He maintained a basic but unstated definition of imperialism throughout his work: imperialism is the forcible conquest and control of foreign peoples. Hobson embellished this basic meaning of imperialism using contrasts with other 'isms'.[2] In his Introduction to the first edition of *Imperialism*, Hobson explored the meaning of what he called the new imperialism by contrasting it with some other contemporary international political 'isms'. In new imperialism, nations were aggressive and exclusive in their relations with one another, unlike the liberal and open nature of nationalism. New imperialism was unlike colonialism, by which Hobson meant what we now call colonisation, because it imposed rule over foreign peoples rather than being, in principle, the occupation of vacant territories. And it was unlike the ancient concept of empire, associated particularly in Western thought with the Roman Empire, because rather than a single global hierarchy, in the new imperialism there were a number of competing and conflicting empires.[3]

Taking these in turn, Hobson noted that in its relations with peoples at a similar level of development, new imperialism was an aggressive and conquering foreign policy, contrasted to nationalism. Hobson cited John Stuart Mill's definition of nationality with approval in *Imperialism*, and described the historical development of nationalism as part of the laws of social growth. Modern imperialism on the other hand was associated with a perversion of nationalism, where the nation was conceived as prior to individual or group needs; with the denial of internationalism because other nations were considered as rivals and competitors rather than as friends; and with the sacrifice of peace, as these exclusive units sought aggrandizement at each other's expense.

'While co-existent nationalities are capable of mutual aid involving no direct antagonism of interests,' he argued, 'co-existent empires following each its own imperial career of territorial and industrial aggrandizement are natural necessary enemies.'[4]

In relations with peoples at a 'lower' level of development, imperialism was a dominating relationship of one people over another, in contrast to colonialism. While imperialism and colonialism were both expansion of the nation beyond its natural limits, according to Hobson, colonialism was marked by the overflow of nationality into vacant or sparsely populated areas of the world. Indeed, Hobson approved of colonialism in principle because the civilisation of the colonising nation was thereby extended across the world. Hobson pointed out, however, that most colonies did not satisfy the conditions of genuine colonialism, but represented instead imperialism. So-called colonies, though populated largely by natives of the territory, were governed by a small, predominantly Western, elite, without any pretence of bringing civilisation to the ordinary people of the colony. Further, the 'colonial' administration only ruled by proxy being themselves directly controlled by the government of their home country.

Not only were the vast majority of colonies' populations native, they were, Hobson believed, frequently unassimilable peoples culturally because of the vast difference in background between the native populations and their imperial masters. The other side of the unassimilability issue, Hobson argued, was that because of the nature of tropical lands, for instance the climate, 'White men cannot "colonise" these lands and, thus settling, develop the natural resources by the labour of their own hands; they can only organise and superintend the labour of the natives.'[5] The structure of imperial rule was superficial yet devastating. It was superficial because the links established by the imperial rulers were loose and temporary, nor did they bring Christianity or civilisation to any great extent. Hobson argued that imperialism extended the area of despotism and exploitation in the world and destroyed ancient or native civilisations.[6]

With regard to the organisation of world politics as a whole, the new imperialism was a struggle between rival empires, in contrast to the vision of internationalism, albeit hierarchical, inherent in the ancient concept of empire. Hobson claimed that '[t]he root idea of empire in the ancient and mediaeval world was that of a federation of States, under a hegemony, covering in general terms the entire known recognized world, such as was held by Rome under the so-called *pax*

Romana'.[7] Such an empire was the realm of peace and of internationalism in so far as each of the nationalities could consider themselves citizens. Many empires competed for supremacy in the new imperialism of the late nineteenth century. Indeed, this was one of the defining characteristics of the *new* imperialism: 'The novelty of recent Imperialism regarded as a policy consists in its adoption by several nations. The notion of a number of competing empires is essentially modern.'[8] These empires competed for territory and were mutually antagonistic. The outcome, therefore, was not internationalism and peace as with ancient empire, but militarism and war.

In sum, the core meaning of imperialism for Hobson was the sustained subjugation of foreign peoples. In the new imperialism, there were additional characteristics, the most marked of which was the international competition of rival empires as well as the progressively dictatorial relationship between imperial power and those Hobson tentatively called the 'backward' peoples.

THE ECONOMIC BASES OF IMPERIALISM

Hobson argued that imperialism was bad business and politics for the nations of the world, both severally and as a group, but beneficial for certain sectional interests within advanced industrialised nations. These sectional interests used their power and influence to push for an imperial policy by which they gained at the expense of the rest of the nation and the world at large. Imperialism was, following Hobson's organic analogy, sectionalism in international society within and between nations. The group Hobson singled out for most, though not all, criticism was the financial sector. His theories of underconsumption and industrial combination explained the economic interests of financiers and investors in imperialism.

In *Imperialism*, Hobson began his development of the theory of imperialism with some empirical work in which he identified some oddities about the foreign policies of the advanced nations, taking the British case as his prime example. He noted the rapid expansion of empire of the advanced industrial nations. Running through the usual economic arguments for empire, Hobson found that empire had neither benefited trade nor been an outlet for excess population.[9] Instead, Hobson identified a number of groups who had an economic or professional interest in imperialism: arms manufacturers, certain trades concentrated in the export sector, shipbuilding, the armed services, the colonial civil service, and certain professions where employees could find lucrative employment in the empire, such as lawyers, teachers, clerics, and engineers. 'These men', claimed Hobson, 'are Imperialists by conviction; a pushful policy is good for them.'[10] 'The vast expenditure on armaments, the costly wars, the grave risks and embarrassments of foreign policy, the checks upon political and social reforms within Great Britain, though fraught with great injury to the nation, have served well the present business interests of certain industries and professions.'[11]

During the period of imperial expansion after 1884, the most significant economic aspect of imperialism was the growth of capital sent abroad from the advanced capitalist states. Hobson noted that investment income from overseas had increased dramatically in comparison to the sluggish performance of the profits from foreign trade. Investment income also was an increasing proportion of the value of imports.[12] While imperial expansion had not benefited the nation politically or economically, Hobson could now answer the *cui bono?* question:

> Aggressive Imperialism, which costs the taxpayer so dear, which is of so little value to the manufacturer and the trader, which is fraught with such grave incalculable peril to the citizen, is a source of great gain to the investor who cannot find at home the profitable use he seeks for his capital, and insists that his Government should help him to profitable and secure investments abroad.

Hobson used the economic theory of underconsumption and his explanation of combination in industry to explain why investors and particularly financiers, the controllers of investment capital, were involved in imperialism. Underconsumption, Hobson had argued, resulted from the maldistribution of income, leaving too much capital in the hands of the wealthy. Unable to spend all of the income they received, the wealthier classes sought to invest their savings. However, because of their own and the workers' underconsumption, there was a correspondingly lower need for capital expansion. The result was, as we have seen, depression in trade, resulting not only in more goods on the market than would sell but especially surplus capital beyond current and future consumption requirements. This surplus capital and depressed market rendered investment opportunities poor, with prices, profits and returns on capital falling.

Underconsumption resulted in a pressure to export capital. Hobson reasoned that investment in the domestic market looked unfavourable and that capitalists seeking to maximise returns from their investments would look to the higher returns available overseas. This would relieve the pressure on the home market. Hobson's underconsumption theory explains why there was a differential, i.e., lower, rate of return on capital in the advanced industrial countries than in the underdeveloped areas.[13] Hobson turned to his theory of unproductive surplus to explain how capital was exported, that is, via trusts and financial institutions. The role that trusts and financial institutions played in Hobson's theory was double-edged: 'the controllers of capital are not only the largest recipients of "surplus" wealth, but the personal embodiment of what is dangerous and wrong in the economic system, regarded from the standpoint of the social good'.[14] In other words, they were both the product of a system in the grip of underconsumption, with its surpluses of capital, and the agents of imperialism who invested abroad and manipulated politics both at home and in the foreign country in order to protect their investments. Trusts and financial institutions were the controllers of the surplus capital that was exported.[15]

According to Hobson, trusts, cartels, monopolies and the financial institutions were the creation of an economic system suffering from underconsumption.[16] Combination was an attempt to avoid the cut-throat competition ensuing from underconsumption crises.[17] In order to avoid the losses from cut-throat competition, firms combined and created powerful trusts that regulated, that is, limited, output to maintain profits either through price rises or the closure of plants or both. Competition had led to waste; combination was an attempt to remedy the situation by substituting regulation of output for reckless overproduction.[18] Unfortunately, 'this concentration of industry in "trusts," "combines," etc., at once limits the quantity of capital which can effectively be employed and increases the share of profits out of which fresh savings and fresh capital will spring', and thus exacerbated the maldistribution of income at the root of underconsumption and the depression in trade. According to Hobson,

> An era of cut-throat competition, followed by a rapid process of amalgamation, threw an enormous quantity of wealth into the hands of a small number of captains of industry. No luxury of living to which this class could attain kept pace with its rise of income, and a process of automatic saving set in upon an unprecedented scale.[19]

The logic of combination in face of trade depression created an alliance between the trust-maker and the financier. It also formed the actual institutional basis of the export of capital.

The profitable management of a trust depends primarily upon regulation of output, which involves a limitation of the employment of capital. It is thus impossible *ex hypothesi* for a trust-maker to find full continuous employment for the high profits he makes by extending the plant and working capital of his own business: such a policy would be evidently suicidal. He must look outside his own business for fields of profitable investment for his profits.

These profits pass ... into general finance, and are thence directed into forming and financing other trusts and large businesses. Thus the process of concentration and consolidation proceeds apace over all the industrial fields where capitalist methods of production prevail. But if a single trust cannot usefully absorb its profits, neither can a group of trusts. The movement, therefore, seems to be attended by a growing restriction of the field of investment. Thus there is a growing natural pressure towards the acquisition of markets outside the present area of monopoly ...[20]

This was the primary economic basis of imperialism for Hobson. He went on to argue:

The economic tap-root, the chief directing motive of all the modern imperialist expansion, is the pressure of capitalist industries for markets, primarily markets for investment, secondarily markets for surplus products of home industry. Where the concentration of capital has gone furthest, and where a rigorous protective system prevails, this pressure is necessarily strongest. Not merely do the trusts and other manufacturing trades that restrict their output for the home market more urgently require foreign markets, but they are more anxious to secure protected markets, and *this can only be achieved by extending the area of political rule.*[21]

As presented so far, Hobson has explained the economics of capital export, giving a reason for the differential rates of return between industrial economies and the undeveloped regions of the world and detailing the institutional means by which capital was exported. My emphasis of the last phrase of the quotation draws attention to the fact that Hobson believed that the extension of imperial control was part of the aims of investors, financiers and industrialists. Intuitively, this might appear somewhat odd. After all, businessmen are usually thought to dislike government interference and prefer a policy of *laissez-faire*, apparently counter to imperialism's extension of state control of territory. Hobson provided three different reasons for the change of attitude towards imperial control among capitalists, as he saw it after the last decades of the nineteenth century. Underlying all of these reasons was the premise that capitalists were eager to protect their investments by the illicit extension, if necessary, of a favourable government's rule.

First, Hobson argued, foreign investment was different from trade in the fixity of interest in the host country that it entailed. For industrialists, the increased connection to a host country of an investment (compared to the temporary and superficial links forged by international trade) led them to push for a policy of increased involvement by government in the internal affairs of other countries to protect their interests over time. This longer-term interest heightened the desire for protection, initially through the governmental provision of law and order by a Western state in the shape of empire. 'Diplomatic pressure, armed force, and where desirable, seizure of territory for political control ...' were the means of this protection, according to Hobson.[22]

Furthermore, industrialists were not in any case always opposed to governmental interference, especially when imperialism secured business for them through monopoly privileges. The new imperialism, Hobson noted, involved imperial protection that excluded potential foreign competition. Protection from rival capitalists from other nations was provided through

> the combined or separate action of capital to obtain the help, financial, diplomatic, military, of the national government so as to secure preferential access to foreign markets and foreign areas of development by colonies, protectorates, spheres of preferential trade and other methods of pushful economic foreign policy.[23]

As a result of the protection provided by the state, Hobson suggested, investors could reap the rewards of an apparently risky investment without the attendant risks: 'Investors who have put their money in foreign lands, upon terms which take full account of the risks connected with the political conditions of the country, desire to use the resources of their Government to minimize these risks, and so to enhance the capital value and the interest of their private investments.'[24]

Financiers, those large institutional investors and the middlemen between investors and entrepreneurs, were especially well placed to benefit from imperialism but the way that they gained differed from those investing in the empire. Hobson argued that financiers' lack of connection to industry (that is, they were portfolio investors rather than investors in the material of the host country) and to the concrete manifestations of an investment led them to push for an expansionist imperial policy.[25] Financiers not only gained as investors but as speculators on the value of investments. 'To create new public debts, to float new companies, and to cause considerable fluctuations of values are the three considerations of their profitable business. Each condition carries them into politics, and throws them on the side of Imperialism.' According to Hobson, financiers made profits from the instability associated with imperialism as opposed to the gains made from the extension of imperial control itself:

> A policy which rouses fears of aggression in Asiatic states, and which fans the rivalry of commercial nations in Europe, evokes vast expenditures on armaments, and ever-accumulating public debts, while the doubts and risks accruing from this policy promote that constant oscillation of values of securities which is so profitable to the skilled financier.[26]

These were Hobson's main arguments that capitalism and capitalists were implicated in the imperialistic foreign policies of, and extensions of imperial control by, the major powers at the end of the nineteenth and the beginning of the twentieth century. Hobson rebutted the idea that capitalism was pacific and had no interest in imperialism. The operation of sectional interests invalidated the claims of the defenders of capitalism. Hobson wrote:

> While it may be true that capitalism as a whole cannot in the long run gain by expenditure on armaments and territorial conquests, this consideration does not dispose of the facts that certain well-organised and politically influential industries gain for a short run by this spirited foreign policy, and that few business men concern themselves with "the long run" or the interests of capitalism as a whole.

Hobson advanced these same arguments to suggest that capitalism was a major source of international conflict and war. While the ordinary investor benefited from extensions of imperial control by their government, Hobson also believed that financiers directly benefited from the wars that resulted from imperialism. He did not, however, argue that they consciously aimed for war.[27] For financiers, war created uncertainty and arbitrariness by which they might gain. This was, however, a matter of degree; too much instability would undermine the system from which the financiers derived their profits. The relationship of capitalists, capitalism, imperialism and war was much more complex than a simple equation of financial greed and imperial wars, however. What is missing from this discussion, as we shall see in the next chapter, is the international context.

THE IDEOLOGY AND PSYCHOLOGY OF IMPERIALISM

According to Hobson, though there were few gainers from imperialism it was a popular policy gathering widespread support from politicians and mass public opinion alike. Hobson explained this apparent irrationality through an examination of the ideology and psychology of the imperial venture that veiled its true nature. There were three parts to Hobson's revelation of imperialism. First, as we have seen above, Hobson linked maldistribution of income in capitalist economies with imperialism and war. This overturned the liberal belief (advanced by Cobden and by Spencer) in the inherently pacific nature of capitalism and economic relations.[28] Second, Hobson demonstrated that a sectional interest's gain was behind imperialism; that there was no gain to society as a whole. Third and finally, Hobson exposed the fallacies in the various ideological defences of imperialism. In his revelation of an economic interest behind imperialism, Hobson did not seek to play down the influence of other honest motivations and reasoning in the initiation of imperial policy. According to Hobson, these other reasons and motivations were functional for imperialism. They were a mask for the economic exploitation of the imperial enterprise and mobilising forces for imperialism, the main reasons why the great majority supported imperialism. Hobson criticised such reasons by showing that these ideas were erroneous and that imperialists' use of such arguments was self-serving. Hobson claimed that any explanation of social events, including imperialism, which relied purely on economic variables was either incomplete or stretched the meaning of economic to include psychological and ideological factors.[29] This claim is fundamental to an understanding of Hobson's theory of imperialism because it demonstrates that what must be examined in order to test the theory are the ideas and beliefs of the time, both well-founded ones and those subsequently discovered to be mistaken.

The supporters of imperialism

Hobson identified a bloc of supporters of imperialism among the political and social establishment whose interests were engaged in imperialism in many ways. He also noted the various vehicles that propounded imperial ideology – the church, the educational system, and so on. He devoted the majority of *Imperialism* to a critical analysis of the contending explanations for imperialism that made up its ideological defence. Hobson saw imperialism as the ideology of the age. Those with a stake in the new colonies or neighbouring areas were disproportionately influential in political circles at home partly because of prevalent ideas about empire. Despite its great cost, imperialism could be put forward as a viable option through phrases such as 'a field of corn does not ripen in a day'. Yet in reality, despite the conflictual visions of the world purveyed by the ideologues of imperialism, Hobson claimed,

> it is only the interests of competing cliques of business men – investors, contractors, export manufacturers, and certain professional classes – that are antagonistic; . . . these cliques, usurping the authority and voice of the people, use the public resources to push their private interests, and spend the blood and money of the people in this vast and disastrous military game, feigning national antagonisms which have no basis in reality.[30]

Hobson argued that trusts and financial institutions used their economic and political power to influence the decisions of their national government, through the manipulation of the press and public opinion as well as directly through some government ministers. They also had the power to manipulate the political, economic and even security situation in the empire or an adjacent area.

Economic interest was not the sole support of imperialism. Far from it. Indeed, an appeal to narrow economic interests would not have been persuasive, Hobson believed. There were also the distinctively political interests of the 'establishment', conservatives and bureaucrats who supported imperialism because it helped to maintain the status quo and their positions at home. Hobson extended his political analysis during the First World War highlighting an interconnected 'circle of reaction' of which imperialism was one part. The circle of anti-democratic forces included imperialism, protectionism, militarism, legalism, distractions, emollients (charity, sport, etc.), regulative socialism, conservatism, state absolutism, authoritarianism (church, school, press, etc.), and bureaucracy; all of which revolved around the pivot of what Hobson termed 'improperty', under which he listed landlordism, capitalism and armaments. Hobson melodramatically used his organic metaphor to describe the connections of the reactionary forces:

> The mechanical analogy of an endless chain is not adequate. For the vicious circle is organic and alive. It is a poisonous co-operative interplay of parasitic organisms, feeding on the life of the peoples by mastering and perverting to their own selfish purposes the political, economic and moral activities of humanity. Political oligarchy, industrial and spiritual authoritarianism, find

natural allies in the servile Press, the servile School, the servile Church, which they utilize to drape their selfish dominion with the gallant devices of national service, Imperialism, 'scientific management' and other cloaks of class mastery.[31]

Political and economic interests were not the only motivations for imperialism according to Hobson. The strength of imperialism derived most fundamentally from the ideology and the rhetoric of those patriots, jingoes and nationalists who, projecting their egos onto their nations, supported imperialism as the extension of national power and prestige. Hobson suggested that children were taught the lessons of authoritarianism learned from the Empire in the schools and that these lessons were reiterated and reinforced in the church. The imperial ideology portrayed imperialism as a Christian mission for civilisation or as a necessary struggle for existence between nations. While being a tool of financial and industrial interests, Hobson claimed that the press also had an interest in the sensationalism of imperial rhetoric, adventures and wars because they sold copies.[32]

The psychology of imperialism related both to the beliefs of politicians and to public opinion. Hobson identified the instincts of pugnacity, acquisitiveness, assertiveness, and most of all, the 'will to power' in statesmen, financiers and industrialists as stimuli to their drive for imperialism. The jingoistic support for imperialism among the masses Hobson attributed to the mob-mind. Hobson applied a crowd psychology in his suggestion that civilised values were submerged in the instincts of the herd. People were credulous and brutal in a way that civilised individuals were not. Pugnacity, bellicosity and predacity, basic instincts supposedly mitigated by civilisation came to the fore, Hobson claimed, in imperialism and war.[33]

Hobson's critiques of the arguments for imperialism

Nearly two-thirds of *Imperialism* is devoted to refutations of various arguments put forward in defence of imperial expansion by those he regarded as the ideologues of imperialism in the press, church, schools, and political circles. Hobson examined the arguments concerning the civilising mission, biological necessity, pressure of population, and the extension of good government. One of the most prevalent and dangerous myths, according to Hobson, was that there was a 'scientific basis of Imperialism regarded as a world-policy', where

[t]he maintenance of a military and industrial struggle for life and wealth among nations is desirable in order to quicken the vigour and social efficiency of the several competitors, and so to furnish a natural process of selection, which shall give an ever larger and intenser control over the government and the economic exploitation of the world into the hands of the nation or nations representing the highest standard of civilisation or social efficiency, and by the elimination or subjugation of the inefficient shall raise the standard of the government of humanity.[34]

Hobson refuted this and other arguments, such as the white man's burden, that posited a mission of civilisation of the backward countries by the most advanced peoples; the idea that the British, for example, had a genius for government and a duty to pass their expertise on to less civilised peoples; and the argument that imperialism is the necessary response to a growing population. According to Hobson, biological and sociological theory supported international co-operation as much as international conflict, as is evident in his use of the organic analogy. The mission of civilisation was a fraud. Under the rubric of this mission, imperialism had, particularly in Asia, destroyed other civilisations rather than establishing any higher civilisation. British 'good government' could not be exported by imposition on unassimilable peoples. Indeed, imperialism had extended the realm of despotism in the world, rather than that of democratic self-government. Finally, Hobson refuted the population outlet argument on three grounds: that economic progress supplied the needs of a growing population, that the new colonies had not in fact taken any greater number of British immigrants and that, with the advance of civilisation, population in the Western nations was not growing that fast anyway.[35]

HOBSON'S PROPOSALS FOR REFORM

Hobson succinctly summarised his remedy for the malady of imperialism: 'Imperialism is the fruit of . . . false economy; "social reform" is its remedy.' This social reform aimed to 'raise the wholesome standard of private and public consumption for a nation . . .'.[36] Hobson's remedies included both domestic and international measures because maldistribution of income and underconsumption were not merely domestic phenomena but occurred between nations and globally.

As we have seen, Hobson's analysis suggested that imperialism was a perverse attempt of one powerful group in society to alleviate its domestic economic problems. The imperialistic foreign policy that was a consequence was, however, only one among a number of policy choices for nations.[37] According to Hobson, the imperial solution would only be effective in the short run as it did not address the root problem of underconsumption. Furthermore, the imperial solution created more problems than it solved: it exacerbated maldistribution of income and stimulated international rivalry and conflict. Exposing the ideology of imperialism, Hobson claimed that the necessity of imperial expansion was a 'popular delusion'; a delusion he tried to dispel.[38]

It is not inherent in the nature of things that we should spend our natural resources on militarism, war, and risky, unscrupulous diplomacy, in order to find markets for our goods and surplus capital. An intelligent progressive community, based upon substantial equality of economic and educational opportunities, will raise its standard of consumption to correspond with every increased power of production, and can find full employment for an unlimited quantity of capital and labour within the limits of the country which it occupies. Where the distribution of incomes is such as to enable all classes of the nation to convert their felt wants into an effective demand for commodities, there can be no over-production, no under-employment of capital, and no necessity to fight for foreign markets.[39]

Hobson's social reform measures domestically aimed at tapping the appropriation of unproductive surplus by the wealthy that was the source of underconsumption. This was more than mere economic tinkering or a taxing and spending policy, however. Hobson claimed that only truly democratic organisation of polity, society and economy would resolve the ethical malady that caused income maldistribution. He specifically advocated fiscal measures to redistribute income through taxation, benefits, a minimum wage and some nationalisation and extensive public works. He also believed that trade union organisation could wrest some of the unproductive surplus from the wealthy.[40] By raising the consumption level of the masses, Hobson believed that this policy would reduce underconsumption and thus remove the pressure to export capital, thereby undercutting the drive to imperialism.

Hobson was aware, however, of the international limits to such high-wage policies. Each national economy was exposed to the vagaries of international economic forces. Faced with the prospect of being undersold by nations where there were lower wage rates, nations could follow one of two courses. They could either rescind the wage rises to avoid being undersold by other nations, or close off the nation from the international economy as much as possible. Hobson questioned both the viability and the desirability of the latter, while condemning the former.[41] The fact that each nation had to consider its place in the international economy was an obstacle to the solution to underconsumption. He thus made proposals for international co-ordination of economic policies, culminating in what he called an international government. This will be discussed in greater depth in the next chapter.

HOBSON'S THEORY OF IMPERIALISM AS AN ECONOMIC DETERMINIST ACCOUNT OF INTERNATIONAL RELATIONS

The theory of imperialism has become something of an industry in itself since Hobson's writings on the subject.[42] Hobson's *Imperialism* has been interpreted and reinterpreted, revised, criticised and defended. A common interpretation of Hobson's theory of imperialism in international relations is summarised elegantly and powerfully by Kenneth Waltz.[43] Here I will concentrate on two areas in which Waltz's criticisms of Hobson are mistaken:[44] first, Waltz criticises Hobson's theory as being economistic, claiming that Hobson saw political outcomes as the result of changes in economic variables; second, he misinterprets Hobson's theory as aspiring to natural scientific status. On the basis of this misunderstanding he charges that Hobson's theory is a monocausal determinist account of the relationship of maldistribution of income and imperialism. However, Waltz's version of Hobson's theory of imperialism lacks the complexity, ambiguities and contradictions of the original and thus his criticisms of Hobson miss the mark. They effectively criticise a theory but not Hobson's.[45] Underlying Waltz's misinterpretation of Hobson is a fundamentally different approach to international relations, exemplified by Waltz's claim that Hobson neglects the 'good' international political reasons for war. For Hobson there were few if any 'good' reasons for war, scientific or normative, international political or otherwise.[46]

Waltz claims that Hobson's theory of imperialism 'can be summarised in one sentence: Uncontrolled capitalist production gives rise to industrial surpluses; from the attempt to market these surpluses an international fight for markets ensues; war results, directly or indirectly, from this struggle for markets.'[47] Waltz has constructed a theory of linear causality where capitalism means the maldistribution of income, which causes underconsumption, which causes excess capital in the national economy, which leads to foreign investment, that causes imperialism, which causes war. This characterisation leads Waltz to criticise Hobson for so-called second image reductionism (that is, a state-level explanation) and economic determinism in his link of a domestic economic condition, surplus capital, to an international political outcome, imperialism.

Waltz seems to be on safe ground with the charge of economism. Hobson conceded in his autobiography that he initially overemphasised the economic elements of imperialism.[48] Yet there are a number of reasons why Hobson's concession need not be taken as an admission of economic determinism. First, Hobson's new imperialism had political and ethical causes. The unfairness of capitalism permitted maldistribution issuing in economic dysfunction. In other work, Hobson stressed the importance of non-economic factors in the determination of economic activity and his theory of imperialism does not deviate from this. Indeed, Hobson believed the creation of a humanistic or welfare economics to be his central contribution.[49] Hobson's opinions on the economic determination of history varied over his lifetime, but usually he condemned it as one of the errors of Marxism, overstretching the meaning of the term 'economics'.[50]

Second, Hobson concentrated on financiers as the beneficiaries of imperialism. But theirs was not a purely economic interest nor an interest moved simply by the pursuit of economic gain. To begin with, those behind imperialism used power, their political power, to influence press, public opinion, parliamentary representatives and even ministers. Hobson emphasised the key role of some economic actors, but their influence in bringing about imperialism is primarily political. Furthermore, Hobson's conception of combination in industry and in social life generally meant that, for Hobson, economic and political interests could no longer be divorced as had been claimed by the proponents of *laissez-faire.*

Third, Hobson's theory of imperialism was an attempt to undermine the liberal belief that economic relations are inherently pacific, a belief that rested on the supposition of the autonomy of economics and politics. Hobson did concentrate on economic factors as a means of subverting this liberal tenet. However, Hobson's analysis reintegrated economics and politics into what might now be described as a political economy of imperialism. Now this reintegration may have been only partly successful, but in essence Hobson, like Marx, was a critic of the idea that capitalism was based solely on economic relations or could be divorced from wider social relations. His portrayal of capitalism as an economic system does not commit Hobson himself to economic determinism.

In sum, the description of Hobson's theory in the previous two sections contradicts Waltz's view. Waltz claims that, in the theory, governments are somehow 'easily drawn' or 'led naturally' into imperialism.[51] Waltz reduces the social, psychological and political context given in Hobson's theory to economic factors and thus derives a monocausal theory of imperialism.[52] Waltz charges that Hobson advanced a simplistic monocausal, determinist theory of imperialism. This metaphysical critique underpins the previous one. Hobson is supposed to have assumed unilinear causation in his theory, from a domestic economic condition to an international political outcome. However, Hobson's theory is not a 'hard', natural-scientific theory of international politics. Waltz, in common with many other international relations scholars, mistakenly interprets Hobson's analogies as if they were assertions of scientific fact.[53] The result of such an interpretation is a hard but brittle theory, a general theory of wide application that Waltz has little trouble demolishing.[54] There are five related problems with this interpretation of Hobson's theory of imperialism.

First, Waltz fails to take account of Hobson's complex formulation of the relationship of international and domestic, political and economic, ethical and social factors. Hobson developed a political economy of imperialism where international and domestic political and economic conditions result in international and domestic political and economic outcomes. He did not claim that maldistribution of income caused all or most wars. He provided the intervening factors of political interest, just discussed, and international structure, to be discussed in the next chapter. Hobson did not claim that imperialism was the sole cause of war or that peace would reign supreme if only imperialism were eliminated.

Second, Hobson developed the theory in the heat of controversy over the British involvement in the Boer War. *Imperialism* is a collection of essays written for different journals over four years from an initial formulation of the theory presented in *Contemporary Review* in 1898.[55] This belies the criticism of Hobson that he generalised his experiences in South Africa just before the Boer War into a general theory of international relations. In fact, it was the 1898 article, 'Free Trade and Foreign Policy', and his contacts in radical circles that led to his being sent to South Africa. The theory generated Hobson's trip to South Africa, not the other way around.[56] The chapter Waltz isolates as the key chapter for his interpretation of the theory was one of the last to be written by Hobson.[57]

Third, the theory continued to evolve over the rest of Hobson's life. It receded somewhat during the decade before the First World War, only to reappear with renewed force in the context of the War and the troubled inter-war period. The changed context of imperialism involved an expansion of its application during the First World War, similar to the imperialism as an international system propounded by Lenin around the same time. Some of Hobson's views on imperialism and its vital elements changed, notably, as we shall see in chapter 7, with regard to the influence of international finance and the role of nationalism.[58] Over his lifetime, in a variety of contexts, Hobson contradicted, revised and refined his early formulation of the theory. The result of controversy, changing historical context and Hobson's exclusion from academia is that his theory of imperialism is considerably less neat than Waltz claims. Waltz simplifies Hobson's theory, making its ambiguities and contradictions invisible. Waltz has not given us Hobson's 'best' theory, however, but has, rather, extracted his own theory from Hobson's writings.

Fourth, Hobson's theory of imperialism is not as straightforwardly determinist as Waltz believes. Hobson's is an explicitly normative theory: social reform is posited as the alternative to imperial policy. He did not see imperialism as an inevitability; rather, he believed that given certain social conditions imperialism was one solution to a series of domestic problems that conditioned the relations of states. That imperialism was a policy chosen by nations implied for Hobson that this was a moral issue requiring ethical analysis. Hobson was conscious of the temporal and geographical limitations of his theory. The notion that imperialism was a necessary part of advanced civilised society was abhorrent to him. He hoped, indeed, that imperialism would be a passing phase in the development of Western civilisation. Hobson's theory of imperialism is not a general theory of Western capitalism.

Fifth, and following from the above, a large part of the purpose of his theory was ideological. He attempted to reveal the delusion of imperial necessity and suggest that imperialism and its deleterious consequences were avoidable.[59] Hobson's theory of imperialism, like much of the rest of his writing, is a conscious attempt to adapt liberal ideology to the changing circumstances of the late nineteenth and early twentieth centuries. It is addressed to 'the intelligence of the minority who are content neither to float along the tide of political opportunism nor to submit to the shove of some blind destiny . . .'.[60] It was a political theory, not a scientific theory.

Hobson opposed the importation of natural-scientific methodology into the social sciences.[61] The notion that Hobson's theory aspires to scientific status is wholly a creation of Waltz himself. The theory of imperialism rests, as does much of Hobson's theoretical writings, on the organic analogy and his theory of unproductive surplus. Imperialism is sectionalism in both domestic and international society.

Finally, there is a sense in which Waltz is correct in his criticisms of Hobson. Though Hobson's theory was not simplistically economic determinist, there is determinism in his theory. While Hobson attempted to expose the illusion of imperial necessity, he appears to have believed that underconsumption was a real problem for the business community with only two basic solutions. His argument was that only radical reform would be successful: in short, given unreformed capitalism, then imperialism. However, the choice for social reform is hardly a choice at all, at least for a civilised people. This means that Hobson did not supplant imperial necessity by choice but merely imposed a parallel necessity for social reform. Hobson's theory is, in this sense, determinist; his argument is that a rational course of action must be adopted if catastrophic consequences are to be avoided. The dichotomisation of imperialism and social reform suggests a necessitarian outlook.[62]

FURTHER CRITICISMS OF THE THEORY OF IMPERIALISM

Besides the interpretation of Hobson's theory in the international relations literature, there have been many attempts to evaluate and to criticise the details of his argument. Regrettably, many of the criticisms of Hobson's theory of imperialism are also based on misreadings of his arguments and yet they remain prevalent as supposedly damning critiques. For instance, in international relations and economic history attempts have been made to expose Hobson's theory through analyses of the economic data concerning the costs of imperialism to states.[63] However, in demonstrating that Britain (or any other nation) did not gain from imperialism, the empirical evidence is supporting Hobson's theory rather than refuting it. As we have seen, Hobson attempted to show that the nation as a whole did not gain from imperialism, but that sectional interests gained at the nation's expense. If the evidence shows that nations did not in fact gain from imperialism, Hobson's case against imperialism is in part proven. Hobson expected a negative balance sheet. Hobson's problematic remains: despite the manifest losses, nations still embarked on imperialism. He argued that this was because of a contemporary delusion of necessity of imperialism and the belief that, for any number of reasons, imperialism was good for the nation and/or the world. The data cited against Hobson are, in short, irrelevant: it is the perceptions of the time, not the statistics as they appear now, that determined imperialism and by which Hobson's theory must be judged.

Some critics have claimed that Hobson believed that most capital exported abroad went to the new colonies. This is a mistake. In fact, Hobson compared the rise in foreign investment with accelerating colonial expansion, but cited no figures showing that a large proportion of overseas investment actually went to the new colonies. He merely denied that the foreign investment figures and the expansion of empire could be a coincidence and provided an explanation of the reasons why it was not so.[64] This is a weaker argument than is usually attributed to Hobson. This reading of Hobson's argument suggests that while underconsumption and industrial combination form the background to imperialism, it was influential people and institutions with investments in certain colonies who asked for and obtained protection for their investments from governments in the shape of imperial law and order who were the real driving force behind imperialism. In this reading of Hobson's theory, there is no necessary correlation between the size of the investment or the return on capital and imperial activity.[65] Perceptions and prevalent beliefs at the time are central to Hobson's theory of imperialism despite the fact that they receive less attention than his economic analysis.

Hobson does not escape this criticism altogether, however. If capital export was going to other industrialised countries, underconsumption could hardly be the real reason, as the receiving country must have been suffering as badly with trade depression as the exporting country. Underconsumption, it might be argued, was itself an ideological product. But this takes us too far from Hobson who certainly believed that while certain social phenomena, such as underconsumption, were not inevitable, they were nonetheless real.

Another misreading has Hobson's theory of imperialism associated with the search for foreign markets and for supplies of raw materials. And it has variously been argued that the evidence shows that the newly opened-up empire and even the established imperial territories were neither good markets nor the most valuable sources of raw materials, and that anyway the foreign markets argument is inconsistent with his theory of underconsumption. However, Hobson specifically linked the new imperialism to the growth in foreign investment. Capital export was primary in this process, the export of goods and the securing of raw materials secondary. Indeed, the search for markets because of conditions of underconsumption at home did not make sense. According to Hobson, the so-called backward peoples lacked purchasing power because of low incomes and thus could not be expected to buy goods at the market price commanded in advanced economies. While they might be potential markets for the future, presently, he argued, undeveloped countries could only be useful as markets in which to dump excess goods at below market prices in order to maintain prices at home. It has since been argued that, in making this argument, Hobson was a forerunner of those who discovered price discrimination and separate markets.[66]

Some accounts of Hobson's theory have seen it as a series of accusations about the activities of a number of people or groups of people as they manipulate governments and popular opinion for their own purposes. Hobson extended the Cobdenite critique of foreign policy to include the businessmen who Cobden applauded.[67] These accounts suggest that Hobson's theory of imperialism is a conspiracy theory, one that has a heritage in liberal radical approaches to foreign policy. Conspiracy theory personalises issues and suggests that the reform of policy will be effected by the removal of certain people or classes from their dominant positions. The evidence for this type of theory could be gleaned from the official statements, private remarks (for example, in memoirs) and actions of the representative actors in the imperial drama. However, Hobson is criticised for providing little evidence to prove that these people actually did conspire and influence policy-makers, even in his strongest case, the Boer War.[68]

There is no doubt that conspiracy theory plays a large part in Hobson's explanation of the Boer War, and that the Boer War was, for Hobson, the classic instance of modern imperialism. In this case, Hobson was not afraid to name names. Nor did he flinch from claiming that a particular race was at the centre of the financial machinations leading to the war, that is, that the war in South Africa was the result of a Jewish conspiracy.[69]

However, the Boer War case was 'only exceptional in the directly conscious nature of its "engineering" ', according to Hobson.[70] Hobson does not provide the documentary evidence that critics charge he should, because conspiracy is not the central feature of Hobson's theory of imperialism. Elsewhere, the conspiracy aspect of Hobson's theory gives way to more general accusations against particular classes or groups.[71] Hobson also queried the idea that the wealthy and powerful who benefited by imperialism consciously sought their interest in an imperial policy. The ideology of imperialism encourages the self-deception, not only of the public, but of statesmen and businessmen.[72] In addition, it is difficult to conceive why Hobson would propose social reform if his theory rested merely on the actions of a group of malefactors.

Bernard Porter has claimed that Hobson had not one but two theories of imperialism, a conspiracy theory derived from his experiences in South Africa and an economic structural explanation derived from his economic studies.[73] While Porter's claim appears plausible, there are reasons to reject it. Structural and conspiracy theories are mutually complementary, indeed, integrally linked, in Hobson's theory. The trusts and financiers could not, indeed would not need to, play the role they do in imperialism if the domestic economy were structured differently. By the same token, Hobson's structural theory is complemented by mechanisms for capital export of which the trusts and the financiers are manifestations. Hobson provided a structural explanation of the power and influence of financial and industrial capital in his economic theories of underconsumption and combination.

Financiers and industrial magnates benefited from the growing concentration of industry and interdependence in the economy, both national and international.[74] There is a double meaning to concentration as Hobson used it in reference, for instance, to industry. It had straightforward political economy connotations, for sure, but it additionally had psychological associations, deriving from his notion of human rationality and also his organic analogy. Concentration meant that businesses have combined and/or become more organised, but it also denoted conscious thought, planning and organisation for Hobson. Concentration of industry and finance made, then, for a powerful interest that knew what it wanted and was able to influence policy-makers. Where this concentrated intention was lacking, disorganisation of opposing interests was enough to permit their manipulation.

The double meaning of concentration has two important implications for Porter's critique. First, there is just one 'structural' theory of imperialism. Concentration joins structural and personal influence.

Second, the double meaning of concentration reinforces the importance of the ideological purpose of Hobson's theory. It was Hobson's attempt, through an appeal to an intelligent minority, to raise the consciousness of the silent majority, to get them to concentrate, as a preliminary to their organisation against imperialism.

Porter also accuses Hobson of basing his theory on 'intellectualist' assumptions, by which he means that Hobson sought a rational source for what he perceived as an irrational social phenomenon.[75] Thus, Hobson showed that while the whole of the imperial enterprise was irrational it was in fact rational for some, i.e., the financiers. This is, Porter observes, fallacious because Hobson has attributed to financiers and industrialists active participation from the gains that they supposedly made in imperialism. It is not implausible, however, that they were not proponents or catalysts but at best third-party beneficiaries or even, as some suggest, losers in imperial adventures.

Porter argues that the strategic concerns of statesmen led to imperialism which was a situation where no-one benefited and no group or individual was specifically to blame.[76] According to this view, substantially supported by, among others, Fieldhouse and Waltz, the security dilemma facing each state forced it to pursue imperial policies.

In his critique of the anti-democratic forces, Hobson also exaggerated the congruence of interests in imperialism. There were numerous differences that divided financiers and imperial entrepreneurs. Financiers had no clear interest in protection, while some manufacturers did and others did not.[77] For instance, the pride and aggrandisement of the imperial politician and entrepreneur were unlikely to find favour with those who believed in the Christian mission of civilisation. In short, Hobson's identification of groups behind imperialism was high on polemic and low on rigorous analysis.

Though it is doubtless accurate to describe Hobson as a rationalist, the problem with this critique is that the security dilemma/strategic interest explanation is dangerously close to being an *apologia* for imperialism and the notion of imperial necessity Hobson sought to expose. The security critique rests on a problematic distinction between political, military and strategic interests and economic and social ones. And while the unity of the imperialist forces might have been overdone, there was some consonance and conjunctures of interests.[78]

A rather more serious criticism is that Hobson failed to develop his concept of finance. He did not discuss or distinguish the different implications of foreign direct investment of physical plant and portfolio investment, foreign investment that takes over already existing businesses as opposed to that which establishes new industries, the repatriation of profits and dividends, nor the issue of the creation of a dependent economy in the host country. For Hobson, '[c]apital invested abroad goes out in the shape of goods, for we have no money to send out, and it is not money but money's worth that foreign borrowers want'.[79] This is linked to Hobson's simplistic notion of investment 'as the process of the distribution of productive energy over an ever-widening area of activity, the movement of capital which it primarily effects being accompanied by a corresponding flow of business ability and labour-power, to co-operate with concrete capital in the production of wealth'. Hobson considered activities 'divorced from the solid facts of business life', that is actual production of commodities, to be pure, wasteful speculation.[80]

He used the term finance to mean both a part of the structure of a world economy and the personnel and managers of financial houses.[81] He oscillated between a view of finance as an overflow created by surplus capital due to underconsumption and the identification of finance as the activities of certain financiers. Other than his observations about trusts and cartels, Hobson did not elaborate on the idea of transnational enterprises.[82] In *Imperialism*, when he discussed finance, Hobson meant the business of financiers manipulating domestically produced surplus capital.[83]

A footnote to the criticisms and rebuttals is necessary. Hobson has been accused by some historians of seeing history through a Cobdenite lens. His view that there was an increase in imperial activity is premised on the idea that there was a mid-nineteenth-century pause, in short, the *Pax Britannica* of free trade and non-intervention. This is an ethnocentric viewpoint to begin with, but is arguably inaccurate even for Britain.[84] However, despite these criticisms of Hobson and because of the 'scientific' interpretation of Hobson's theory, international relations has uncritically accepted his statement that there was a period of increased imperial activity at the turn of the century. This appears in Waltz's reformulation of the theory as the 'imperialism of great power', but even more significantly in hegemonic stability theory. In short, international relations scholars have viewed Hobson's interpretation, including his ideological assumptions, as history.[85]

CONCLUSION

I have presented Hobson's arguments concerning the domestic determinants of the imperialistic foreign policies being pursued by a number of Western states at the end of the nineteenth century and the beginning of the twentieth. I have also suggested that Hobson's theory of imperialism has been stylised and caricatured in the international relations literature. There remain a number of serious ambiguities and lacunae, of course. It is a complex and sometimes contradictory political theory, a political diagnosis of the social pathology of imperialism, rather than the scientific theory it is usually understood to be.[86] Hobson tried to expose the self-deception of the ideology of imperial necessity and to restore imperialism as a definitively political foreign policy option for Western nations.

Indeed, the theory of imperialism was Hobson's attempt to expose a series of fallacies. First, the liberal doctrine of *laissez-faire* had been invalidated by the facts of increasing political and economic combination both nationally and internationally. Second, the trend to combination invalidated the view that politics and economics were autonomous spheres of social life. Both in fact and in theory Hobson argued this was an untenable view. Finally, Hobson unseated the liberal conceit that capitalism led to peaceful international relations – capitalism was now exposed as a cause of war.

This chapter has been devoted mainly to the domestic context of an imperialistic foreign policy as Hobson saw it. This is often taken to be the sum total of his theory of imperialism. The next chapter demonstrates that this is not the case and that therefore it is incorrect simply to extrapolate Hobson's arguments presented so far into international relations. The international context does appear in Hobson's conception of imperialism, as we saw at the beginning of this chapter, and it is to this context that I now turn.

CHAPTER 6

The international relations of imperialism

Hobson's theory of imperialism is considered a theory of international relations. Despite this, the international aspects of the theory are ignored in descriptions in international relations that use instead an extrapolation of Hobson's account of domestic variables into international relations. As Kenneth Waltz points out, to make sense of imperial expansion, control and consequent wars, an account of the international context is required. Hobson provided this, although often rather briefly and in passing. Hobson's theory is not economic determinist because, for Hobson, the international relations of imperialism was the cause of the political manifestation of the new imperialism. The source of imperialism internationally was global political and economic competition between states for territorial monopoly and between financial and industrial trusts for commercial/financial monopoly. Underlying his discussion, Hobson understood imperialism to be a consequence of

> the confident belief that no real solidarity of interests exists between the various units of humanity, and that, therefore, it is possible for each person, class, or nation, to make a separate gain for himself by seizing and utilising the political and economic resources at his disposal.[1]

It was a product of sectionalism, not only domestically or in economics, but in international politics.

Specifically, the new imperialism was the result of the political and economic competition of rival empires superimposed on the competition of trusts and cartels struggling to avoid the logic of underconsumption. This is discussed first. I then turn to the protectionism, militarism and war that result from competitive political expansion and the imposition of imperial rule on unassimilable backward peoples. Additionally, protectionism, militarism and war all had their impacts on domestic politics. In his later writings, Hobson also became concerned with the transformation of imperialism into inter-imperialism, where the competition of the imperial powers was replaced by their collusion in the exploitation of the rest of the world. Given the international scope of imperialism's causes and consequences, Hobson proposed reforms of the international system as well as domestic social reform. (We noted in the last chapter the international limits to certain aspects of Hobson's social reform programme.) The chapter proceeds to a consideration of two substantive aspects of imperialism where Hobson's criticisms are in some respects muted, that is, in the advent of a global financial network and the development and allocation of the world's natural resources. In conclusion, Waltz's criticisms of Hobson's theory of imperialism are revisited.

TERRITORIAL MONOPOLY AND GLOBAL UNDERCONSUMPTION

The new imperialism was defined as an international phenomenon by Hobson, as we saw in chapter 4. One of the four defining features of imperialism after 1884 was the conflict of imperial powers for control of the rest of the world. This new imperialism meant that 'nations trespassing beyond the limits of facile assimilation transform the wholesome stimulative rivalry of varied national types into the cut-throat struggle of competing empires'.[2]

As we have already seen, one reason for the formal conquest of territories was the perception that they provided outlets for surplus capital. Territorial acquisition was required because several advanced industrial nations were suffering the condition of underconsumption simultaneously. Hobson's discussion was marked by the prevalence of competition and the absence of central control in the international system. He drew analogies between the monopolisation of national economies and monopolisation of the world by the imperial powers. As we saw in chapter 3, Hobson believed that the era of *laissez-faire* was drawing to a close. This was true also in international politics and economics. International politics was entering a phase of cut-throat competition as the imperial powers increasingly monopolised territorial control of the world.[3] World politics was transformed as the remaining uncontrolled territorial areas were divided between rival empires and those empires were closed off from foreigners.[4] Any further changes in territorial control could only come, as Lenin noted, through war between the imperial powers.

Global underconsumption

Hobson claimed that underconsumption affected all advanced capitalist states as they embarked on industrialisation and mechanisation. According to Hobson,

> the system prevailing in all developed countries for the production and distribution of wealth has reached a stage in which its productive powers are held in leash by its inequalities of distribution; the excessive share that goes to profits, rents and other surpluses impelling a chronic endeavour to oversave in the sense of trying to provide an increased productive power without a corresponding outlet in the purchase of consumable goods.[5]

In an argument strikingly similar to his any/every paradox explanation of underconsumption, however, Hobson extended his argument beyond the plurality of capitalist states to the international competition of states. Underconsumption and the competitive economic expansion that resulted from it had international dimensions. In a passage that is worth quoting at length, Hobson argued that though each nation separately could industrialise and adopt a capitalist system of distribution, it was not possible for every nation to follow this path without conflict:

> The members of any single nation, taken as an aggregate, may ... save an indefinitely large proportion of the national income, provided that other nations, saving less themselves, will borrow and apply to productive purposes or to increased consumption the savings thus made available. This was the position of Britain during the greater part of the nineteenth century. No limit was set upon the savings of her people when most of the world were insufficiently provided with capital. But when the whole Western world and large parts of the hitherto undeveloped lands of Asia, America and Africa had been equipped with modern machinery of manufacture and transport, while agriculture in many staple branches was passing under machine-economy, the problem of the proportion of saving to spending stood out in its true significance. When the United States and Germany, with some smaller European countries, equalled or passed England in the use of machinery and power, and competed for the export of capital-goods, while Japan cut into the Asiatic markets heavily, the restriction upon the effective saving in England and other advanced industrial countries began to be manifest. It appeared first in a strong competitive drive towards imperialism, the acquisition of exclusive or preferential areas for markets and for capitalist development in the remaining backward countries.[6]

This competition explained the territorial expansion aspect of the new imperialism. Underconsumption alone only explained pressure to export capital; the global dimensions of underconsumption underpinned the increasing monopolisation of territory that marked the new imperialism. For example, Britain's nineteenth-century economic expansion had little need of formal political control because there were no challengers to British supremacy. Once Germany and the United States had become industrial powers comparable to Britain, however, competitive economic expansion ensued, of which formal imperial control had to be a fundamental part. The imperial rivalry following 1884 posed a dilemma for Britain, argued Hobson:

> The spread of modern industrialism tends to place our 'rivals' on a level with ourselves in their public resources. Hence, at the very time when we have more reason to fear armed coalition than formerly, we are losing that superiority in finance which made it feasible for us to maintain a naval armament superior to any European combination.[7]

The international logic of imperialism was simple and straightforward. Without international competition, underconsumption in one nation might issue only in capital export not imperial expansion. Once many developing nations embarked on this course, however, imperialism, the international political enclosure of economic activity, appeared to be necessary. The corollary was, as for economic monopolisation, a reduction in the areas of profitable exploitation as each imperial power sought to obtain and secure areas exclusively for itself in spheres of influence. International political and economic conflict intensified as areas of the world set aside for exclusive exploitation diminished and expansion was restricted, Hobson suggested.

War was not the only possible outcome of the system of globalised underconsumption; worldwide trade depression was another possibility. In the Great Depression of the thirties it was clear that trade depression was not merely a domestic economic problem. At this time, Hobson resurrected his theory of underconsumption as an explanation of global economic dysfunction. He had in any case examined the international economic dislocations of the post-war period according to his underconsumption theory. Hobson denied other economic analyses that suggested that international economic woes, including the Great Depression, were due to the tumult of the First World War or its aftermath. He also dismissed theories that posited monetary or credit explanations for depression. By contrast, he claimed that the First World War and the Great Depression both had a common cause in the developing social relations of capitalist international economic relations, that is the appropriation of the social surplus and consequent maldistribution of income.[8]

Hobson's root-and-branch solution to the Great Depression of the thirties was international government to co-ordinate economic policies and directives to ensure a just distribution of wealth, thus dealing at the global level with underconsumption.[9] Hobson argued that

> as full productivity implies international co-operation in industry, commerce and finance, so the provision of an adequate expenditure upon consumption goods involves, if not a fully planned international policy, at any rate the adoption by all advanced industrial nations of a common economic strategy of high wages, public services and increased leisure, in order to secure a right equilibrium between productivity and consumption.[10]

THE ECONOMIC CHARACTER OF IMPERIAL COMPETITION: PROTECTIONISM

As we saw in the last chapter, Hobson believed that an increasingly interdependent global economy was emerging. Industrialisation was transforming the world, making possible the extension of the division of labour and specialisation across the entire globe.[11] By the same token, open national economies rendered each vulnerable to trade disruption by its trading partners. Hobson noted a common perception: 'When a nation depends for the supply of its daily bread upon the economic activity of other nations, its political independence is felt to be imperilled.'[12] With the problems of trade depression due to underconsumption making the need for markets abroad appear compelling, growing economic interdependence made control of external areas for investment and trade also appear necessary. Protectionism, wrote Hobson, was 'an endeavour to struggle against certain dangers inherent in the world-economy of Free Trade, and to keep within the territorial limits of the nation [or Empire] a sufficient volume and an adequate variety of industry'.[13] It was an attempt to defend the nation against the apparently 'disintegrating influences of commercial internationalism'.[14]

Imperialism thus appeared as one means of securing a nation's economic future. The new imperialism, Hobson argued, was naturally allied with protectionism, the exclusion or discrimination against foreign goods and capital. National firms called for protection of their home markets and for preferential access to imperial markets. This alliance of imperialism and protectionism flew in the face of the traditional opposition, particularly in the British discourse, between those who argued for Empire as a way to open markets to trade and the so-called Little Englanders, but was a product of the international relations of the new imperialism.

Hobson opposed the tendency to imperial protectionism. He followed Cobden, believing in the economic and pacific benefits of free trade and openness to global interdependence. The argument was that openness to trade, participation in the global division of labour and specialisation would lead to economic gains for all nations and would encourage friendly relations between trading peoples. Openness and free trade was the route to peace and prosperity.[15] Part of the reason that imperialism was a bad policy for the imperial nation and for the world as a whole was that it entailed the abandonment of free trade.[16] Hobson's first article concerning imperialism addresses the refutation of free trade in British foreign policy. He argued that:

> In total contravention of our theory that trade rests upon a basis of mutual gain to the nations that engage in it, we undertook enormous expenses with the object of 'forcing' new markets, and the markets we forced were small, precarious and unprofitable. The only certain and palpable result of the expenditure was to keep us constantly embroiled with the very nations that were our best customers, and with whom, in spite of everything, our trade made the most satisfactory advance.[17]

Furthermore, protectionism was simply 'economic militarism', claimed Hobson.[18] It reinforced a view of the world as a dangerous place, composed of hostile, exclusive empires each attempting to keep trade to itself,

> where a nation is exposed to have its foreign trade cut off during war, common prudence, it is held, must impel the State to make arrangements enabling the nation to be as self-sufficing as possible in supplies of the requisites of civil existence and military use ... Protection is urged, not as an instrument of national wealth, but of national defence.[19]

Imperial protection was the policy of keeping the imperial and home markets closed to rivals' trade, achieved in the last resort by military force. Hobson criticised imperial protection as economically unsound and politically dangerous, whether presented simply as a scheme for gathering revenue, for excluding foreign goods through a system of imperial preferences, for the creation of a customs union, or even as the concept of an imperial federation. Free trade was preferable to any policy of forcing markets open or keeping them closed to other competitors. The costs of a protectionist policy were prohibitive due to the administrative and military cost of maintaining imperial exclusion and also of dealing with the strained relations with erstwhile trading partners now made imperial rivals.[20]

Hobson argued that imperial protection was not only costly, it was bound to fail. Imperial self-sufficiency was an impossible end. Even large political entities, such as the British Empire, were not self-sufficient in food, could only pursue a policy of self-sufficiency at great cost, and would in any case remain vulnerable in time of war. The final fallacy of imperial protection, then, was that it was a viable alternative. Rather, imperial rivalry created a perverse form of interdependence, that of the competition of an arms race: 'Imperialism ... has brought a great and limitless increase of expenditure of national resources upon armaments. It has impaired the independence of every nation which has yielded to its false glamour. Great Britain no longer possesses a million pounds which it can call its own; its entire financial resources are mortgaged to a policy to be dictated by Germany, France, or Russia.'[21]

THE POLITICAL CHARACTER OF IMPERIAL COMPETITION: MILITARISM AND WAR

For Hobson, militarism was 'the organisation of physical force by the State, so as to be able to compel members of another State, and some members of the military State itself, to act against their will'.[22] It entailed a constant preparedness for war. The new imperialism created militaristic international relations because it was a policy of forcible territorial expansion and used military force to exclude commercial rivals from markets.[23] Militarism meant '[t]he hostile grouping of nations for superior strength in a balance of power, the failure alike of economic and of military disarmament, the open preparations for a future war ...'.[24] Imperialism fostered exclusive and aggressive nationalistic 'close state' that attempted to secure for itself national or imperial self-sufficiency.

In international relations, militarism became self-reinforcing, claimed Hobson in a crude formulation of the security dilemma:

> The very existence of this militarism, by stimulating the fears, suspicions and hostility of other States, similarly dominated and directed by their group-interests, appears to justify itself by helping to create a dangerous world in which strong martial force is a necessary precaution.[25]

Hobson claimed that militarism further chilled international intercourse because international relations were conceived totally or primarily in terms of the military relations of states rather than the cultural and economic exchanges of people(s). It was a retrograde step for humanity because an international system in the grip of militarism was ruled in the last instance by force rather than claims of reason or justice.[26]

While militarism was the normal result of imperialism, Hobson argued that war was also a likely consequence. Instability, mutual suspicions and the sense of injustice made for a system constantly on the precipice. While Hobson did not assume any single cause for the new imperialism, war appears to be a consequence of the international manifestations of militarism engendered by imperial competition. Unfortunately, militarism and war were not only caused by the direct competition of imperial states. Increasingly, imperial conflicts were being fought by proxies for imperial powers. Hobson forcefully condemned this: 'The expansion of our Empire under the new Imperialism has been compassed by setting the 'lower races' at one another's throats, fostering tribal animosities and utilising for our supposed benefit the savage propensities of the peoples to whom we have a mission to carry Christianity and civilisation.'[27] Furthermore, the 'kilometritis' of imperial expansion and the compulsion to stiffen imperial control bred bloody conflicts with backward peoples. The international system's war-proneness was worsened by the tendency of imperial powers to arm 'friendly' 'backward' peoples. The result of this tendency was a militarisation of African and Asian societies.

Hobson also identified, in his 1938 'Introduction' to *Imperialism*, a major conflict in the international system between the 'have' and 'have not' nations, meaning those that had empires and those that did not. The 'have nots' claimed their own right to areas of the world for their exclusive exploitation. These nations were given the pretext for imperial expansion and war by the actions of the 'have' nations that had already obtained substantial empires. They were also prompted to aggressive, competitive action because the international system of competitive empires was based on militarism and force. Hobson was perturbed by the implications of this analysis. Developing these ideas in the thirties, Hobson realised that Germany, Italy and Japan could justify their aggressions on the grounds that the earlier imperial powers had done the same.[28] This made for an extremely dangerous situation. However, Hobson remained cynically optimistic that the wealthy ruling classes in the 'have' nations would prefer to settle the 'have'/'have not' issue peaceably.[29]

In his argument that war was to a certain extent functional for the capitalist system, Hobson had to counter the liberal argument that capitalism favoured and benefited most by peace. His rebuttal was forthright. The old liberal argument neglected the role of sectional interests. Indeed, it was not only the preparation for war but war itself that was beneficial for certain sections of society. Once again, Hobson turned to his underconsumption argument to find the culprits:

> Capitalism no doubt favours expenditure on armaments as a profitable business proposition. But it needs armaments because it needs war. War is a profitable business policy. Its destructiveness is the other way out of the plethora of peaceful productivity. If foreign markets do not expand fast enough to take off the surplus of capitalist production, an era of destructive waste is the only acceptable alternative.[30]

Resuscitating an argument he first made with Mummery in 1889, Hobson did claim at one point that capitalism as a whole benefited from war because it did 'for the time being rectify the balance between productivity and consumption and give prosperity alike to capital and labour in the uninvaded and the neutral countries'.[31] For the most part, however, Hobson argued that 'though war, with its revolutionary aftermath, may well seem dangerous to the capitalist system, it is open to argument whether such risks may not appear worth running in view of the alternative piling up of unsaleable surpluses which the extension and improved methods of modern capitalism involve'.[32] The problem with saying that capitalism preferred peace was that it was individual capitalists rather than the interests of capitalism that made the decisions.

While Hobson initially criticised the financiers as the sectional interest gaining most by imperialism and resultant militarism and wars, during the First World War he turned his attention to the arms manufacturers. These manufacturers had a positive interest in the strife of nations and were parasites on an international system based on military force. He remarked ironically that the arms industry, an industry in the business of the destruction of civilisation, was an increasingly global enterprise.[33]

THE DOMESTIC REACTION OF IMPERIALISM

The protectionism, militarism and war that characterised imperial rivalry in international relations impacted on imperial societies as well as the conquered peoples.[34] According to Hobson, imperialism reinforced anti-democratic forces in three ways. First, following the nineteenth-century radical critique, Hobson accused establishment vested interests of using foreign policy as a distraction from important political issues at home. Involvement in international and imperial politics diverted time and money away from domestic social and economic causes:

Whenever real issues of 'the condition of the people' grew insistent, they were edged aside by one of those stage monsters of foreign or imperial policy, the menaces or the misdeeds of France, Russia, Turkey, or Germany kept for the purpose. In the early seventies the political wizard of the day invented Imperialism in order to keep the people quiet for a generation.

To 'stay giddy minds with foreign quarrels' has long been a recognised expedient for threatened home despots, and a certain admixture of plausible economic incentives is found useful in order to turn the emotions of a confused popular mind away from dangerous attacks on property.[35]

Second, Hobson claimed that the despotic style of government in imperial dependencies was reimported into and corrupted the political institutions and traditions of the imperial state. This was a direct consequence of the return of imperial administrators and military officers used to autocratic rule in the empire. Hobson wrote, '[i]t is, indeed, the nemesis of Imperialism that the arts and crafts of tyranny, acquired and exercised in our unfree Empire, should be turned against our liberties at home'.[36]

Third, Hobson argued that the requirements of controlling a huge heterogeneous empire resulted in centralisation of political power. Additionally, the centralisation of government was reinforced by the need for secrecy in dealings with foreign powers.

The cumulative domestic impact of imperialism, then, was to oppose democracy and encourage autocratic and centralised bureaucratic government.[37]

Hobson claimed that protectionism was a producers' policy:

[O]rganized financial, industrial, and trading groups within a nation strive to direct its political and economic policy so as to secure for themselves as large a share as possible of the world's wealth 'under the name and pretext of the commonwealth.' Thus a protectionist, imperialist, militarist system is maintained in order that these interests may make profits by isolating the home market and taxing 'the consumer,' ...[38]

At the expense of the mass of consumers, powerful industries and firms able to get the attention of government sought the protection of their profits through import controls and tariffs. Cartels could use their sheltered status to make large profits. Protection was itself an encouragement to the creation of national monopolies. It funded imperial expenditure at the expense of the less well-off because it was a tax on consumption and such indirect taxes were regressive.[39] Finally, Hobson asserted that, despite the claims of its proponents, the aim of an imperial policy of protection was economic nationalism premised primarily on national defence or imperial efficiency rather than national or imperial economic welfare. Protection was a central pillar of an economic nationalism that encouraged wasteful military spending, withdrawing workers from productive employment to put them into the armed services, he argued.[40] Gains from social organisation were wasted not only by the costs of militarism and war but by the expropriation of the surplus by the ruling classes and the aura that the First World War had given to force in the settlement of disputes.[41] International competition also limited the possibility of raising the standard of living of the workers because of the prospect of being undersold by cheaper foreign goods.[42]

Hobson's critical opinions of the domestic impacts of protection, militarism and war have to be qualified by his support for social planning, which, though he did not acknowledge it, entailed interference in the market tantamount to protection. He was also impressed by the progress made towards social control and planning of the economy during the War, claiming that this demonstrated the gains from social organisation.[43] Nevertheless, militarism restricted civil liberties. It destroyed democracy and reason in politics and society, according to Hobson. State autocracy, Hobson wrote, flowed from militarism short of war because

peace hath her emergencies no less than war, and the economic emergency, the creeping paralysis, which has seized the world during the past few years may seem to call for the suspension of the ordinary processes of government. Liberty and equality under such circumstances must give place to an enforced fraternity called the 'Corporate State.'[44]

The imperatives of militarism and protectionism created an exclusionary, dictatorial state, Hobson argued:

Not only the material life of the people but its soul would thus be nationalised and militarized under the closed State. Democracy could have no place in such a State. In industry, as in politics, the Government, dominated in all matters of importance by considerations, not of general human welfare, but of national defence qualified by business pulls, must impose the arbitrary will of the political and business rulers and their paid agents upon the people.[45]

The impact of war was similar only more extreme. While he conceded the necessity of some restrictions in time of war, Hobson objected strongly to the imposition of arbitrary rules over civil conduct, such as the suspension of habeas corpus. 'War necessarily cancels liberty, forcing obedience to imposed authority, and the war mentality is not unnaturally carried on into the emergencies of an unstable and dangerous peace', argued Hobson. He refuted the argument that,

The personal rights good for peace are bad for war. By this argument have been defended military and industrial conscription, the persecution of conscientious objectors, the repression of liberties of speech, Press and meeting, the imprisonment upon suspicion and without trial by administrative action, and, in short, the claim of absolute power by the Executive.[46]

In short, the effect of imperialism on societies was what might be regarded, following Spencer, as a 'moral degradation' from military and industrial ethics. In the inter-war period, Hobson played down the significance of the First World War as a unique cause of international economic troubles. The problem, Hobson observed, ran deeper: the Great War, that is, was itself a product of the conflict engendered in international relations by imperial rivalry. While the War had buttressed the use of force in the settlement of industrial and social disputes, Hobson argued, it was easy to overemphasise the importance of the War's dislocating effect on the world's economy and the economic relations of Europe in particular, rather than looking for the common cause of the economic problems and the War in capitalist economic organisation.[47]

Hobson neatly summarised the domestic effects of the new imperialism on democracy, peace and justice, in a passage once again worth quoting at length:

It is a constant menace to peace, by furnishing continual temptations to further aggression upon lands occupied by lower races and embroiling our nation with other nations of rival imperial ambitions; to the peril of war it adds the chronic danger and degradation of militarism, which not merely wastes the current physical and moral resources of the nations, but checks the very course of civilisation. It consumes to an illimitable and incalculable extent the financial resources of a nation by military preparation, stopping the expenditure of the current income of the State upon productive public projects and burdening posterity with heavy loads of debt. Absorbing the public money, time, interest and energy on costly and unprofitable work of territorial aggrandisement, it thus wastes those energies of public life in the governing classes and the nations which are needed for internal reforms and for the cultivation of the arts of material and intellectual progress at home. Finally, the spirit, the policy, and the methods of Imperialism are hostile to the institutions of popular self-government, favouring forms of political tyranny and social authority which are the deadly enemies of effective liberty and equality.[48]

HOBSON'S PROPOSALS FOR REFORM

With underconsumption being both a common problem for capitalist economies and one that prompted competitive economic policies between nations, Hobson's proposals for reform had to include a significant international aspect. The international limits of his social reform policies have already been noted in the previous chapter. However, more fundamentally, because the scope of imperialist malady was international, Hobson believed that the remedies also needed to be international. Hobson had four proposals for international relations, all of which except the first entailed the creation of a global authority that Hobson called international government. Hobson suggested that, to begin with, nations should not come to the aid of their nationals in their dealing with foreign countries. A policy of non-intervention here would reduce the friction between nations, Hobson believed.[49]

Second, he proposed an international government to arbitrate the claims of the Great Powers. An international government which could put down wars and suppress imperial competition would allow for the healthier competition of nationalities and permit nations to pursue policies for advancing national welfare rather than military preparations for war. International rivalry such as there was would be conducted on what Hobson regarded as a 'higher' level.

Third, Hobson hoped that an international government would institutionalise the norms of an international economic order of free trade, thereby undercutting imperialism's drive to protection. He acknowledged that international interdependence had proceeded too far to permit a return to a system of *laissez-faire*, because this would merely result in the reinstatement of the imperial conflicts. Hobson believed that free trade and the Open Door could thus be made to apply to all nations, a condition conducive to global welfare.[50] Hobson was suggesting an international government as a neutral beneficent instrument that would enforce the rules of free trade, decide imperial claims and direct the development of the world in terms of global welfare. I discuss this in greater depth in the next chapter.

Fourth, he suggested the need of an international government to supervise the development of natural resources in the backward countries. Mandate policy would be a system whereby international government would be the arbiter of the rival claims of the Great Powers. The international authority would have the power and duty to monitor the respective mandated power to ensure that development policies were not prejudicial to the welfare of the native population or the interests of other nations or humanity as a whole.[51]

THE PROBLEM OF INTER-IMPERIALISM

After writing *Imperialism*, Hobson became increasingly concerned by the possibility that the competition of national empires might be transformed into collusion and combination, much as had the cut-throat competition of firms. Hobson initially discounted the idea.[52] Increasingly, however, he came to accept the possibility of what he called inter-imperialism, 'an economic international co-operation of advanced industrial peoples for the exploitation of the labour and the undeveloped natural resources of backward countries, chiefly in Africa and Asia'.[53] Pitting the rich nations of the world against the poor, this was the final twist of logic of Hobson's analysis: following the theory, national imperialism could not be the final stage of combination because national capitalisms could collude and bring their national states together, solving the problem of imperial strife in order that the imperial system be maintained.[54]

Inter-imperialist combination was a possibility created by the internationalisation of cartels and the growth of global finance.[55] 'As capitalism generated imperialism,' Hobson wrote, 'this intercapitalism will generate an inter-imperialism.'[56] He argued that by substituting a race cleavage for the class cleavage at home:

> Western industrial civilisation, organised internationally under industrial, commercial, transport, and financial cartels, would exploit the tropics, and other backward countries containing or receiving supplies of cheap submissive labour, for the benefit primarily of profit-making syndicates, but, secondarily, of the skilled white labour in the final manufacturing processes and other economic services still retained in the Western world.[57]

That is, inter-imperialism, like imperialism before it, bought off domestic opponents of imperialism by creating resources for high wages in imperial states. The workers as well as the capitalists in the advanced countries could then live comfortably off the sweated labour of the rest of the world. The difference was that under inter-imperialism, all the workers of the Western capitalist states would be implicated rather than just the section in, for example, the arms industries.

Inter-imperialism, according to Hobson, would be a 'world-order' where 'the ruling classes of the most powerful Western allies undertake in the name of pacific internationalism the political government and the economic exploitation of the weaker peoples and the less developed countries of the world'.[58] While the Berlin Conference on the partition of Africa between the Great Powers was the first inkling of an attempt at inter-imperialism, early on Hobson was most concerned with the fate of China as it was divided up between the imperial powers. With the fervour for a new world order after the First World War, however, Hobson argued that the new League of Nations might also become a vehicle for inter-imperialism. It would be

> a League from which all non-European States, except perhaps the United States and Japan, were excluded, would be exceedingly likely to develop a wide conscious 'imperialism' which would in the long run prove not less dangerous to the peace of the world than the national antagonism of the past, in that it was the expression of the joint ambitions and pretensions of a group of powerful white nations masquerading as world government.[59]

Hobson thought that inter-imperialism might give capitalism a lease of life for a generation but that it was ultimately doomed to fail.[60] However, the inter-imperialist system was to be the final world conflict of clashing economic interests. The sectional interests within firms, trades, industries and nations would in inter-imperialism be projected onto and replicated at the international level: 'The conflicts of economic interest ... between capital and labour within the single business and industry, between sheltered and unsheltered industries within each nation, between Western national capitalisms, struggling for a restricted world market, will now have given place to a final conflict between the interests of the advanced and backward peoples.'[61]

Inter-imperialism could only delay the day of reckoning for the imperial organisation of international relations, he believed. Though the problem of inter-capitalist rivalry would have been transcended and the possibility of war between the Great Powers reduced, the underlying conflict in the capitalist system worldwide engendered by the appropriation of surplus value would have reached its climax.[62] This system would ultimately collapse because, as with industrial and financial combination, it failed to address the root problem of the unjust system of maldistribution of income. Increasingly the profits extracted from this 'huge "sweating system"' would fall because of the insufficiency of demand, as it had in the competitive and monopolised national economies and also in the competitive imperial system.[63] Furthermore, like imperialism, inter-imperialism stimulated exclusive nationalism in the exploited backward peoples, potentially creating the bases for a global conflagration involving both the advanced and backward countries.[64]

IMPERIALISM, FOREIGN INVESTMENT AND INTERNATIONAL FINANCE

As I noted in the last chapter, Hobson's conception of finance was rather undeveloped. This led him to move between different conceptions without acknowledging it. It has been argued, by Peter Cain among others, that Hobson's attitude to foreign investment changed after his denouncement of the role of capital export in *Imperialism*, leading him into self-contradiction. In the initial theory of imperialism, finance was a national and international sectional interest causing national and international conflict. But, in the decade before the First World War, Cain argues, Hobson held a more simplistic and sympathetic view of the effects of foreign investment on international relations, believing that international finance was the developer of the world and therefore beneficial in terms of both peace and prosperity.[65] According to Cain, the underconsumption theory that underpinned Hobson's theory of imperialism is founded on a rejection of Say's Law, but his critique of imperialism *per se* rests on a Cobdenite argument that must validate Say's Law.[66] Cain goes on to claim that Hobson remedied this contradiction in later writings but at the cost of minimising his critique of international financial capitalism. Peter Clarke refutes Cain's arguments and points out that Hobson was both less consistent at any one time and more consistent over time than he is given credit by Cain. Both Clarke and Cain consider Hobson a Cobdenite on international economic issues.[67]

Cain's criticism is invalid because throughout his writings Hobson conceived finance as potentially playing a functional role in the world economy while also having the potential to be a powerful sectional interest. In *Imperialism*, Hobson offered three reasons why capital export, as opposed to the export of goods, should lead to pressure for extension of imperial control: first, investors wanted to secure or enhance the value of their investments; second, investors hoped that the new colony would make possible new speculative ventures; and third, financiers as an international class benefited from the instability and public debt created by imperialism.[68] In the first two cases, the reason for imperialism was the pressure of *national* capital on its governmental representatives to secure investment opportunities. In the last, Hobson's explanation of the sectional interest behind imperialism was that '[t]he wealth of these houses, the scale of their operations, and their cosmopolitan organisation make them the prime determinants of imperial policy'.[69]

The problem is that there is a difference between national, international and global finance that is crucial for Hobson's theory, yet is not spelled out by Hobson. He was consistent, however. Investment abroad 'binds members of different political communities more closely by bonds of plain business interest' and is 'a powerful interest in the peace, well-being and progress of those foreign countries [where capital is invested]'.[70] What Hobson objected to in *Imperialism*, and continued to object to, was the pressure to invest created by trade depression at home as a result of underconsumption.[71] There was, on the other hand, nothing inherently malevolent about foreign investment. Hobson argued that 'the cross-ownership among nations is by far the most substantial guarantee of the development of a general policy of peace'.[72]

The root of Cain's mistake is his overemphasis on the importance of Say's Law; he mistakenly attributes a chronology to Hobson's thought where there is not one. While there was, as Cain points out, some contradiction in Hobson's imperialism theory between his Cobdenism and his underconsumption theory within the domestic context, his later writings on economic internationalism were not fundamentally different. It should be noted that Say's Law applies to a closed economy and Hobson drew attention to Say's Law in the national context in his

Imperialism. However, despite the omission of a reference to this in his analysis of economic internationalism, Say's Law must here be applied to the international economy, the economic system that Hobson was discussing. The conclusions may be different but that is because the context rather than the analysis is different.[73]

Furthermore, according to Hobson, so far as finance is truly international, it will be a harbinger of peaceful international relations. There is a fundamental difference between foreign investment, i.e., national surplus capital financing of production overseas, and international finance, the collection of nationalities involved in cross-national financing of production and trade. Additionally, Hobson believed that 'international will continue to gain upon purely national finance, and that this will help to secure peace and order over all areas of international investment'.[74] With improvements in transport and communications, the world was truly a single economic system. In this system, finance had an important role to play as 'an automatic apparatus for the application of economic stimuli and the generation of productive power at points of industrial efficiency . . . '.[75] Deprecating the defects of modern finance (which I shall discuss shortly), Hobson claimed that 'genuinely international finance' would be a pacific force:

> Where the international character of an investment has been further marked by the substantial participation of investors of several nationalities, there will not be either the same temptation or the same ability to induce a government to bring pressure upon a foreign state in the interests of financiers, many of whom, are not its own subjects.[76]

Hobson also considered the cosmopolitan as opposed to international aspects of finance. Investors abroad became 'cosmopolitan capitalists', true 'men [*sic*] of the world', i.e., they lost their truly national characteristics.[77] However, the truly cosmopolitan figures were the financiers. While they had a functional role in the world economy 'using skilled foresight, so as to direct the flow of industrial capital into the most serviceable channels',[78] they could also become a powerful sectional interest, a global financial interest exploiting the products of world industry. Hobson's condemnation of cosmopolitan finance was often based on an anti-Semitic jibe, as in *Imperialism*, but he also acknowledged the positive role played by financiers in oiling the wheels of the new world economy.[79] Cosmopolitan financiers were 'in a unique position to manipulate the policy of nations'.[80] They promoted companies, were the unproductive middle-men between investors and entrepreneurs, and through their control of finance, particularly credit, they could manipulate prices. Their interest in public debts and in financial fluctuations threw them on the side of risky and conflict-ridden ventures such as imperialism.[81]

Hobson continued to be a critic of imperialism after the publication of *Imperialism* in 1902. His criticisms of finance's role in imperialism can be found, even during his support of international finance in the years before 1914. During and after the War, Hobson returned to his critique of imperialism, yet maintained his belief in the importance of economic internationalism of which international finance was a central element. For Hobson, there was no contradiction between the deleterious impact of foreign investment as a root of imperialism in practice and the beneficial impact of international finance in economic internationalism in principle! The first derives from national sectionalism in international relations; the second is a part of the development of an organic world economy. The difference between his opinions in *Imperialism* and in *Economic Interpretation of Investment*, so often referred to, is traceable to differences in immediate and contemporary social contexts rather than being rooted in theoretical inconsistency. *Economic Interpretation of Investment* was written with a capitalist investor audience in mind. Hobson moderated a number of his criticisms of investment activity because of the audience. In the pre-First World War period, there was a good deal of optimism concerning international economic and social relations – this was the high tide of Norman Angell's influence, especially in his book, *The Great Illusion*, which Hobson cited at length.[82]

THE DEVELOPMENT AND ALLOCATION OF THE WORLD'S NATURAL RESOURCES

The issue of how to develop the world's natural resources was to be one of the most serious problems for economic internationalism, Hobson claimed. Development was central to the attainment of welfare on the way to higher levels of civilisation. Yet the exploitation of resources by imperial countries had also led to international conflict. Hobson's partial defence of the control of the Third World's natural resources has the scent of imperialism about it and has been described as such by at least one commentator.[83]

Hobson was keenly aware of the problem of exploitation of 'backward' peoples by the advanced countries – this was a central thrust of his *Imperialism.* By keeping the benefits to themselves the imperial nations deprived the rest of the world of the benefits of the diffusion of wealth throughout the economic system. The result was that the distribution of the benefits of the development would be unjust and 'inefficient' in terms of global welfare. The waste of imperialism, despite the gains from development in the advanced industrial world, was in the exploitation of the native population and the stimulation of conflict between the Great Powers in their rivalry to gain areas for exploitation.

By the same token, Hobson was not persuaded by the contrary arguments made by socialists or nationalists for the absolute right of nations to do what they wanted with 'their' natural resources. Hobson rejected these on the grounds that there was no such absolute right to property. He refuted the right of nations to do with their territory and what's in it, under it, etc., as they wish, just as he denied that individuals have an absolute right of private property. The criterion for national as well as individual property was, for Hobson, the ability to use it. Thus, for example, any backward people occupying territory that could be exploited for the common good of humanity had no right to stand in the way of that development.[84]

Some interference in the business and government of 'advanced' nations and 'backward' peoples was inevitable, however, because of the increasing connection of the international economy. It was the responsibility of Western governments to make sure that the process of opening up developing countries' resources was not overtly exploitative as it would be if left to private business interests.[85] To counter imperialist or nationalist discourses, Hobson looked to his touchstone of human welfare. His approach on natural resources can be construed as unalloyed global utilitarianism: Hobson supported interference in other countries to exploit natural resources in principle because this was a route to maximise human welfare. Many of these resources were in backward countries populated by peoples unable or unwilling to exploit the resources. Under such circumstances, advanced countries could benefit all of humanity, and not just themselves, by developing these resources. Accordingly, advanced nations which could exploit these resources should do so, even if this was at the expense of the inhabitants of a particular area.[86] Thus, 'all interference on the part of civilised white nations with "lower races" is not prima facie illegitimate' and 'civilised Governments *may* undertake the political and economic control of lower races – in a word, ... the characteristic form of modern Imperialism is not under all conditions illegitimate' because '[t]he natural resources of the soil belong to nobody'.[87]

Having said that imperialism to develop natural resources was not in principle illegitimate, Hobson placed several conditions on such activity. First, 'every act of "Imperialism" consisting of forcible interference with another people can only be justified by showing that it contributes to the "civilisation of the world"', that is, humanity-wide welfare.[88] It followed that such interference must be premised on access for all people(s) to natural resources. This is an international concomitant of Hobson's principle of equality of economic opportunity derived from his views on distribution. No preferential access was permitted: 'If all backward countries, whether under the political control of some European or other "advanced" State or still politically independent, were formally recognized by Conventions of the civilised Powers as similarly open to the trading and investing members of all countries on a basis of economic equality, with adequate mutual guarantees for the enforcement of treaty obligations, the greatest step towards lasting and universal peace would have been taken.'[89] Second, the rights of, and benefits to, the native population should be of primary importance in the consideration of whether intervention to exploit natural resources might take place. These rights would most likely be upheld not by the 'backward' nations themselves but by international agreement.[90] Third, there must be international agreement to permit the interference. Hobson argued that advanced nations should only be allowed to develop the natural resources of a backward country with the permission of an international government and if monitored by that international government so that it abided by the first two conditions above.[91] In other words, imperial countries should not intervene on the basis merely of their own claim that their self-interest accorded with the global good or that their self-interest had priority. Such self-assertion was indeed, for Hobson, the 'radical moral defect' of imperialism.[92]

In proposing international permission and monitoring of 'imperialism', Hobson was one of the early proponents of the mandate system that was subsequently set up in the League of Nations. There is a problem, however. While such mandates might seem a perfectly reasonable suggestion on practical grounds, it throws the whole of Hobson's suggestions with regard to economic equity on the international level into doubt. Hobson conflated the issues of the global utilisation of natural resources with the unequal relationship of the advanced and backward nations. Hobson's concern with the development of natural resources as an international issue was skewed through this conflation. The issue of natural resources poses the problem of the rival claims of humanity and nationality, that is, universal versus particular claims. Hobson addressed this almost exclusively as an issue in the relationship of the backward and advanced nations. While he tried to counter the imperialist arguments for the rights of the advanced nations to exploit the resources of the undeveloped countries, this conflation only led him to advocate a form of international paternalism. Hobson left the allocation of resources in the advanced countries out of his discussion of mandates. Because of this conflation, we are faced with the notion that backward peoples were to be the subjects of paternalism, to be led to development by the advanced West – presumably for the benefit of all, but with little choice, it would seem, for the large proportion of the world population that formed the backward nations. Hobson did not defend the underlying presumption to all this: that the status quo of resource utilisation was to be taken as given.

Hobson did not spell out what part the mandated territories would play in the international government. If they were not to be represented, international government would be merely an institutionalisation of the inter-imperialism of advanced nations Hobson hoped to avoid. If mandated territories were to be represented, interference by other states and by the international government would give them a lower status than that of advanced nations. Hobson was apparently untroubled by such contradictions and blatant paternalism in his ideas.[93] This is a strange conclusion for someone who was supposedly so concerned about questions of welfare and just peace in the relations of advanced and backward peoples.[94] Hobson condemned the inter-imperialism of the League of Nations as it was established, yet his own proposals seem to imply the same conclusions.[95]

In his ideas on natural resource development, Hobson also apparently forgot the distinction between material and human welfare that he was usually so careful to draw. For instance, one of the most startling and stark contradictions in his work is his eulogy of the development of natural resources by Western capitalism in *Economic Interpretation of Investment*:

> The development of a backward country by foreign capital is always beneficial to the country itself, to the industrial world at large, and to the investing country in particular.

Compare this with his opinion ten years earlier:

The successful exploitation of certain sources of material wealth might, for a time, be taken as tokens of success, and as constituting a service to the world; but a wider range of vision would show that these material gains were purchased by great racial disturbances, which made the price too costly.[96]

Thus, while Hobson advanced a new approach to natural resource development involving an embryonic mandate system, it is not at all clear that he understood the complexities of the issue or overcame his Western bias.

CONCLUSION: WALTZ ON HOBSON REVISITED

While the problems of Hobson's theory of imperialism with regard to the concept of finance and the development of natural resources are serious, most criticism in international relations relies on a reading of the theory similar to that of Kenneth Waltz. It is time to revisit Waltz's attack on Hobson's theory in the context of the international relations of imperialism. Once again, Hobson's ideas are a good deal more sophisticated than is usually given credit.

Waltz criticises Hobson's theory of imperialism for being a 'second image analysis' or 'reductionist theory' of international relations. Specifically, Hobson is accused of having attempted to construct a general theory of international relations on the basis of a theory about, and experience from, British domestic economic conditions. However, as the discussion in this chapter shows, Waltz has illegitimately extrapolated a theory of international relations from Hobson's theory of an imperialistic foreign policy. It is Waltz rather than Hobson who focuses solely on domestic conditions. He is then able to reduce these to economic factors and extrapolate them into a theory of economic imperialism. Waltz's version of Hobson's theory of imperialism thus completely neglects Hobson's discussion of the international context of the new imperialism. Moreover, Waltz is not alone in this omission: while Lenin's concept of uneven development has been adopted in the international relations literature, Hobson's discussion of the monopolistic competition of empires has been completely ignored.[97]

Hobson explained government involvement in imperialism through the superimposition of widespread underconsumption on international political rivalry. While Waltz considers underconsumption to be a domestic phenomenon, Hobson identified it as a general problem for all capitalist countries. Imperialism, Hobson could argue, was the product of many nations' similar attempts to deal with common problems of underconsumption.

Furthermore, it is only in his discussion of an international system of rival empires creating protectionism and militarism that it makes sense to talk of Hobson believing that imperialism caused war at all.[98] Hobson wandered beyond strictly domestic analysis when he suggested that the international system of competitive empires impacted on domestic institutions and policy-making. Such international determination of domestic policies has been labelled 'The Second Image Reversed' because it turns the direction of causation of Waltz's second image upside down.[99] Finally, in his reform proposals, Hobson advanced a classically third image – that is, international system level – solution to imperialism in the shape of an international government. In short, as this chapter has shown, *contra* Waltz, Hobson did provide a theory of the international relations of imperialism.

CHAPTER 7

Economic internationalism, free trade and international government

This chapter explores the apparent contradiction in Hobson's writings on economic internationalism between his defence of free trade and his advocacy of international economic government. The way in which he did or did not face this apparent contradiction is important because Hobson's arguments became the basis for the transformation of liberal internationalism that is reflected in the difference between the nineteenth-century radical Richard Cobden, on the one hand, and twentieth-century liberals, John Maynard Keynes and David Mitrany, on the other. Hobson himself did not consider his opinions on free trade and his advocacy of a redistributive international government to be in contradiction. On the face of it, though, his ideal vision of an international economic government directing capital, labour and natural resources as well as his proposals to restore the European economies after the Great War through inter-governmental co-operation compromises the central tenets of free trade doctrine.

The chapter deals with the underlying themes and theory in Hobson's economic internationalism rather than his specific policy proposals and his constantly changing outlook on international economic issues.[1] Hobson's free trade internationalism is set out first. The second section looks at the rules and institutions that Hobson felt were needed to maintain free trade. Third, Hobson's ideal of an international economic government is considered. While certain suggestions for international government do not contradict his defence of free trade, many of his arguments run counter to the spirit of free trade. The chapter turns to an examination of Hobson's proposals with regard to the free movement of people that highlights the contradictions within his economic internationalism. The chapter concludes with a critical assessment in light of his ideas on the evolution of international relations.

HOBSON'S FREE TRADE INTERNATIONALISM

Free trade was the cornerstone and abiding concern in Hobson's economic internationalism. He wrote of his perspective on international economic issues:

As an economist, steeped in the principles of Cobden and his British school of liberals, my predilections (prejudices if you will) have always been in favour of the freest possible movement, alike of trade and persons, and against fiscal protection and immigrant restrictions.[2]

Hobson defended the validity of liberal free trade principles, as passed on from the texts of classical political economy from Ricardo onwards, arguing that 'liberty of exchange benefits a whole society and each of its members where complete mobility of capital and labour and equal access to natural resources of the land exist'. For Hobson, division of labour and greater specialisation created benefits not only within national boundaries but between nations. 'The wider the area,' Hobson claimed, 'the freer and more secure the nature of this intercourse, the greater is the net gain, both to those parties directly engaging in each act of commerce and to those who indirectly profit by doing business with parties thus enriched.'[3]

In *International Trade* and *The Science of Wealth*, Hobson used parables of a small trading community to illustrate the benefits of free exchange between communities and, by extension, nations.[4] Free-trade principles showed that the division of the community of traders into two separate political communities did not alter the gains from the division of labour and specialisation through exchange:

Freedom of exchange would still tend to make each person on either side dispose of his labour-power and his capital in a manner which conduced to the maximum productivity of the two villages, regarded as an economic group ... The political separation of the two villages could not itself affect the economic gain of maintaining old relations. Except where political interference with these trade relations is expressly contrived, there is no plausibility in the mistaken notion that villages, towns, or nations engage in trade with one another.[5]

Hobson claimed that this logic applied to the nations of which these smaller political communities were a part; national boundaries could only be a harmful interference to the gains from free exchange so far as nations were part of a single economic system. He claimed that with a single world economy of trade, nations could not be considered economic units because international trade was not trade between nations acting as single entities but trade between the individuals, households, groups, firms and industries within nations.[6] Competition in and for international trade did not imply conflict between nations, because 'no such collective competition exists at all. So far as trade involves competition, that competition takes place, not between nations, but between trading firms, and it is much keener and more persistent between trading firms belonging to the same nation than between those belonging to different nations.'[7]

According to Hobson, a single world economy where flows of investment were of greater importance than trade in goods would make the nations of the world still more interdependent. Hobson argued that international economic relations could be understood through the same laws of economics as applied to the domestic economy because interdependence meant that there was increasingly one single global economy rather than a series of separate national economies. For this reason he extended the free trade argument to apply to factors of production as well as goods. This altered the normal notion of free trade handed down from Ricardo because this form of trade was no longer 'arm's length' because businesses might now be owned cross-nationally.

Free trade, for Hobson as for all liberals, was more than a good economic idea, however. It was the basis of international co-operation. 'International trade is the incipient form, the true utilitarian condition, of international morality: trade intercourse is the beginning of human fellowship.'[8] Hobson claimed that free trade was part of an 'economic internationalism [which] is an essential feature of civilization'. Free trade was, for Hobson as it had been for Cobden, the foundation of peace and prosperity: 'commerce has always been the greatest civilizer of mankind. All other fruits of civilization have travelled along trade routes ... Cut off commerce, and you destroy every mode of higher intercourse.'[9] The exchange of goods of free trade was only part, but an essential part, of the exchange of ideas and the cross-fertilisation of cultures that was so important to the future development and the current sensibilities of the human race. It is the wider meaning of exchange, of interdependence and openness that gives free trade the moral high ground, according to Hobson, again following Cobden and also Spencer. Free trade was not just a policy for prosperity, but one of peace. Furthermore, according to Hobson, '[t]he larger meaning of Free Trade ranks it as a phase of social evolution by which, on the one hand, militarism is displaced by industrialism, and, on the other hand, political limits of nationalism yield place to an effective internationalism based upon identity of commercial interests'.[10]

Hobson's critique of protectionism and economic nationalism

Hobson's economic internationalism and its affirmation of free trade was reflected in his rejection of arguments for protection and economic nationalism. Protection, for Hobson, was a futile attempt to close off a national economy from the effects of internationalisation. Protection lowered world prosperity as a whole by introducing artificial barriers to trade and investment. Besides this point, however, the main force of Hobson's argument was that the protecting nation (that is, for Hobson, Britain) could not benefit by protection. He argued, for instance, that capital would flow out of the protected area, because '[e]very fresh barrier against freedom of exchange, rendering less effective the division of labour among nations, causes the capital and labour in the country which imposes it to be less productively employed than it would otherwise have been'.[11] This would lead to inefficiency and thus a rise in prices, and less wealth and employment. According to Hobson, government interference with trade, not only in the form of tariffs but in such apparently innocuous (and today common) practices as national accounting, created the impression that nations traded as single entities and popularised the view that nations were economic competitors.[12]

Hobson was well aware of the various justifications and rationalisations of protectionism as an argument against free trade. He discussed and dismissed the arguments for protection of key industries, of infant industries, protection as military necessity, and the argument that defence comes before opulence. In each case, Hobson attempted to show that the arguments fall for both political and economic reasons. Protection neither enhanced economy, nor did it help defence.[13] Hobson's rebuttal of protectionist arguments can be taken in two parts: first, his rejection of protection on economic grounds, relying on free trade arguments; and second his reflections on the politics of protection.[14]

Hobson claimed that import taxes could not both protect and keep prices down. To the extent that a tariff protected a national area, the good on which there was a tariff was being excluded. Revenue could only be raised if goods came into the country, Hobson pointed out.

Revenue-raising and protection were contradictory goals. Hobson also argued that protection would retard rather than encourage economic development. This was because protection would lead to a misallocation of capital to inefficient firms and industries. The overall deterrence of (foreign) capital caused by protection (as a result of limiting the division of labour and thus reducing profits overall) would also hinder development.[15]

Hobson argued that proponents' claims regarding the economics of protection did not include the deleterious effects brought on the protecting country by other nations' retaliation and imposition of similar tariffs. Retaliation was not only a bilateral problem, however. With growing protection, as in blocs of imperial preference, a climate of economic nationalism spread, poisoning the trading and investing environment of the entire world economic system. The idea that trade had to be fought over would be a self-fulfilling prophecy, Hobson warned, reducing the world to economic warfare.

Hobson suggested that the arguments against protection also applied to imperial preference systems and regional customs unions. According to the free trade argument, it was clear that any barrier to exchange would result in a loss of the benefits from the division of labour. Thus, while '[i]t is true that the possibility of economic self-sufficiency is greater as the group is larger and admits more division of labour ... this does not cancel the damage of erecting barriers. For every extension of the area of free markets secures a more effective division of labour, and a larger absolute share for each free participant.'[16] Hobson wrote that 'Free Trade has nothing but commendation for proposals for closer or more effective trade relations between allies, provided they are not intended, and do not in fact work out, as a policy of exclusion and hostility to other countries.'[17] Thus in practice, though customs unions could mean the reduction of tariffs within the union, they actually entailed exclusion of other nations' goods. According to Hobson's free trade arguments, in each case there would be a loss in terms of a potential global division of labour, and a loss to productivity and hence welfare. Exclusion also brought with it the economic consequences of retaliation.

Regarding the politics of protection, Hobson noted that all protectionist arguments appealed to separate interests within society. Each group was told by protectionists that they would benefit. However, Hobson argued that this benefit was always at someone else's expense and that the economics of protection could not be applied generally to the economic system.[18] Hobson described protection as a sectionalist policy because it could only benefit the protected firms or industries, while harming other unprotected firms and industries, through lowered incomes, higher prices and less employment. It was in short a producers' policy. Hobson claimed that powerful business interests were calling for a policy of protection to defend their interests at the expense of the rest of the nation and indeed of global welfare as a whole.[19]

Besides the domestic pressure for, and implications of, a protectionist policy, there were international political consequences. Retrogression to economic nationalism would lead to the deterioration of international relations which would have its own costs above and beyond those resulting from the reduction in trade and economic activity, Hobson believed. There were costs to setting up the protective system both in terms of civil government and the need for military expenditure. Imperial protection involved the constant preparedness to fight for markets, to force doors to trade open and to protect any exclusive or preferential trade routes and markets from the encroachments of competitors.[20] To Hobson, protection implied militarism and political isolation, as we saw in the last chapter.

Hobson's attack on protection went still further, however. Should there be war, protection was a feeble instrument of national defence both before and during war, he claimed. Hobson denied the opposition of defence and opulence, claiming that this was a fallacy of those in favour of protection. Free trade, he countered, made for economic strength, the basis of military power. Free-trade policies also did not antagonise neutrals to the conflict, thus helping the free trade country to obtain supplies for its war effort.[21] In sum, for Hobson, protectionism enfeebled the nation economically and estranged it from others politically – it was a menace.

The exception: unemployment

Hobson deployed these arguments against protection and for free trade in contemporary disputes over British foreign economic policy. For example, he opposed Joseph Chamberlain's British tariff reform movement at the end of the nineteenth century. He argued that the tariff reform policy proposed served the interests of producers; would reduce the incomes of the least powerful sections of society, especially workers in unsheltered industries; and would stimulate conflict between Britain and its economic rivals.[22] He opposed a later campaign for a system of preferences to goods within the Empire and attacked the idea of imperial federation as an abandonment of what he considered Britain's successful policy of free trade. While the impact of these policies would be to reduce global welfare and make for international strife, Hobson pointed out that the goal, imperial self-sufficiency, was an impossibility and, anyway, was against the interests of the colonies.

During the First World War, Hobson opposed the proposals, made at an Allied conference in 1916, for a post-war blockade of enemy nations, the curtailing of trade with those nations and with certain neutrals, and the proposals for a trade bloc of the Entente powers after the War.[23] Such actions would be, according to Hobson, the continuation of the war by economic means and would inevitably result in what they were aiming to prevent, that is, the restoration of a balance of power in Europe with Germany once again powerful. He was also a vociferous critic of the Versailles peace settlement, especially the reparations forced on Germany, the failure to cancel war debts, and also the implications of the creation of new states in Eastern Europe. He argued that the defeated Austro-Hungarian Empire had in the past at least permitted the relatively free flow of goods across a large part of Europe. On the other hand, the new states created out of the Empire, being weak economically and founded in nationalism, attempted to control their economies with state direction of the economy and high tariffs. Along with the rise of protectionist sentiment in Europe, this meant that the new boundaries in Eastern Europe were a hindrance to trade between nations.[24]

However, after the First World War and especially during the Great Depression, Hobson became increasingly disaffected with the pure (or unilateral) free trade argument.[25] Circumstances must qualify free trade theory, said Hobson, because 'the irrational condition of general unemployment during a world depression throws out of gear the simple logic of Free Trade . . .'.[26] Hobson argued against those who claimed that the economic troubles following the First World War were solely the result of deviations from free trade policies or of dislocations brought on by the War. Economic woes were, for Hobson, more fundamental than a maladjustment of international economic relations. They were a result of underlying economic conditions of the nations of the world, particularly the advanced capitalist nations. Because of these economic conditions, free trade was inoperative and protection might be a short-term, national solution, according to Hobson.

Contradicting his usual attacks on protectionist ideas, Hobson claimed that protection might benefit a nation when there was general unemployment. He had in the past argued that free trade logic determined that no individual nation's level or configuration of employment could be guaranteed. Indeed, temporary unemployment of certain persons as they changed jobs in response to changing patterns of trade was a part of the free trade argument. The dynamics of competition led to the creation of new products, giving the advantage to those countries that exploited the new products and innovations in production techniques.[27] It followed that in normal economic conditions free trade could not guarantee a nation full employment at any particular time. Nevertheless, adherence to liberal trading policies was the long-run route to national prosperity as well as being the policy for global welfare, according to Hobson. The unemployment discussed here is not generalised, systemic or persistent, but rather, in economic parlance, simply frictional. Briefly, full employment, excepting frictional unemployment, was assumed in free trade doctrine.

Depression, however, undercut the full employment assumption of free trade doctrine. 'Given a general depression and unemployment in the industrial world, a tariff might be used to distribute the aggregate volume of employment for the time being favourably to the political area which set it up,' because, with a margin of unemployment in the national economy, a tariff could exclude foreign competition and redirect production to national industries. According to Hobson, protection would increase national employment and 'export' unemployment to other countries, if 'the tariff [kept] out foreign goods and so [substituted] domestic goods, increasing the total volume of goods made in this country and reducing the volume of goods made in the foreign exporting countries'.[28]

Hobson rationalised this attack on pure free trade doctrine with an appeal to Adam Smith. If all trade was equally beneficial, Hobson reasoned following Smith, domestic trade was to be preferred over foreign trade because there was a gain 'at both ends' of the exchange, that is, both buyer and seller were nationals rather than one being a foreigner as was the case with foreign trade.[29]

This defence of protectionism was not a systematic part of Hobson's economic internationalism, however. He also advanced reasons to think that protection would not remedy unemployment. These mirror his free trade arguments made earlier. First, while a protectionist policy would maintain employment and incomes for the nation setting up tariff barriers, tariffs only redistributed unemployment to other countries. They did not reduce the world level of unemployment. Indeed, further barriers to trade would tend to reduce the productivity of capital and labour, thereby creating more, rather than less, unemployment in the world economy. Second, there was the possibility of retaliation and 'beggar thy neighbour' policies. If other states also raised tariffs, then unemployment would effectively be re-imported into the country that imposed the first tariff. Worse still, with more and higher barriers to trade, unemployment would rise, particularly in the protecting nations but also worldwide. Third, once established, tariffs tended to be difficult to remove. Politically, strong interest groups behind the tariffs argued for their maintenance. Economically, protection encouraged the dependence of industries on protective measures and an 'appropriate' time for the removal of protection never arrived because there were always reasons not to remove the tariffs. Tariffs, then, tended to persist into periods of 'normal trade' with all their deleterious effects. Fourth, a protectionist policy would only create employment if the redirection of production did not involve large increases in domestic prices. The redirection of funds to protected industries might well result in the failure of unsheltered industries in the protected national economy, again resulting in a decrease in employment.

Hobson concluded that free trade was the best foreign economic policy for each nation to pursue and the best policy for the world economy in the long run, even in periods of general unemployment.[30] Though free trade could not deal with the depression at the root of general unemployment, this did not mean that its opposite, protection, was the solution to trade depression. Though free trade principles faltered during periods of unemployment, Hobson was not convinced that free trade was itself the source of the problem of unemployment. Even if free trade had no short-term solution, protection only addressed the symptoms rather than the fundamental causes of the problem: 'Protection is a bad palliative,' Hobson argued, 'because it does not increase the capacity of consumption to keep pace with production.'[31] Indeed, during the 1920s and 1930s he suggested that foreign trade measures were not the answer to economic instability or global trade depression. He asserted that what was needed was a policy of national (and international) wealth redistribution. This policy prescription follows from his analysis of the cause of trade depression. For Hobson, trade depression and consequent unemployment could only be explained by underconsumption that was the direct cause of the failure of effective demand in capitalist economies. The remedy to unemployment was to remove underconsumption.

As we saw earlier, underconsumption was caused, according to Hobson, by the maldistribution of income in capitalist economies that gave too much to the wealthy and too little to the poor. As such, protection did not just miss the mark regarding unemployment, it might actually make matters worse, he claimed. In so far as tariffs restricted international competition, they encouraged the formation of national cartels which in turn restricted competition and production, worsening the unequal income distribution and reducing employment. Furthermore, protection as a form of indirect taxation hit the poorer sections of the nation harder than the rich, exacerbating the maldistribution of income, the root cause of unemployment through underconsumption.

INSTITUTIONALISING FREE TRADE

Even during the Great Depression Hobson remained a free trader, certainly more than, say, John Maynard Keynes. However, as we have seen, Hobson was not an unthinking adherent of free trade principles. Free-trade principles are often considered the international analogues of *laissez-faire* doctrine or as part and parcel of the ideology of *laissez-faire.*[32] According to Hobson, on the other hand, national economic policy geared to redistribution was not only the remedy for unemployment but was the route to the full and just operation of free trade. Additionally, he suggested that the norms of free trade could only work properly through international co-ordination of national policies.

During Hobson's lifetime pure free trade policy ceased to be implemented or even advocated by governments. Even if free traders were winning the theoretical argument, Hobson wrote, they were nonetheless losing in the struggle to implement their policies. Free-trade theory and practice were beginning to look like distant ideals, irrelevant to the contemporary world economic situation, particularly, as we have seen, during the Great Depression.[33] The spirit of the age was the end of the liberal century and the opening of an era of protectionism and imperial rivalry so well dissected by Hobson himself in his *Imperialism.*

Hobson's analysis of free trade and his modifications relied on his critique of the operation of *laissez-faire* nationally and internationally. The role of governments in national and international economic affairs was growing, as was industrial combination in the form of national and multinational trusts and cartels.[34] As he argued in his theory of imperialism, underconsumption had undermined free trade because it compelled capitalists to seek foreign trade and capital exports as a way of avoiding trade depression at home. International trade was transformed by combination, underconsumption, and governmental intervention, from co-operative and mutually beneficial exchange to conflictual struggles to exclude competitors from privileged markets, that is, the 'irrational' policies of protectionism and imperialism.[35]

In such circumstances, Hobson wrote, *laissez-faire* solutions and simplistic advocacy of free trade doctrine provided neither effective nor just alternatives. Rather they would allow powerful cartels and the so-called advanced industrial nations to exploit the poor, the weak and the unorganised.[36]

In short, pure free trade had been transcended by the monopolistic developments of modern industrial economies.[37] *Laissez-faire* could not operate as free traders such as Cobden had envisaged because the view of the economy on which it rested, that of a large number of relatively small firms competing fairly, had ceased to exist.[38] In the context of the growing combination and interdependence of a world economy marked by imperial rivalry, free trade doctrine far from being a universally applicable maxim, had become a Victorian illusion and an ideology, a pretext and rationalisation for (British) imperialism.

For Hobson, the need for new liberalism to transcend Cobden's analysis also applied to international economic affairs:

> What Cobden's analysis [of free trade] failed to recognise was that an appeal made, as was his, to the collective self-interests of whole nations, is only completely effective where the government expresses the aggregate interests of the nation, that it is liable to fail where the interests of special classes or industries within the nation arrogate to themselves the power of government.[39]

Free trade through national economic reform

Hobson's ideas on the basis of free trade in the new conditions of the world economy mirror his proposals for the reform of imperialism. Hobson proposed national economic reform to lay the basis of the proper operation of free trade. We have seen that his new liberalism opposed *laissez-faire* doctrine, suggesting instead that governments could be the creators as well as the destroyers of liberty.[40] Hobson rejected the argument that state intervention was an international analogue to protection and that it compromised freedom of trade. Protection of disorganised labour, he argued, could not be equated with the protection of powerful capital. 'Industrial and social legislation, by helping to raise the physical and mental status of the workers, has helped them to secure the liberty and mobility which underlie the true economy of *laissez-faire*.' Such freedom, guaranteed by government intervention, would be the basis for true free trade.[41]

Hobson's new liberalism was to be the basis for his reaffirmation of the desirability of free trade, but free trade without its *laissez-faire* underpinning. He claimed that state intervention in the economy to mitigate the maldistribution of income in the advanced industrial nations would undermine the underlying compulsion to maintain trading relations by force rather than free exchange. National economic peace, that is, an end to the class war of the capitalists and the workers, was an essential part of peaceful economic internationalism, according to Hobson.[42]

Hobson only briefly dealt with the ramifications of domestic economic intervention as a basis for economic internationalism. In the thirties, when the prospects for international co-operation and the League looked bleak, he considered the idea that nationally planned economies would trade with one another as corporate entities. More usually he hoped that state intervention in domestic economic affairs would not disrupt the freedom of individuals and groups in their commercial and financial relations across state boundaries and was generally against the exclusionary practices involved in creating a nationally planned economy.[43] He was not in favour of large government projects but rather preferred fiscal measures for redistribution through the taxation and benefits systems, as well as social legislation to defend the rights of workers, i.e., through trade unions. Nationally planned economies might well behave as monopolists in the world market: corporatist states' industries might, Hobson admitted, compete with each other, replicating the imperialism and protectionism he was seeking to remove.[44] He also hoped that his scheme for national redistribution if married to a parallel international policy would avoid the deterioration of international relations associated with closed systems of national planning such as was taking place in the thirties in the Soviet Union particularly.

Free trade through international government

Hobson realised that domestic and international reform to permit the proper functioning of free trade had to come together. The increasing interdependence of the world economy meant unilateral national policies had international repercussions. He had diagnosed that competitive imperialism and rising protectionism made any isolated national arrangements (including those just mentioned) a fragile basis for free trade. In the disorganised world economy each nation pursuing its own immediate self-interest would culminate in global rivalry, uncertainty and impoverishment. In such a climate of distrust, Hobson argued, free trade could only be maintained through an international institution or, at the very least, the co-ordination of national economic policies that established certain 'rules of the game'. Hobson loosely called this range of proposals international government, meaning a process for international control rather than a formal international structure.

International economic government had two functions in creating the basis for free trade. The first function was the maintenance of, and monitoring state adherence to, certain rules of free trade, particularly the 'open door' to trade and investment, that is, free and fair access of each nation to the natural and human resources of the whole world. Reasserting that '[t]he effective liberty of every people demands freedom of commercial intercourse with other peoples ...', Hobson claimed that an 'International Government ... representing the commonwealth of nations ... would seek to remove all commercial restrictions which impair the freedom of economic intercourse between nations.'

According to Hobson, if the international government could enforce an open-door provision, then the 'sting' of national imperialism would be drawn and needless wars averted.[45] The matters to be dealt with by an international authority included freedom of access to trade routes, admission to markets, equal opportunities for investors, and an international commission to oversee the development of the backward countries.[46] This openness and equality was most commonly applied by Hobson to the relations of the advanced nations with the backward peoples, but he was quick to point out that the aim of openness and equality applied to relations between advanced nations as well.

The second function of international government was to instil certainty and stability in the world economy so as to enhance economic performance by reducing the role of chance and uncertainty in economic decisions. 'Let international government put down wars and establish Free-Trade', he claimed, and 'the truly vital struggles of national expression will begin.'[47] He hoped that political stability would be improved with an international government. On the economic side, he suggested that an international government might, for instance, be a gatherer and disseminator of information on the world economy.[48]

Hobson's view of the international government as a means of institutionalising free trade was quite limited. It was merely to make sure free trade operated properly. However, there were wider implications: Hobson hoped that 'so far as the needs and interests of the peoples can find expression in foreign relations, the deep constant underlying identity of human interests will constantly react in efforts to mould international institutions that are favourable to co-operation'.[49] An international economic government would, Hobson believed, reveal this underlying harmony in free exchange.[50]

When looking at the development of economic internationalism during his lifetime, Hobson thought that intergovernmental conferences, agreements and institutions would widen in scope and become increasingly institutionalised. He was especially hopeful with regard to international co-operation on labour and working conditions in the newly formed ILO. He thought that some form of international bank and financial controls should be set up. The need for co-ordination of national policies to maintain free trade was also urgent during the immediate post-First World War period. Hobson argued that an institutionalised free trade regime was necessary if anarchy in Europe, as each nation sought to restore its war-torn economy, was to be avoided.

INTERNATIONAL ECONOMIC GOVERNMENT

The level of intervention by governments in international economic relations envisaged in Hobson's proposals for the institutionalisation of free trade was modest in comparison with his proposals in the domestic arena. On the one hand, Hobson toned down his interventionist proposals for an arena that was on the face of it less susceptible to such reform. Free trade was the minimal requirement for international economic (and cultural) co-operation and exchange, he argued pragmatically, and was a bulwark against imperialism and protectionism. For Hobson, international economic co-operation and exchange were well in advance of primitive international political relations. In the relatively primitive social realm of international relations, free trade was a progressive ideal compared to nationalism, mercantilism or imperialism.

Openness to trade and freedom of exchange would be the precursors of more organised and rational forms of co-operation once the time was right, however. This was explained by the evolutionary theory of co-operative surplus, the basis of his proposals for state intervention. Superimposed on international economic relations, the theory of co-operative surplus mapped out for Hobson the logical development from free trade to interventionism in international economic relations. However, this logical development had to await the slow historical development of the conditions for international co-operation. As the global economy became more organised through the nineteenth century, though, there was a growing need for central rational control of international economic relations. Such control was absent in the contemporary world market, Hobson noted. He suggested that what was ultimately needed was what he called constructive internationalism (as I have labelled it in chapter 4, new liberal internationalism): the rational administration and efficient organisation of the world economic system by an international government.[51]

Hobson's constructive internationalist ideal was an interventionist international economic government. Parallel to his pronouncements on domestic matters, he extended the meaning of equality of opportunity beyond mere freedom from hindrance in exchange, advancing a conception of 'positive liberty' as equality of opportunity in international relations. 'Equality of opportunity for commerce, for investment of capital, and for participation in the development of the world's resources', argued Hobson, 'is the first condition for the progress of national civilization in the world. In the fruits of such progress every people should get its share, and the co-operation in this common task is the surest bond of peace among nations.'[52] His proposals for the economic functions of an international government were not, then, limited to the negative conception of the role of removing obstacles to free exchange or stabilising contemporary international economic relations.

Hobson, therefore, proposed an international government that was rather more expansive and interventionist: 'social control ... must in the long run be international, so as to correspond with the area of the economic system itself'. Ideally an international government would manage international economic relations rather than be merely the guarantor of free trade. International government would provide '[t]he world's wealth for the world's wants'.[53] In a passage extending his human law of distribution to humanity at large, Hobson posited 'the authority of some international government competent to deliver "the economic goods", i.e., to control the development of world-resources in the interests of humanity'.

If the world for economic purposes could be organised upon this principle, its natural resources, assigned to the cultivation of the inhabitants of the various countries, according to their capacities, and supplemented where necessary by suitable drafts from other countries: a broadcasting of the pooled skill and technique and organising power available from all world-sources, a central distribution of capital, a common saving fund, available according to the industrial needs of different countries and industries, the world would then be raised to the level of its highest productivity. If also, this greatest economic product were able to be distributed, or rationed, according to the diverse needs, or capacities of enjoyment of the members of this world community, such an economy of production and consumption would yield a maximum economic contribution to human welfare.[54]

Hobson only made a few scattered and sketchy remarks concerning the specific functions and shape of his international economic organisation directing the global economy. He was more specific on the policies needed to assure rapid reconstruction of Europe in the emergency immediately following the First World War. He called for international co-operation to aid the devastated countries. In particular, he called for the United States with its relative gains from the War to transfer some of its surplus to destitute Europe.[55] Hobson was cautious to note, in his discussions of the need for an international economic government during the twenties and thirties, that this phrase did not necessarily mean centralised international control and planning, but the extension of some already existing common national principles to the international economy and a federal economic authority to monitor national policies.[56] He believed rather that the nascent international functional institutions, such as wartime inter-Allied arrangements and post-war novelties like the ILO, would be forerunners of and subsequently agencies of a new international economic government.

THE INTERNATIONAL MOBILITY OF LABOUR

Hobson's suggestion that free trade and international government were not incompatible, a view that is defensible within his theory of co-operative surplus, is certainly controversial. His argument allowed him to paper over some serious contradictions between an interventionist international government and a more *laissez-faire* vision of the global economy, and also between international relations driven by economic forces and an international government aiming to raise the general level of human rather than economic welfare. Hobson avoided these contradictions by staying with general principles and abstract analysis, except for his policy recommendations on tariff reform. However, they emerge in his writing on international labour mobility, which thus makes for an interesting case study in Hobson's economic internationalism.

Given his interest in human welfare, it is perhaps not surprising that Hobson's economic internationalism involved not only trade of goods and transnational flows of capital but also the international mobility of labour. The logical conclusion of free trade doctrine was that maximum economic welfare would be achieved with free mobility of both factors of production, labour as well as capital. Hobson believed that internationalisation of labour would parallel the internationalisation of capital, though he had a number of hesitations regarding the process of internationalisation and its ultimate outcome in terms of human (as opposed to economic) welfare.

Improved communications and transportation made international mobility of labour desirable and in the final analysis inevitable, Hobson believed.[57] Already loosened national and local affinities and personal attachments would become weaker, he claimed. The competition of foreign labour in national labour markets would be beneficial in global welfare terms but would also mean that workers could not be certain of finding gainful employment in one locality for the whole of their working lives. Labour could and should be more mobile.[58]

Hobson was alive to the fact that labour was not made up of 'economic men', nor was it a fluid, infinitely divisible factor of production; indeed it was a much less fluid factor than capital, though he criticised the view that saw capital as a fluid factor, too. Personal attachments and other cultural and individual aspects of welfare were important. These conditioned and compromised the fluidity of labour. The idea that there was a single world labour market was false and would remain so.[59]

International mobility of labour created problems for states with social policies aimed at improving the quality of life for the national workforce, that relied upon the exclusion or limitation of immigration.

An influx of foreign labour, prepared to work for less, in less safe conditions, and so on, tended to undercut policies such as legislation to maintain a minimum wage, improve working conditions and terms of employment, and so on.[60] Hobson had some difficulties here. On the one hand, he criticised the policies of states, like Australia, which had large undeveloped natural resources, yet sought to exclude immigrants.[61] He admitted, however, that this would be a difficult issue for an international government to resolve and suggested that the advanced West was unlikely to welcome unlimited numbers of immigrants. Hobson rather vainly and optimistically hoped that a reformed capitalism would render flows of labour unnecessary as each nation developed its own resources and traded goods and services. Neither absolutely free mobility nor nationalist exclusion seemed to Hobson to be the best policy for the achievement of the greatest human welfare. Instead, he fudged.[62]

Yet, in his attempt to compromise on this issue, the taint of bias attaches to Hobson: why should the West with its riches of economic development be permitted to exclude poorer workers from other countries? Why should they be permitted to evade a policy that, according to Hobson's own arguments, would be for the benefit of humanity (and even specifically for the national welfare) in the long run? Seen in this light, welfare legislation was a protection scheme for Western labour. Indeed, as some have argued, it was a concomitant of imperialism and potentially of inter-imperialism as Hobson envisaged it.

Hobson also mistakenly believed that freedom of movement would for the most part lead to flows of labour from the developed to the undeveloped world. In fact, job-seeking immigrants flow to the wealthiest parts of the world – a conclusion an economist versed in *laissez-faire* doctrine would find obvious, but one which Hobson, hoping for overall development of the world according to global welfare, apparently did not.

Hobson's mistake concerning the direction of flows of labour was only one part of his rather contradiction-ridden attitude to international labour mobility. As we have seen, Hobson proposed as an ideal, an international economic government to direct the world's labour force to where it was needed rather than where it would desire to go:

Such a World-Government, devoted to the best development of Earth's resources for the benefit of mankind, would find its chief task in the direction of migration from over-populated into under-populated areas, and the selection of fit types of immigrants, having regard to racial, climatic, and other conditions.[63]

Though Hobson discussed this ideal in abstract terms, it is all too easy to see an implicit authoritarianism in the direction of a mass labour force over the entire face of the earth.

Hobson's arguments for free trade in labour and the global direction of labour both collide with his humanistic conception of welfare because they both rely on a narrower economic calculus. Early in his career, Hobson advanced a humanist critique of the emphasis in free trade on economic (that is, material) values to the exclusion of wider notions of welfare, such as the quality of life.[64] He claimed that specialisation degraded producers, that the division of labour divided not just tasks but the people doing those tasks. Hobson used this argument to claim that Britain's place in the international division of labour had removed British workers from clean air and pleasant scenery to put them into crowded towns in unhygienic conditions.[65]

However, in contrast to Ruskin, Hobson believed that, 'the one great "economy" which modern science has most powerfully impressed upon us as a means of progress [is] the division of labour, or "differentiation of functions"'.[66] And he believed that the Industrial Revolution was indeed progress and that machines could improve productivity, allowing more time for welfare-enhancing leisure.[67] In the international context, Hobson also acknowledged, yet failed to deal with, the difficult issue of cross-cultural valuation of work, that is, how do you value labour in economies at various levels of development and in different cultural contexts?[68]

Hobson was often in two minds on the advantages and disadvantages of the international division of labour. He cautioned that 'division of labour is only a true economy when a sound principle of co-operation underlies and dominates division, maintaining the unity and harmony of the whole process'.[69] The resolution of this tension lies, as we noted in chapter 3, in Hobson's hope that specialisation and machine production in industry would allow for more leisure and progress in human civilisation. Nevertheless, his defence of free trade and international economic government are based on material rather than his much vaunted human welfare.[70]

CONCLUSION

Compared to his writings on imperialism, Hobson's work on economic internationalism has been rather neglected in terms of academic attention. This is unfortunate, since Hobson's proposals were, if general in character, an important contribution to the transformation of liberal internationalism in the early decades of the twentieth century. They also reflect an elaboration on his ideas for reform of imperialism as well as presenting the dissonance between a harshly realistic assessment of imperialism and his optimistic views on economic internationalism.

As a set of economic ideas, Hobson's economic internationalism by itself was nothing terribly profound and is hardly considered relevant today. His defence of free trade was relatively crude and not much of an advance for liberalism beyond Cobden or Angell, though he was ahead of his time in his appreciation of the economic globalisation. His theory of international trade and his discussion of international finance have been superseded both by subsequent developments and by more sophisticated theory, notably in economics. His discussion of international trade did not include an analysis of the effects of non-tariff barriers to trade, a significant obstruction to the operation of free trade in the later decades of the twentieth century. Though he acknowledged the role of international investment, Hobson did not grasp the idea of a multinational company or the internationalisation of production. For example, there is no discussion in Hobson's work of intra-firm international trade, that is, trade across international borders between branches of a single multinational firm, and thus of the problem of transfer pricing. However, in his defence, Hobson's view of Cobden is particularly appropriate: 'The element of truth in this criticism is for the most part attributable to economic developments, the character and pace of which neither Cobden nor any other statesman of his time could have foreseen.'[71]

Hobson also overemphasised the harmful impact of protection on international relations, suggesting that civilisation was at risk. More recently, Susan Strange has argued that the effect of protection in world politics is negligible. States maintain reasonable relations during periods of high tariffs and other protective measures because these relations, political, military-strategic, and so on, are more important than mere trade.[72]

Finally, in the criticisms of Hobson's potential relevance (or otherwise) for international political economy, there is something of an anomaly in Hobson's writings on the increasing importance of international trade. Hobson believed in the increasing internationalisation of the economy in absolute terms, but at the same time admitted that:

When a modern nation has attained a high level of development in those industrial arts which are engaged in supplying the first physical necessaries and conveniences of the population, an increasing proportion of her [*sic*] productive energies will begin to pass into higher kinds of industry, into transport services, into distribution, and into professional, official and personal services, which produce goods and services less well adapted on the whole for international trade that those simpler goods which go to build the lower stages of civilization.[73]

Unfortunately, he did not trace out the implications of the anomaly of an internationalising economy happening at the same time as a growth in importance of domestic relative to international trade. Though this is an intriguing point, Hobson's belief that tertiary sector services and commodities were less suitable for international trade has been proven mistaken by the internationalisation of financial services, the international media and information networks and the growth of tourism.

More seriously, for Hobson's new liberal vision of international relations, arguments that Hobson rejected elsewhere in his writings appear in his economic internationalism. For instance, he put economic advance well ahead of social justice in international relations, restoring the autonomy of politics and economics that he had rejected in nineteenth-century liberalism. Economic internationalism reveals more clearly than elsewhere in Hobson's work the materialist, economistic aspect of his evolutionary theory of co-operative surplus and its divorce from his organic conception of human welfare. Even as he proposed the need for political control in international economic relations in parallel to the national control of economy, he argued a secondary role for political relations: 'international economics must be supported and sustained by international politics'.[74] For example, Hobson claimed that nations were not economic units. This sounds plausible until it is asked, what then is an economic unit? Hobson's implicit answer was that the individual or the firm is the unit in the global market. This, though, is an answer dangerously close to the individualism of *laissez-faire* dogma.

In Hobson's defence, his proposals were meant to be general rather than specific and to sketch the outline of what was needed rather than analyse a particular aspect of international economic relations or construct a global economic blueprint. In the longer term, Hobson's contribution to international political economy is the development of a new context for theorising about international economic relations. Hobson was part of the transformation of the liberal perspective on international economic relations from the dogmatic assertion of free trade of Cobdenite radicalism towards a functional approach to international economic organisation. Hobson's approach foreshadows the work of scholars concerned with the development of international institutions to stabilise economic relations, to mitigate the effects of the world market and to alleviate poverty.[75]

Living through a period of major international economic dislocation, Hobson's proposals reflected his hopes, fears and realistic assessments of the contemporary international economic outlook. He was growing more and more confident of the importance and beneficence of international financial relations before the Great War, and was, naturally, less hopeful about the benefits of untrammelled free trade during and after the First World War. He was, nevertheless, ambitious in his plans for economic government during the War and immediately afterwards. He believed that economic government would be a central pillar of any workable League of Nations, and that if it did not address economic issues the League experiment would fail. With this failure regrettably becoming increasingly obvious in the thirties, Hobson once again became more cautious in his advocacy of international economic government, at the end of his life calling for domestic social reform in order to remedy international economic ills.

This very brief exercise in placing Hobson's free trade arguments in their historical context reveals one final intriguing shift in his arguments. Hobson's theory of imperialism was a liberal's response to Britain's relative economic decline. Under increasing pressure from the industrial competitiveness of the United States and Germany, British policy-makers and industrialists were considering a move away from the hegemonic policy of free trade. Hobson, however, argued against protectionism for Britain, because at the turn of the century Britain maintained trade supremacy. Turning from the benefits of free trade was folly for a great power which had the most to gain anyway from this policy, especially with its dominance of shipping and other transport, he argued.

Yet, in the post-war period, when Britain's position in the world had clearly declined, Hobson argued that Britain could not afford protectionist measures because to do so would be to cut off the trade, e.g., in food and raw materials, that Britain was dependent on. Hobson shifted from the argument that free trade was beneficial to a hegemon to an argument that it was essential to smaller powers compelled to be in foreign trade. The question that Hobson did not address is whether middle powers (for want of a better term) might indeed benefit from protectionist policies, as the United States and Germany had done.

In general, however, Hobson's ideas on economic internationalism are significant for his move from *laissez-faire* to interventionism in international economic relations. In this respect, Hobson was one of the earliest contributors to the ideological transformation of liberalism that culminated in the post-1945 world order compromise of 'embedded liberalism'. Still more important, Hobson's writings provide a theory explaining why such a transformation was necessary and how it came about.

CHAPTER 8

International government and the maintenance of peace

International government as the rational organisation of international relations appears to be a logical extension of Hobson's new liberalism, specifically his theory of co-operative surplus and his organic analogy. In fact, however, Hobson's most detailed proposal for international government appeared during and as a reaction to the First World War rather than any growth in international co-operation. In *Towards International Government* and the Union of Democratic Control pamphlet, *A League of Nations*, Hobson addressed the questions of international peace, security and order, and suggested international government as an alternative to the balance-of-power system which, he believed, had been a major cause of the First World War.[1]

Hobson hoped that his proposals would fulfil three requirements for international peace: the consolidation, extension and addition of sanction to international law, the establishment of a method of just and peaceful settlement, and the reinforcement of methods for constructive co-operation.[2] He argued that peace could only be achieved by centralising force to strengthen international law and methods of peaceful resolution of international conflicts. Hobson justified his ideas on centralised force through an appeal to the surplus and organic concepts. His discussion of international government as the culmination of the growth of international institutions and his broader proposals for an international federation are also couched in terms of these concepts. However, Hobson's reliance on a centralised force sits uneasily with his evolutionary discussion of international relations.

This chapter explores the tension between Hobson's idea of an international government maintaining the peace, outlined in the early chapters of *Towards International Government*, and his more general ideas on the emergence of peace through international co-operation. The first section examines Hobson's proposals for an international government involving extended provisions for arbitration and conciliation and the establishment of an international force. Hobson's broader conception of international government as a federation of nations united by a network of international functional institutions is discussed in the second section. The subsequent section considers Hobson's reaction to the formation and travails of the League of Nations during the inter-war period. Next, Hobson's proposals for an international government are placed in the context of his surplus and organic concepts. After some critical remarks, the conclusion suggests Hobson's proposals for centralised force in international government were illiberal and that his new liberal, proto-functionalist analysis was sounder.

THE LOGIC OF INTERNATIONAL GOVERNMENT: COLLECTIVE SECURITY, LAW AND PEACE

Hobson argued a simple, logical case for international government. He did not detain himself with the intricate details of how such an institution might actually operate, claiming that it would be bad intellectual economy to get bogged down in the details.[3] Hobson argued that an international government must have extensive powers and functions ceded to it by states. He proposed that arbitration and conciliation should replace war as the means to resolve disputes between states not settled through diplomatic means. The kernel of his proposals, however, was that nations should use their joint pressure to ensure that disputants agree to go to peaceful settlement and comply with subsequent decisions. Members of the new international organisation would deter aggression both from within and outside the organisation through the threat of the use of their predominant force in joint action against an aggressor. Hobson believed that collective force would not only enhance peaceful settlement but would encourage nations to disarm.

Arbitration, conciliation and the extension of international law

Hobson approved of the development of arbitration agreements in the Hague Conferences and in bilateral treaties before the First World War. He argued, though, that the War had exposed their flaws as means of peaceful settlement. Arrangements for arbitration were weak to begin with because there were a multitude of separate treaties with different rules. There was little consistency among them to permit the extension of the rules of arbitration into general principles of international law.

While agreements on arbitration varied widely in scope and application, Hobson decried two common features. First, honour and vital interests were usually excluded from arbitration treaties. Second, dispute settlement procedures generally utilised a tribunal format which was putatively balanced through the appointment of an equal number of partisan judges. For Hobson, the first created a loophole for aggression; the second mistook 'balanced' partisanship for impartiality. Hobson also condemned arbitration arrangements before the War for their lack of sanction, that there was no penalty for not abiding by arbitration or conciliation judgements.[4]

As his alternative vision, Hobson proposed a single arbitration treaty to be signed by all states. This universal treaty would standardise international legal procedure. He argued that submission of disputes and observation of arbitration awards to an International Arbitration Cout be compulsory. He called for a sanction to be attached to failure to submit disputes or to honour awards.[5]

Hobson acknowledged that not all disputes were amenable to arbitration. Disputes that could be arbitrated were those involving legal interpretation of treaties or international law, disputes that could be settled within international law, and disputes concerning facts that could be scrutinised according to the legal rules of evidence.[6] Non-arbitrable disputes were those that involved political issues and economic and other interests. These were by their nature more controversial, but also were likely to be a greater source of international strife. To deal with these disputes, Hobson suggested drastic changes to the Hague's International Commissions of Inquiry to transform them into what he called a Conciliation Commission. Hobson's proposals for the new Commission parallel those for the Court of Arbitration. There was to be a general treaty adhered to by all states, including provision for the compulsory submission of all disputes without reservations. The proposal that the restructured Commission should be permitted to discuss all non-arbitrable disputes also widened the scope of the Commissions of Inquiry considerably.[7]

Hobson further proposed that the Conciliation Commission should not be limited to making reports based on their inquiries and attempts at conciliation. It would, like the Court of Arbitration, make awards. Awards would propose resolutions to disputes which would have to be abided to by the disputants.[8] Hobson suggested another major innovation: he hoped that the Conciliation Commission could have a preventive as well as a curative role in dispute resolution. To this end, he recommended that the Commission should have the power to initiate inquiries into disputes or potential areas of conflict, even if the case had not been submitted by the disputants. Hobson hoped that the Commission might intervene in the early stages of disputes, thus facilitating peaceful resolution of conflict and avoiding the outbreak of hostilities.[9]

Hobson also advanced the idea of 'cooling off' as an aid to peaceful settlement.[10] For Hobson, halting a state's pursuit of its cause by military means gave 'the opportunity for a full rally of the resources of informed public opinion on the side of peace'. He claimed that:

> Delay, the statement of the case and the consequent appeal to justice, will, therefore, insensibly and not slowly undermine the absolutism of the modern State, by enabling statesmen to perceive that the reasonable self of a nation can only be maintained by membership of a Society of Nations, and that such membership involves a submission of its private arbitrary judgement on international matters of conduct to the rational will of the whole Society.[11]

In short, rational thought would prevail, given time, and the pacific influence of world and national public opinion would have time to assert itself.

Finally, Hobson wished to support the activities of the Commission with a sanction to enforce submission of disputes and compliance with its awards, if required.[12]

To summarise, Hobson proposed measures to facilitate and enforce legal settlement of disputes between states. These measures were to replace war and mitigate states' attempts to be the judges in their own cause. To effect these proposals, Hobson insisted upon two fundamental changes in the nature of contemporary international law. First, treaties for peaceful settlement of disputes through arbitration and conciliation had to be made wider in their scope and have (near) universal adherence by states. Second, submission of disputes to the Court or Commission was to be compulsory and without reservation, as was the observation of awards handed down. Hobson tried, then, to close the loopholes through which states had been able to avoid arbitration and fight aggressive wars, such as the First World War, by non-adherence or non-compliance.

Considering all the elements together, Hobson's proposal for peaceful settlement of disputes entailed a treaty setting up an international organisation of which all states would be members:

The Treaty establishing a League of Nations would, ... in the first instance, bind the signatory Powers, not to a particular mode of settlement by Arbitration or otherwise, but to submit all issues on request to a Joint Committee of Investigation, empowered to determine whether the particular issue was by reason of its nature, or the point of its development suitable for settlement by Arbitration or Conciliation, or by a preliminary process of Inquiry by the Council of Conciliation with a view to subsequent reference to Arbitration.[13]

Collective force, an international executive and disarmament

Resolution of disputes by arbitration and the rules of international law instead of war rested ultimately on the ability of the international community to compel disputants to come to arbitration or conciliation and to observe awards. The third major change in international law Hobson called for was that there be sufficient sanction to enforce submission and compliance with awards. Hobson claimed that arbitration and conciliation would come to nought if there was no adequate sanction for non-compliance with the obligation to submit disputes or honour awards. Without a credible sanction, Hobson argued, states would not be able to trust in arbitration or conciliation. He asked 'If no provision is made for enforcing the acceptance of the recommendations of [the Conciliation Commission], what measure of security has been attained?'. States would fear that others would 'defect' (to use recent game theory terminology), that is, continue to use war as an instrument of national policy and not abide by international decisions. They would therefore continue to rely on traditional means of providing for national security. This fear, Hobson pointed out, was at the root of the arms races between states and was a major source of international conflict.

Collective military force involved a cession of certain sovereign powers by states to back up the international organisation of arbitration and conciliation. Hobson recognised that states would be reluctant to undertake to make an international force that could conceivably be used against themselves. He hoped, however, that the manifest failure of international mechanisms lacking such central power to back up the law would persuade states that collective force was the only way forward.[14]

The emphasis on the necessity of force is a novelty in Hobson's discussions of international relations.[15] Hobson both defended and criticised the arrangements for peaceful settlement derived at the Hague. The Hague arrangements failed, he claimed, not because they were fundamentally mistaken but because they were not backed up by adequate military sanctions. According to Hobson, the first essential of the international government was to keep the peace. It must therefore be strong enough to do so.[16] Prior to the First World War, in *The Case for Arbitration* and *Imperialism*, Hobson had argued that public opinion and a sense of justice were sufficient for the operation of international arbitration. Arbitration was the peaceful alternative to settlement of disputes by war. By contrast, his view in *Towards International Government* showed something of a realist turn towards the use of force in the face of the failure of such moral sanctions in the race to war and its cataclysmic course once begun.[17]

Hobson argued that a sanctioned scheme would encourage peace because it would be an incentive to disarmament. A collective force as a sanction for arbitration decisions would break the cycle of fear of one state of another's aggression, Hobson believed. Such an arrangement would only work, though, if all states were convinced that there was no gain to be made from aggression. Under such conditions, it might even attract states initially outside the treaty: 'If the united strength of the Treaty Powers remained so great as to render the pursuance of [a state's] aggressive designs impossible or too dangerous, the lawless Power might learn the lesson of the law, and abandoning its hopes of aggression, come into the League.'[18]

Hobson wrote that alliances were notoriously short-lived and an inadequate means to provide for national security. The collective security mechanism of international government would reverse the motives of national policy, he believed, dissolving the particularistic ties that made for the shifting pattern of international alliances.[19] Hobson hoped that states would calculate their security gains in the international government and be convinced to abandon their old alliances, intrigues and arms races, trading their national attempts to provide security separately through development or augmentation of their own military forces for the security of international law backed by an effective collective force.

In terms of the shape of the collective force, Hobson dismissed the idea of creating an independent international force or permanently allocating national units to a joint force. Instead, he advocated a formal arrangement whereby member states in a collective security arrangement would take joint action as decided against an aggressor.[20] He also proposed that, as a result of increasing international interdependence, an economic blockade of an aggressor could be a weapon in the collective security mechanism. However, he counselled that boycotts were prone to evasion by those supposedly implementing them and liable also to rebound on the initiators. Nonetheless, he particularly approved of the idea of a financial (as opposed to trade) boycott. A financial boycott, he suggested, would be facilitated by the creation of international financial institutions as part of the international government.[21]

While he conceded that a Joint Standing Committee would be sufficient to direct the collective force of a minimal League of Peace, Hobson claimed that more extensive international arrangements for peace were required. An international council representing the member-states was required, so as to act as the executive of international decisions.[22] 'Without such a representative body in permanent being,' he argued, 'a deep sense of unreality will continue to attach to the Court of Arbitration and the Committees of Conciliation and to the treaty which shall claim to establish them as authoritative modes of settlement'.[23] The international council would embody the universality of the arbitration and conciliation agreements as well as the collective security mechanism. Being a permanent international body, the international council could take action to prevent as well as remedy international conflicts.

The membership and structure of the international government

Hobson used terms like 'international government' and 'society of nations' loosely, as we have seen. By world state, for instance, Hobson meant 'any body of political arrangements to which most of the principal nations of the world are parties, sufficiently stable in character and wide in scope to merit the title of international government'.[24] He is not even consistent in his use of the phrase 'society of nations', which sometimes appears to mean the collectivity of the nations of the world, and sometimes the government of that collectivity.[25] The binding together into a treaty for arbitration, for Hobson, was the basis for confederation.[26]

The primary institutions of international government were, Hobson believed, an international court overseeing arbitration and conciliation and an international executive council. Hobson did not discuss an international secretariat or administration to any great degree, except to assume that there should be one to support the operations of the new international institutions. He did propose that there should be an international legislature to go with the executive and judiciary. An international council would be an inadequate response to the constantly erupting international conflicts arising as a result of rapid pace of global change. An international parliament would make and amend international law and treaties to facilitate international co-operation and avoid potential conflicts. It would also reflect changes in global 'public opinion'.

For Hobson, an international legislature was a logical consequence of his analysis. He had allocated the Conciliation Commission the power to initiate inquiries into disputes and potential conflict situations. He acknowledged that the awards and inquiries of the Commission would amend old international law and create new ones. A legislative body was thus necessary in order to oversee the modifications and development of international law to ensure its coherence and relevance to contemporary international conditions.[27]

Hobson argued that membership of the international government should be as universal as possible; all willing nations were to be admitted into any new intergovernmental arrangements. There were both immediate and practical as well as long-term reasons of principle for Hobson's arguments for universality. After the First World War, the exclusion of the defeated powers, particularly Germany, would mean that the international government was effectively a continuation of the victorious alliance. Ultimately, Hobson believed, a League only of the war-time allies would bring about the reassertion of the balance of power. Inclusion of Germany would, he believed, aid the reduction of lingering resentment of war between the combatant nations. While Hobson hoped that the new international government would be the international manifestation of democracy, he argued that non-democratic states, such as Russia, should be included. Similarly, the inclusion of non-European states such as Japan and the USA was required because 'an attempt to treat Europe as a separate political system would be mischievous'. Furthermore, in the long term, international justice and the 'wider task of preserving world-order could only be performed with equity if all the nations were represented in the League'.[28]

In his discussion of voting power in the international (executive) council, clearly the hub of the international government in Hobson's eyes, he argued against 'one state, one vote'. To begin with there was a huge disparity between states. There was little prudential need for formal equality of nations in an international government, as there was with the individual representation in national government that guaranteed the integrity of persons. Hobson argued, further, that setting voting rights according to sovereign statehood would have a deleterious impact on internationalism. He speculated that population might be a basis for representation and voting, and later that standard of civilisation might be an important qualification to a strict population measure. Hobson claimed that the utilitarian principle of votes per power or per head of population was not entirely theoretically sound but was nonetheless the most likely to be adhered to by the Great Powers that would be the ones most needed in the establishment of the new organisation. Anyway, 'putting the matter at its worst,' he argued pragmatically, 'it would be better for the interests of the great nations to prevail than for those of the small nations, not because a great nation is more likely to be in the right, but because it is better for a larger number of human beings to have their way than for a smaller'.[29]

Hobson was concerned about the matter of the type of person who should participate in the activities of the international government. 'Men of legal eminence' were appropriate appointments for the Court of Arbitration and, to a lesser extent, the Conciliation Commission.[30] The Executive Council should be made up of representatives from the member-states. These representatives, Hobson hoped, would be men of public affairs, such as politicians, literary figures, and so on, rather than the career diplomats who represented and espoused what he regarded as the old order. He hoped that democratic nations would elect their representatives. Democratic representation would give legitimacy to a representative and ensure that he was respected at home. Democratic election would also, Hobson believed, encourage the participation on the Council of men imbued with the spirit of internationalism. To operate effectively, Hobson believed that the Council would have to be made up of permanent representatives. These men could devote their time and energy to the international government and avoid the distraction of national commitments.

The issues of the character of international personnel and (where possible) democratic representation were critical in Hobson's eyes. It was essential to remove the diplomats of the old order if the experiment in internationalism was to have a chance of succeeding. The old ways of the diplomatic corps would cramp internationalism and infuse international co-operation with the tradition of suspicion that had predominated in the past, he felt. In the long run, election of representatives to the international government was considered by Hobson a step towards a truly democratic international government, accurately representing 'the international mind'.[31] Though he later admitted that the notion of democratic control of foreign policy was harder to pin down than many (including Hobson himself) had thought, he stressed, in *Towards International Government*, the importance of public scrutiny and input from democratically elected representatives to the main lines of foreign policy, including the signing and amending of treaties.[32] First, in the early stages of the international government, democratic control would prevent a swift return to the old politics by ousting the personnel of that era. Second, democratic control was part of Hobson's larger vision of a democratic federation of nations; in other words it was a part of the triad of peace, democracy and internationalism.

INTERNATIONAL GOVERNMENT, CO-OPERATION AND PEACE

According to Hobson, while the institutional arrangements of arbitration, an international council and collective force were mechanisms to prevent conflict arising, they did not solve (or cure, as Hobson wrote, utilising a medical variant on his organic analogy) the problems leading to the conflict. International government could do more than simply keep the peace. It could, he argued, help to resolve some of the underlying tensions that led to the outbreak of hostilities. It had a positive role to play in encouraging international co-operation that was the route to a more fundamental and durable peace than could be achieved merely through institutional innovation for arbitration and so on. This was Hobson's ideal of an international federation with associated functional agencies outlined in chapter 4.

Hobson's suggestions for international government-led co-operation follow from his theory of co-operative surplus and his organic analogy. He hoped that the international government would be able to tackle international economic problems and especially to address the issue of international economic inequality. He claimed that international institutions had grown over the course of the nineteenth century, largely to deal with international issues raised by commerce, transportation and communications, and other technical matters. Hobson believed that '[w]e possess already the beginnings alike of the legislative, judicial, and administrative apparatus of international government' and advocated building on these rudimentary organs of international government.[33] Hobson envisaged an international government growing from its beginnings as a minimal arrangement to secure peace, such as he had proposed, to one that would forward human welfare through constructive co-operation and positive internationalism.

Hobson argued for international regulation of the rapidly changing and increasingly complex technical co-operation across national boundaries. An international body to monitor and oversee these new developments was required. Regulation effectively created new law, implying a role for the international legislature. He argued that the benefits of central organisation of technical and commercial international co-operation would lead to a steady growth in functions for the international government, because 'an immensely enhanced economy would be given to this co-operation if its various branches could be gathered into a single centre and placed under a single international supervision and control'.[34] This centralising tendency had been manifest in all smaller areas of society, and Hobson believed that the same would apply to the society of nations.[35] At the same time, international functional agencies would be delegated specific functions.

Hobson believed that an international federation was the ideal political form for international government, it having a single overarching structure to match the scope of the world economy, while also reflecting the diversity of the political and cultural world. An international federation was an expression of the development of civilisation, giving substance to the emerging international mind, that is, the spirit of internationalism, that was growing among civilised peoples. Federalism was, according to Hobson, 'the international aspect of democracy'.[36] Besides the federal structure, Hobson's ideal involved democratic states with the people in control of foreign policy, along the lines of Kant's scheme in *Perpetual Peace.*[37]

Federalism was, for Hobson, a functional mode of government, a means of enhancing global welfare and avoiding international conflict. For Hobson, it also incorporated a prototype of the principle of subsidiarity that has since emerged in the context of the European Union:

> Federalism implies everywhere the subordination of the absolute sovereignty of one political area to the claims of a wider rule on the ground that certain

> aspects of local or national government vitally affect the wider area. It may be regarded as an economy of government, each area, from the family through the widening areas of local and national government to internationalism, practising free self-government in such matters as fall predominantly within the compass of its own knowledge, interest and capacity.[38]

The international government would be concerned with matters of international peace, security, economy and so on, but would delegate many of the other functions to national governments, which in turn would deal with their particular concerns and delegate the rest to local governments.

Hobson did not hold that all these elements were required for any experiment in international government, such as the League of Nations, to be worthwhile. However, he did believe that an international federation of democratic nations was the political arrangement of the world to guarantee a true, lasting peace. This is where some problems arise: the driving force behind Hobson's scheme for peace is centralised force; behind his ideas for constructive internationalism, it is democratic organisation.

Hobson's conception of the international federation differed in kind from his idea of the League as a collective security mechanism. The latter involved a strong central government with decisions being made at the centre in order to be authoritative. The international federation, on the other hand, would have to delegate authority for many political decisions to the respective national states, and on industrial, financial and commercial matters to what he called 'federal functional bodies'.[39] The contrast between these two approaches is the subject of the fourth section.

THE LEAGUE OF NATIONS

It would be something of an understatement to say that Hobson was not impressed with the League of Nations as it was actually established. He poured scorn upon the new international arrangement, 'this sham league', as he called it. The experiment in internationalism provoked some of Hobson's most visceral writings on international relations. The League of Nations was 'oligarchic', 'a conspiracy of autocrats', 'a League of Governments', 'a travesty of internationalism' and 'a Holy Alliance of the Entente Powers'. Most explicitly, it was 'a League of the Foreign Offices of the Governments of the victorious Allies'. The League was a sham because it was not a League of Nations or Peoples but a 'League of Conquerors'.[40] The tenor of Hobson's criticisms of the new League can be indicated in a few words: it was an inadequate international government. All this, despite the fact that he had initially dismissed the idea that a League of Nations could become a New Holy Alliance![41]

Hobson wrote a stinging critique of the peace negotiations at the end of the First World War and the creation of the League within that framework. He exposed what he called the idealism of the peoples and the politicians, and demonstrated how this idealism was exploited by powerful cliques of politicians and businessmen who had an interest in the re-establishment of the old aristocratic and state-centric order of international relations.[42]

Hobson criticised the creation of new nationalities at the end of the First World War.[43] He decried unfair application of the principle of national self-determination. The principle was qualified by 'military necessity', 'historical right' and 'economic need'. The principle and its exceptions were invoked in such a way that they worked against the defeated central European powers, he argued accurately. The new states in central and eastern Europe created new German minorities. The most stark abuse of the principle of national self-determination, however, was the refusal to allow the newly truncated Austria to join Germany, despite the express wish of the Austrian population to do so. The pandering to nationalist sentiment elsewhere in Europe and especially the creation of new national boundaries to trade in the break-up of the Ottoman and Austro-Hungarian Empires fostered resentment in the defeated nations, stimulated aggressive nationalism across Europe and stored up economic troubles for a stricken continent following an exhausting war.[44] The implications for the League were disastrous. With few provisions for sound economic internationalism in the League Covenant, Hobson correctly predicted that the League would preside over an increasing level of nationalist animosity and economic exclusion.

The critique of the League of Nations

So much for Hobson's criticisms of the peace settlement at the end of the First World War. The first problem with the League of Nations was that it was linked to that settlement. 'Instead of being founded on the broad basis of peaceful equality of nations', Hobson observed that the

League was 'an appendage to a dictated peace, thus absorbing the principle not of equal justice but of force in its very origin'.

This was not just an unfortunate accident, however. Hobson accused the makers of the League of seeking to perpetuate the Entente Powers' supremacy at the end of the war by institutionalising their position in the new international organisation. According to Hobson, the Covenant was 'an extended War Alliance impudently masquerading as international'.[45] The League was formed by the victorious allies and was composed of that alliance plus 'good' neutrals. Bad neutrals (those who were considered to have sided with the Central Powers or with Communist Russia) and enemies from the War were excluded from the new international organisation. This injustice was magnified by the provision in the Covenant that subsequent accessions to the League would be accepted only on a two-thirds vote of the League Assembly. Even then, new member-states joined at the status of a small power. Hobson pointed out that the terms for Germany's accession to the League meant that it would rank with Siam and Newfoundland rather than France or the United Kingdom.

Hobson was deeply worried by the exclusion of Germany and Soviet Russia and the refusal of the United States to take part in the League. The lack of universal membership, particularly the absence of a number of great powers, rendered the justice of its arbitral decisions and the activity of its collective force problematic. It also created another complication: possible League intervention in non-member states' affairs. Hobson argued that any such collective action would be tantamount to ruling without consent. The League Covenant should apply only to those states that signed it, he argued.[46]

The domination of the victorious Great Powers in the new international arrangement was most clearly exemplified by their control of the Council, the most powerful decision-making body in the League's structure.[47] Hobson also criticised the allocation of votes in the League Assembly to the self-governing dominions of the British Empire. Hobson denied that these dominions were self-governing, particularly in the all-important area of foreign relations. The votes of the self-governing dominions were in fact British votes. He argued that this violated any pretence to democratic representation as it gave Britain six votes to every other state's one.[48] But all talk of votes was, Hobson suggested, 'futile' anyway, because amendments to the League's constitution could only be effected with a unanimous vote of the membership. Hobson scoffed that this gave every member-state a veto on internationalism, effectively reinstating state sovereignty as the organising principle of the international experiment.[49] Hobson expected League collective action to follow sporadically when certain Great Powers wanted it and when their own military power was deemed to be unequal to the task.

According to Hobson, the League was designed not as a mechanism for disarmament but as a second line of military defence for the Great Powers. The first means of defence was the retention of full national forces.[50] Hobson pointed out that the retention of large national forces by League members would render disarmament impossible, because the arms race would continue.

He later criticised the League for failing to acknowledge underlying tensions that were major causes of international instability, such as imperialism and exclusive nationalism. League supporters had, claimed Hobson, overemphasised narrow concerns with peace and disarmament to the neglect of the positive, constructive co-operation required as the basis of a true, lasting peace.[51] Disarmament and arbitration had failed and would continue to fail, he argued, if the international antagonism and fears that caused nations to build up their armouries were not removed. In this vein, Hobson attacked the mandate system instituted in the League as 'a thin veneer for the distribution of colonial spoils among the Big Five'.[52] League mandate provisions were to apply to derelict empires and territories unable to govern themselves. However, this was a pretext for the division of the Ottoman and German overseas empires between the Allies, especially favouring the British dominions. The division of mandates had been decided by the victorious allies at a conference before the creation of the League. This division of mandated territories was then imposed on the League and the vanquished empires by the Allies.

Hobson claimed that '[t]he mandatory clauses of the Covenant furnish the political machinery for the completion of the process by which Western Europe has absorbed in colonies and protectorates so large a section of the earth'.[53] According to Hobson, the League mandates constituted a new phase in imperialism where the ruling classes of certain powers would govern the entire world under the cloak of internationalism. He was outraged at the provision only for 'equitable' (as opposed to equal) treatment of all trading and investment concerns in mandate territories. The mandatory power was thus effectively accorded economic privileges that it could hand to its nationals, excluding or restricting other nations' firms and entrepreneurs. The transformation of the mandate idea, which Hobson supported as beneficial to internationalism, into a new form of imperial control was most obvious for Hobson in the absence of effective monitoring of the mandate territories by the League.[54]

A qualified defence of the League

Hobson was not all criticisms, however. He reserved a few kind words for the League as the first tentative step towards organising international co-operation and, ultimately, to the creation of an international government. He interpreted and defended the League as the permanent embodiment of an internationalism that had been evolving since the nineteenth century.[55]

Before the War, Hobson had argued that '[t]he insistence upon freedom to make war and bring havoc into the social order of the world, is a right not to rational liberty but to anarchy'.[56] He continued his opposition to the unreserved rights of state sovereignty after the War. Indeed, the failure of the League was making 'manifest the urgent peril of an anarchy of States as an alternative'.[57] Rampant sovereignty resulted in international anarchy, for which international government was the only solution.

> An ill-constructed State is generally better than anarchy. Now, the present alternative to a League of Nations, however unsatisfactory in its personal control, is a return to international anarchy.

This might appear a rather conservative idea, Hobson observed, being the defence of an unsatisfactory status quo. However, the League was a flawed but still vital institution in the creation of international peace and human welfare.

Hobson approved of the League's acknowledgement of the principle that 'effective self-government requires that the area of such government shall be related to the particular groups interested in the objects of such government'.[58] The League thus incorporated national interests as part of internationalism. While wary of assertions of nationalism and sovereignty, Hobson viewed a cosmopolitan government or unitary world state as unnatural in the context of contemporary international relations.[59]

Hobson even accounted for the League's failure to make significant advances in international co-operation by pointing to the uniquely bad context for progress in international relations after the First World War. The slow progress arose, according to Hobson, because of the tying of the new international organisation to an unjust peace treaty. Furthermore, in the post-war period there was, according to Hobson, an unparalleled atmosphere of antagonism and desire for revenge in international relations. The suspicions of France, the exclusion of Soviet Russia, the isolation of the United States, the feeling of betrayal and disillusionment in Germany and the struggles of new European nation-states contributed to a renewed militarism and nationalism. Effectual operation of the League's economic agencies was precluded by the dislocation created by national economic insecurity after the Great War, the fall-out of indebtedness and monetary instability from the War and the onset of the Great Depression.[60]

Hobson proposed a series of reforms to improve on the League's feeble performance and reduce its biases. Reiterating the requirements of a successful international government, he listed the following conditions:

> The inclusion at the formation of the League of all willing nations, the detachment of the constitutions and functions of the League from all war associations, the adoption of open diplomacy and popular representation in the League government, effective international control over the relations between advanced and backward peoples, the application of the Open Door policy to all backward countries and new areas of economic development . . .

He also called for the immediate inclusion of Germany with status equal to the other Great Powers, a truly representative international parliament with deliberative and legislative powers, a fairer basis for representation on the League Council, the replacement of the unanimity provision by majority rule, and the creation of an international commission reflecting the interests of labour to decide on international standards for working conditions.[61]

In *Towards International Government*, Hobson was cautious enough to admit that his more extensive proposals could not be expected to happen overnight.[62] In his calls for reform immediately after the establishment of the League, however, he demanded immediate changes to the League that went far beyond merely remedying its defective origin; mechanisms for constructive co-operation should be enacted as soon as possible.

The League and internationalism in the twenties and thirties

Hobson continued to advocate reform in the cause of the progress of civilisation through peace, democracy and internationalism, though he claimed that the First World War had shaken his conviction in the rationality of man. While he was concerned during this period with the problems of a new world, as he called it, there were new opportunities as well as looming dangers.

Hobson's tone on international issues changed during the thirties. He became increasingly disillusioned with the League and the prospects for internationalism. The thirties were a period of instability and crisis, to be sure. Hobson was by now an old man who had outlived most of his life-long friends. The difficulties were greater still: the failure of the League as a system of collective security, the rise of Fascism and the Great Depression confronted Hobson and his liberal and radical friends with the apparent failure of all they had hoped for. 'Can democracy survive?' was a central question in Hobson's *Democracy and a Changing Civilisation.* He even asked whether, in its present form, it should survive. His answer was (as ever), more or less, yes.[63] Internationalism and peace, the other two parts of the triad of political causes to which Hobson applied himself, also appeared to be suffering secular decline. For Hobson, the League manifestly failed in the crises over Abyssinia, Manchuria and Spain. His belief in the League as an instrument of international co-operation waned.[64]

Hobson changed his opinion on the need for a single international force as the hard end of collective security. In the thirties, he called for an international air force to deter aggression and keep the peace, a proposal similar to that by David Davies. This rather fantastic suggestion for reform can be seen simply as another variant of the centralised force, advanced in *Towards International Government.* However, there is a tone of desperation here. The suggestion strikes one as the outdated view of a Victorian who considered bicycles revolutionary.[65] Hobson closed his discussion of an international air force on an alarming note that sums up one of the problems with the idea of an international force: 'can we look forward to an early time when humanity will triumph over nationality – or when the bombing of a city will be accounted a defence of humanity?'.[66]

Hobson's renewed emphasis on the importance of domestic reform further reflected his withdrawal of support from the League. The 'hard saying' of 1915 became the only way forward in the late thirties:

It is impracticable to hope for peace and justice in international affairs unless the conditions for internal peace and justice within the nations have already been substantially obtained.[67]

Internationalism, democracy and peace were still intimately linked. However, now Hobson believed that democracy within the nation-state had to come first, controverting his warnings about the 'Close State' being of necessity militaristic. Though Kenneth Waltz has suggested that Hobson's was generally a state-level analysis of international relations, this was the first time that Hobson clearly placed a temporal priority on domestic reform over international reform.[68]

What remained of Hobson's commitment to practical internationalism became a defence of the achievements of democracy against the rise and aggression of the Fascist powers. He conceded the necessity of a limited organisation for collective defence. No doubt, he admitted, this would reinstate the balance of power, but such were the circumstances that this policy was necessary. For instance, Hobson approved of Clarence Streit's plan for the union of the democratic countries.[69] At the beginning of the Second World War, Hobson hoped for US intervention in the war in the hope that the war would thus be prevented from escalating or made shorter. His gloomy conclusion was that the Second World War could end in a victory for Fascism or, even if the Western powers were to win, a re-run of the iniquities of Versailles.[70]

In his wartime proposals, Hobson hoped that the peoples would lead internationalism. He closed *Towards International Government* in a confident mood:

[The peoples] will insist that the obsolete rhetoric of Power and Sovereignty, with the ideas of exclusiveness and antagonism which it sustains, shall be swept away, and that the affairs which concern nations shall be set upon the same footing of decent reasonable settlement that prevails in every other human relation.

With his growing disillusionment with the League, Hobson admitted, however, that '[t]he sentiment of humanity, human sympathy, still lags far behind the requirements of a sound World Government' and also behind the actual facts of economic and political internationalism.[71] In his last writings, Hobson argued that what was needed was a spirit of internationalism, not more rational arguments why internationalism was sound, or institutions claiming to represent the international interest. While this spiritual internationalism was a theme common to many of Hobson's writings, here he contrasted it with the failure of the practical experiment rather than hinting at their dialectical relationship. There is the suggestion that true internationalism would have to wait until the distant future and that no amount of international institutional reform would change that. In many ways, Hobson's writings in the late thirties reflect the crisis of liberal internationalism of the time. The previously reinforcing relationship of theory and practice, of domestic and international reform and of spiritual and material elements in internationalism had broken down.

THE LOGIC OF INTERNATIONAL GOVERNMENT AND HOBSON'S EVOLUTIONARY APPROACH TO INTERNATIONAL RELATIONS

Hobson deployed the organic analogy and his theory of co-operative surplus as rationalisations for international government. Unfortunately, his proposals for the extension of international law and an international force, though he claimed them as a part of his scheme for a fully democratic international government, do not fit well with his evolutionary approach to international relations.

A central feature of Hobson's proposals for an international government in 1915 was his emphasis on the need for a central force. Hobson claimed that peace was the first function of government. In international relations, he argued that the international government had to use force to maintain peace. The collective international force would impose justice and enforce decisions of the international court, as well as deterring aggression. He made the case for a centralised force by appealing to an argument analogous to the theory of co-operative surplus.[72] According to Hobson, force could not be done away with entirely, because society or the world was neither entirely rational nor entirely just. However, with advances in civilisation, force was a diminishing element in social relations. Legitimate force had become more or less monopolised by a central agency representing the whole of society, i.e., the state, creating what Hobson called the economy of force in the progress of civilisation. Force (nearly) monopolised by the central agency resulted in an aggregate reduction in the use of force in society.[73] Furthermore, Hobson argued, along the lines of his organic theory, that physical force *per se* was not a bad thing. It was only a malevolent factor when used disproportionately to ends secured or for an irrational purpose. For example, war in the international system was a bad thing because of its sectional nature. International force, representing the will of the international society, would be more likely to be just. Nonetheless, Hobson argued, other rational methods of altering behaviour were to be preferred over force if these were available. Opponents of a world super-state, 'moral force anarchists' as Hobson called them, opposed Hobson's arrangement on the grounds that as states were tyrannical, a super-state would be super-tyrannical. Hobson argued against this that central force had been needed in all societies, large and small, throughout history, and that it was highly irresponsible to abjure the use of force in a society where morality was as yet undeveloped. 'It is idle to imagine', he argued, 'that a society starting with so little inner unity of status and purpose can dispense entirely with the backing of physical force with which the most highly evolved of national societies has been unable to dispense.'[74]

In *Towards International Government*, Hobson was hoping for a revolutionary change, exemplified by significant institutional innovation, in international relations. He described this (again in organic terms) as a 'rapid mutation'.[75] At the end of the First World War, he expected that the peoples of the world, tired of war, would call for a drastic change in international arrangements to avoid a recurrence of the Great War. He appears to have believed that such a rapid transition was possible, indeed a necessity, because of the unusual and traumatic conditions of the War and its immediate aftermath. He believed that the dread of the alternative, that is, a return to the war system of the balance of power, would be sufficient to convince people to support an international government.[76]

Hobson's economy-of-force argument for international government rested on a presumption derived from his evolutionary approach to international relations: international relations was a backward realm of social organisation when compared to domestic society. As we have seen, Hobson believed that the morality of international relations was primitive, but developing with the advance of internationalism. The economy-of-force argument suggested that force was necessary even in an advanced and civilised society such as Britain. How much more, Hobson maintained, did international relations require central force to maintain peaceable and just relations in the primitive, predominantly egoistic, morality of the society of nations.

Hobson's conception of the primitive nature of international relations gave rise to an anomaly in the first half of *Towards International Government*. Though he condemned the use of the term 'Power' when referring to the relations of nations, Hobson used this term throughout his discussion of his proposed League as an arbitration treaty and a collective security system, and in his sketch of the structure of an international government.[77]

The anomalous use of the term 'power' indicates that there is something awry. Though adopting some of the rhetoric of an evolutionary approach, the force-oriented perspective of Hobson's international government proposals is not compatible with the evolutionary perspective on international relations embodied in his broader suggestions for an international federation. In the latter, Hobson recognised that government's role goes beyond peace-keeping, as he had shown in the domestic context. Hobson argued that the constructive co-operation of nations, rather than simply preventive measures, was integral to a durable and meaningful peace.[78] International government, like national governments, could encourage and direct co-operation. If international relations were developing and becoming more integrated, particularly in international economic relations, it would be appropriate for an international government to fulfil the role of the international co-operative institution representing the interests of the society of nations as a whole. The underlying premise here is that co-operation rather than centralised force brings peace. It follows that international government reflects not the economy of force but the economy of organisation. The argument for centralised force suggests that peace and order need to be maintained in international relations for the achievement of improvements in human welfare to be possible; the argument for constructive internationalism suggests that the satisfaction of human welfare involves human interaction and institutions that will bring peace and order to international relations.

The organic analogy and theory of co-operative surplus tend to support incremental change rather than the revolutionary change Hobson called for in his blueprint in *Towards International Government*. In contrast to his centralised international government as a collective security mechanism, Hobson's ideas on international government as an international organisation performing welfare functions and reflecting the federal nature of international political life are evolutionary, gradualist and devolutionary. They rest not on dramatic changes of political opinion grasping international institutions and bending them to their will, but on gradual change in international organisation as a response to the underlying conditions of global welfare requirements. International relations were backward, but were evolving; the emerging internationalism brought a more developed sense of morality for international relations. The standard-bearers of the developing morality of civilisation were the democratic, advanced nations of the world, often smaller states such as Switzerland or the Scandinavian countries, rather than the powers that currently ruled international relations to whom Hobson had turned in his force-oriented collective security proposal. The contradiction between the economy of force and the economy of organisation appears additionally in Hobson's proposal for an international economic boycott and financial pressure: such economic coercion sits uneasily with Hobson's economic internationalism and his belief in the benefits of international co-operation.

How did Hobson make this mistake? His arguments for a central force appear to be illiberal and anti-democratic. The incongruity results from an error by Hobson. He mistook an emergency measure, the last resort of established authority, for the foundation of that authority. International force was an emergency measure both at the end of the First World War and in the face of the threat of Fascist aggression. The international force was a way of stabilising international relations in a time of chaos. However, Hobson did not question the premise of this stabilisation sufficiently; it was not a basis for a democratic federation of nations. For instance, Hobson hoped for the inclusion of all the nations of the world, yet his international structure strictly only required the adherence of the Great Powers for its successful operation.[79]

Hobson's specific proposals for international relations varied over time, as we saw, and the contradictions in his work emerged in his response to international change. Yet his analysis of international relations as a backward social realm remained the same. What actually changed was his estimation of the current potentialities and progress of international relations. His force-centred analysis reflected a deep pessimism about the morality and altruism in the relations of states. This pessimism is not surprising considering the state of the world in 1915 when *Towards International Government* was written, in the period immediately after the War when Hobson described the world in such negative terms in *Problems of a New World*, and during the crises of the thirties when Hobson wrote a piece called 'Force Necessary to Government'. Pessimism led Hobson to emphasise the need for central force as the vanguard of a more constructive internationalism that was to follow later. At these times, Hobson's attitude seems to have been that the poor condition of international relations required an immediate, revolutionary change. This contrasts with the optimism about the progress of civilisation that predominated in his discussion of constructive internationalism as the pinnacle of his evolutionary scale for world order, where gradual change was nevertheless inevitable and indeed already in progress.

A CRITICAL LOOK AT HOBSON'S PROPOSALS FOR COMPULSORY ARBITRATION AND COLLECTIVE SECURITY

Hobson's proposals for a centralised international government for compulsory arbitration and collective security suffered from the problems common to such schemes.[80] Additionally there were contradictions between Hobson's visions of collective security and his prescriptions for democratic governance in the international system. For instance, in a world of diverse nationalities and states, and their respective interests, Hobson's desire for a universal international organisation conflicted with his emphasis on the need for a coherent and coercive international government punishing non-compliance. Hobson understood the problem: the heterogeneity of nations meant that an international government would need a long list of aims. Hobson preferred a wider membership, but admitted that this would result in a looser union.[81] Yet a looser union must mean the absence of mandatory sanctions, compulsory arbitration and the centralisation of force. Surely, by Hobson's own logic, his scheme must fail.

Hobson tried to close the loopholes in his scheme with compulsory arbitration and conciliation backed up by a military sanction to punish non-compliance. Unfortunately, if the sanction and compulsion of the treaty were to be made credible, it would more than likely have deterred states from joining the arrangement, as even Hobson admitted.[82] And even if this was not the case, Hobson's assumption of the justice of international force rested on an assumption that the international authority or common international interest existed and was apparent to all. This was a leap of faith on Hobson's part, though, and without it the justice of international action appears problematic: what one nation regarded as the international interest would be regarded by other nations merely as that first nation's interest.

In short, Hobson's proposals were contradictory: on the one hand, he hoped that a universal organisation would be the forum to forge and articulate an international interest, while on the other hand the international force proposal presumed a readily apparent international interest already existed. Hobson could only avoid this dilemma by ignoring his own criticism of political thought, that 'we do not believe in ideas as we believe in force'.[83]

Hobson's hopes for disarmament rested on the creation of a preponderantly strong international organisation with near universal membership. Any non-universal organisation would have to retain arms to defend itself from potential aggression from an outsider. This might, as he argued, result in a reinstatement of the balance of power. Hobson believed that the League also had to be strong enough to continue should one of its members defect from the organisation.[84] Such precautions suggest that swift arms reductions would be unlikely to result from Hobson's version of international government. Indeed, the dispersion of forces in the collective security arrangement he envisaged would make matters worse because co-ordination of the international force would reduce the gains from the economy of force.

More generally, a rather simplistic domestic analogy seems to underlie Hobson's proposal that peace required international law to look more like domestic law in terms of its compliance and sanctions mechanisms. Hobson's proposal for some form of sanction to deter states from engaging in aggressive war is analogous to the role of the police and the courts domestically. Hobson relied on an analogy of states or nations to persons in domestic society in his discussion of international arbitration, national self-government, and the role of an international legislature. A domestic analogy also underpinned his argument that international government must be based on consent, as well as arguments against the private right of states to wage war, absolute national property rights and the right of rebellion in international relations.[85]

An interesting case of domestic analogy is the principle of representation in the international government. Hobson argued that domestic equality in voting, that is, one person one vote, was maintained not on the principle of equality but for prudential reasons. In international relations, with the patent inequality of states and fewer prudential constraints, the principle of equality could be dropped in favour of, what Hobson considered the more fundamental maxim, treating only equals equally.[86]

Criticisms of the impracticality of Hobson's proposals came from other reformers, among others, Leonard Woolf and J. M. Keynes. Lowes Dickinson, for instance, argued that Hobson's project was too ambitious and far-reaching to be achieved. He even suggested that Hobson's revolutionary scheme would scare governments from any of the less ambitious international schemes. In short, Dickinson argued, Hobson was making the best the enemy of the good. Hobson replied that the logic of international government demonstrated that smaller proposals were themselves unworkable.[87]

CONCEPTUAL AND PRACTICAL PROBLEMS IN THE SCHEME FOR AN INTERNATIONAL FEDERATION

Most of the criticisms of Hobson's new liberal vision of international relations centre on the level of generality at which he conducted his analysis. For instance, Hobson was impressionistic on the role of a global authority supervising international economic and cultural exchanges. This is indicated most clearly in his lack of specification of the meaning of federalism. The term is made so general that it becomes meaningless. This is even more the case in his use of the related term, confederation. For example, in *Towards International Government*, Hobson argued that there should be confederation of states rather than a single federal state, without specifying what differences were entailed.[88] New liberal internationalism looked forward to the rational management of international affairs, especially international economic relations, through some form of institutionalisation, and the organic analogy implied government at the appropriate level, whether local, national or international. Yet the very comprehensiveness of the organic analogy and Hobson's theories of surplus value meant that he could cobble together a collection of contradictory proposals. Such general prescriptions were a poor foundation for a substantive proposal on international government. For instance, Hobson did not consider the problems associated with the creation of novel functional and federal agencies and with the level of government in his scheme. He did not demonstrate the direction of institutionalisation in international relations apart from vague references to some new quasi-functional international organisations, such as the ILO.

Hobson frequently wished away problems with his proposals with an assumption of an implicit harmony of national interests. However, states do indeed have conflicting interests that are a product of their circumstances rather than a result of the irrationality of statesmen. Hobson did not see, for instance, that the role of an international representative, who had to represent both the national and international interest at the same time, could not simply be solved by correct, that is, democratic, representation. Hobson also assumed that a cooling-off period would encourage rational consideration by the parties of the issues in a dispute, thus facilitating a peaceful settlement. Unfortunately, a cooling-off period could also be exploited in order to build up forces.

Hobson believed that democratic control of foreign policy would bring peace because 'the people' would be more pacific than their governments, despite the fact that he also cited the 'mob mind' of mass public opinion and the manipulations of the press whipping up bellicosity and xenophobia as primary causes of war![89] In any case, he turned out to be wrong on the transformative impact of public opinion at the end of the First World War. The peoples of Europe carried the resentment and nationalist fervour of the War into its aftermath. Hobson recognised this and later described the change of ideas necessary to bring international government as being akin to a religious conversion. Where he had once hoped for the rational expression of a desire for peace among the peoples of the world, he later believed that a leap of faith (in internationalism) by civilised humanity was required.

Hobson's commitment to the theory of co-operative surplus and his reliance on the organic analogy gave him a pro-organisation bias that blinded him to a number of inadequacies of his proposals. He defended the League as the only alternative to nationalist anarchy and an important contribution to the struggle for national democracy against militarism. It could be argued on the contrary that, for many peoples, an oligarchic League dominated by the Great Powers would be worse than a less-ordered alternative.[90] Hobson himself had argued in *Imperialism*, for instance, that the division of Africa between the Great Powers at the 1884 Congo Conference was the starting-point of the modern period of imperialism, and elsewhere had agonised about this being the early indicator of the emergence of inter-imperialism. In *A League of Nations*, however, he claimed that the Berlin Treaty (that followed the Congo Conference) could have been a basis for pacific internationalism![91]

Hobson attacked the oligarchic nature of the League of Nations, yet his proposal for an international government would have been very similar.[92] His ideas on voting according to population and size, and later some measure of the level of civilisation and contribution to internationalism, were certainly controversial.[93] The application of a civilisation test, especially tied to the contribution to the advance of internationalism, would be biased in favour of the Western nations.

Hobson's self-consciously utilitarian proposals would have trampled the rights of minorities and would effectively have set up a 'tyranny of the majority'.[94]

The organisational bias also contributed to Hobson's ethnocentric blindness to the integrity of cultures other than Western civilisation. Hobson's proposals would have continued and indeed systematised the tyranny of the powerful Western nations and the subordination of the colonial peoples. Such territories and the peoples living in them were not to be represented by their own appointees but to be trusts of the international government. There is even a linguistic aspect to Hobson's paternalism. Hobson never referred to backward peoples as nations. This is because a reference to nationhood would be an admission that these peoples were civilised and should be part of the international government on an equal basis.

Following his theory of co-operative surplus, Hobson interpreted past efforts in internationalism, such as the Hague institutions and conferences as well as private international co-operation, as the rudiments of an international government. This linear conception of international history prevented Hobson from considering internationalism on its own merits rather than as some form of prototype international government conceived as national government writ large. This led him both to deprecate the diverse functions of international institutions and law and also to advocate changes inappropriate to the peculiar circumstances of contemporary international relations.

In Hobson's defence, a blueprint for an international government is easy game for a realist critic. Realists simply assert the primacy and logic of the contemporary states-system and point to the eternal verities of international politics, such as the struggle for power and the pursuit of national interest.[95] However, the realists' challenge to reform is based on an assumption of recurrence and repetition in international relations that is as unwarranted as an assumption of harmony and progress. Hobson was aware of many of these realist criticisms and at more than one juncture wondered if international government over-extended the world's 'enthusiasm for humanity'.[96] His argument that consciousness of kind extended beyond national states, for instance, was a plausible retort to realist emphasis on national over international interest, and it suggested that the previous failures of internationalism need not be repeated because economic and social conditions had changed.

CONCLUSION

In sum, Hobson's proposals for international government have two logics within them: the logic of centralised force and the logic of central organisation. These involve different and incompatible routes to internationalism. While the logic of organisation fits with Hobson's theory of co-operative surplus, the logic of centralised force is an anomaly for Hobson's new liberal approach to international relations.

In the context of other proposals for the reform of international relations, Hobson's was admittedly quite bold. At the end of the War a considerably watered-down version of the League idea was instituted, indicating that Hobson's proposal was too much for statesmen and other reformers of the day. Plans for international government have since fallen out of favour, making Hobson's ideas appear rather quaint. A number of Hobson's criticisms of the betrayal of the internationalist ideal in the League of Nations still have considerable purchase, however.

In terms of the development of international theory, Hobson's extension of the logic of the increasing co-operation of people and peoples to humanity at large prefigures the functional approach to international relations. For today's reformers, however, the main lesson to be learned from Hobson's discussions of international government, like so many others of its kind, is that international peace and global welfare cannot be fabricated simply by innovating institutions based on a domestic model without some critical examination of the original and the new (i.e., international) contexts. Specifically, international institutions must have legitimacy if they are to contribute to the progress of justice and civilisation.

CHAPTER 9

J. A. Hobson and liberal internationalism

This concluding chapter examines Hobson's contribution to liberal international theory. Hobson's approach is presented first through a look at his ideas on sovereignty, diplomacy and the balance of power. Hobson is then placed in the context of the liberal tradition of international thought, specifically with reference to Richard Cobden, Norman Angell and David Mitrany. Next, the effect of the First World War and war in general on Hobson's liberalism is considered. There follows a comparison of Hobson's new liberal internationalism with Robert Keohane's neoliberal institutionalist approach to international relations. I conclude with a discussion of Hobson's contribution to international thought.

Hobson was a major figure in the transformation of the liberal tradition of international thought. It should be noted in passing that he would have considered the term 'liberal tradition' an oxymoron.[1] Liberalism, for Hobson, was a rationalist (constructively) critical political philosophy that challenged the oppressive traditions and customs of society. In any event, Hobson's part in the transformation of liberalism has begun to receive scholarly attention of late. We are no longer in the dark as to how the liberalism of Cobden, J. S. Mill and Gladstone (to take a rather diverse group of nineteenth-century liberals) became the liberalism of today, associated with the welfare state and intervention in the economy. Unfortunately, the parallel change in liberal international theory, from the non-interventionism that underpins Cobden's and Mill's approach to international relations to the institutionalism and welfare orientation of many of today's liberal approaches has remained under-researched. In the story of the development of international theory, the liberal approach leaps from Cobdenism to functionalism apparently with no stage in between. What would, on the face of it, appear to be a crucial period in the development of international relations, the years just before and after the establishment of international relations as an academic discipline, is omitted. Hobson had an important role in this transformation; a role that this study has attempted to lay out. Following Freeden's argument regarding the new liberalism, it is notable that Hobson was, nevertheless, only one among many authors who transformed nineteenth-century liberal internationalism into its twentieth-century institutionalist variant.

The silence on early twentieth-century liberal international theory is attributable to both international relations specialists and the intellectual biographers of Hobson and the new liberalism. The latter have either considered Hobson a Cobdenite or have been perplexed by his apparent theoretical schizophrenia, oscillating between Cobdenite free-tradism, on the one hand, and organically inspired institutional reform, on the other.[2] This study has argued that it is as incorrect to label Hobson a Cobdenite in international relations as it would be to label him a Cobdenite in domestic affairs; that his approach to international relations is best understood as a new liberal internationalism that parallels his new liberalism. The problem with the studies of the intellectual biographers has been exacerbated by the dominance of historians and historically oriented research on Hobson. The commendable concern with where Hobson's ideas came from, who his intellectual predecessors were, and so on, underplays Hobson as a producer as well as a consumer of ideas. In short, Hobson himself was an intellectual forebear in the liberal tradition, and not just of G. D. H. Cole, Harold Laski, R. H. Tawney and their like, but also indirectly to later liberal internationalists such as David Mitrany.[3] The scent has been lost, so to speak, in tracking liberal internationalism just as we go beyond Hobson to those who built on his ideas. Hobson's true significance for international relations is thus hidden by the historical emphasis of the studies on his work, because it was to be other scholars, particularly Mitrany, who built on his achievements within liberal internationalism and fleshed them out into more systematic and detailed proposals and analysis.

Hobson scholars have also tended to stick to the immediate context of Hobson's theories. These most clearly apply most often to the domestic context in the first instance, i.e., the British state and British society. Yet while the concrete instances to which Hobson's theories applied were critical and an important part of understanding his work, the theoretical framework that Hobson developed was of more general application than merely nineteenth- and early twentieth-century

Britain. Liberals like Hobson prescribed not only for the unique moment and conditions of one society at one period but with the whole of humanity, or at least its vanguard in liberal democratic political communities, in mind in one way or another. For the Hobson scholars, Hobson's interest in international relations becomes an application of theory to practical policy comparable in status to his discussion of taxation, unemployment or poverty. The consequent reduction in the theoretical significance of international relations for Hobson's work has contributed to the silence on the shift in liberal international theory made by Hobson, one that parallels closely the ideological shift domestically.

As we have seen, there has been a skewed understanding of Hobson in the international relations literature as well. The problem here goes beyond the theory of imperialism. It turns rather on the current understanding and categorisation of theories in international relations. In terms of the history of thinking in international relations, Hobson has been labelled an idealist. However, idealism is too general a term to describe Hobson's international theorising accurately. His writing was too sophisticated and too varied to fit comfortably into this pigeon-hole.[4]

Hobson's international theory does not comfortably fit into any of the so-called paradigms of international relations – realism, structuralism or pluralism. For realism, international relations is the relations of states. Hobson regarded this as derived from earlier *realpolitik* theories, that he criticised as forms of the separatist fallacy. Hobson was very critical of views of the world based, as he saw it, on the outdated notions of Machiavelli and Hobbes, particularly as promulgated during his time by certain German historians and political philosophers as well as social Darwinist imperialists in Britain.[5]

Though the theory of imperialism is the foundation of the structuralist paradigm, Hobson does not fit this category well. This is because the structuralist paradigm has been developed from neo-Marxist critiques of the Leninist version of imperialism. Hobson was not a Marxist. He strongly criticised the labour theory of value, the Hegelian dialectic and the doctrinaire aspects of Marxist socialism as he saw it. Further, for Hobson, the opposite of organic harmony was disorganisation rather than structural inequality. Inequality derived from disorganisation. This is a different approach to that in Marxism, which can be illustrated by the contrast of Hobson's understanding of the imperial international system with that set out in *Imperialism, the Highest Stage of*

Capitalism, where Lenin uses an idea of 'uneven development', a concept alien to Hobson, to explain the conflicts of capitalism.

Hobson's concern with the dynamics and interconnections of the social world appears to bring him close to the pluralist paradigm. However, this paradigm is also concerned with the relations of separate things, people, groups, international organisations and also states. These separate entities are related to the whole of world society in the shape of networks, but primacy in this paradigm is still with the unit level rather than system-wide.[6] Hobson's approach to international relations as to social life in general is holistic. His emphasis on the interconnectedness and unity of the world system seems to emphasise the system-level over the separate units. Hobson was constantly attempting to transcend what he considered to be anarchic pluralism, to see the whole beyond the parts.

Hobson's liberal international theory is best appreciated by placing him in the development of liberal thought on international relations from the nineteenth century onwards. Pluralism understood as one recent aspect of the liberal tradition and not some sort of axiomatic categorisation of thinking in international relations comes closest to being the category to which Hobson's international theory would belong.

Finally, the lacuna of each discipline might have been remedied had it not been for the relative lack of exchange of ideas between international theorists and intellectual and economic historians. Hobson scholars have not studied the development of international theory, especially after Hobson; international theorists have hardly studied the development of liberalism.

HOBSON'S LIBERALISM AND HIS CRITIQUE OF CONTEMPORARY INTERNATIONAL RELATIONS

Hobson's liberal internationalism was manifested in his rejection of the current arrangement of international relations. His reforming spirit sought to grapple with perceived problems in international affairs, for example, war, and the realisation that the international context prevented the solution of perceived domestic problems. Hobson was profoundly dissatisfied with contemporary international relations. He criticised a number of the central elements of contemporary international theory: sovereignty, international law, diplomacy, the balance of power and the use of force. Hobson's assessment of these elements of international theory differ from much contemporary analysis and subsequent realist theory. His critique of the 'old', 'traditional' or 'obsolete' ideas highlights his rationalist or idealist, liberal conscience.[7]

Sovereignty and international law

Hobson argued, as we have seen, that sovereignty was associated with a power-oriented view of the world, that had contributed to the creation of international anarchy.[8] Claims to sovereign independence were instances of individualism in international relations, a failure to acknowledge the increasing connectedness and interdependence of the society of nations. Sovereign independence was outdated, he argued, because it was tempered by obligations under international law and because of the growth of interdependence brought on by trade, travel and other communications.[9] Sovereignty no longer reflected the true interests of the several national elements of mankind. Privileging national interests over the global common good, it was an obstruction to international co-operation and an international government.[10] It was thus an obstruction to civilisation, educating habits of thought opposed to the developing co-operation of humanity.

Sovereignty, according to Hobson, legitimised the practice of states acting as if they could be a law unto themselves. He denounced the absence of a central enforceable sanction and called the legal rules of international relations 'a loose code' of 'so-called international law'.[11] According to Hobson, peace and justice in international relations depended on the further extension and strengthening of international law, so that nations could no longer plead 'vital interests' or 'honour' to evade their obligations. International law could no longer be merely 'voluntary' for states. The lawlessness, as he saw it, of contemporary international relations prompted him to offer suggestions in terms of backing up law with sufficient force.[12]

Hobson believed that domestic law should be the model for all law. In common with much contemporary opinion, Hobson believed that international law was at a primitive stage of development. Insofar as international law failed to measure up to the standard of domestic law, it was not law at all. The progress of international law could be measured by its increasing similarity to domestic law, through the growth of universal rather than bilateral treaties, conferences on international legal matters, an international judiciary, and the strengthening of sanctions. While international law was still feeble, Hobson was hopeful that the mechanisms of peaceful settlement and of functional co-operation set up in the latter part of the nineteenth and the early part of the twentieth centuries would be a basis for future development of true law internationally, paralleling the supersession of the priority of individual over social interests domestically.[13]

Hobson's view of international law and sovereignty is at odds with the common view today. Sovereignty, as understood in much of the international relations literature, is a category of legal status, a badge needed to participate in international relations.[14] According to this perspective, Hobson's critique, based on the facts of interdependence, is a critique of the consequences of sovereign statehood not of the concept *per se*. His idea that international law qualifies sovereignty misunderstands the nature of both sovereignty and international law. Sovereign statehood is the basic qualification for a state to be party to international law. International law is, then, by definition the law between sovereign states, not over them. Thus, so this argument goes, as states have to consent to be bound by international law, it is difficult to argue that international law is a limitation on states.

While the view just outlined might be too restrictive for current international law, with the inclusion of rights of self-determination and of human rights becoming more salient, Hobson's view is definitely flawed. Hobson's mistake with regard to sovereignty is compounded by his flawed conception of law. International law is usually considered distinct from domestic law by virtue of its different enforcement measures and the structure of the society within which it is placed. Nevertheless, international law is law, not just a primitive set of rules or pre-law.[15] To suggest that international law is not law because of its lack of enforcement mechanisms is to mistake the basis of law in authoritative rules of the international system for the means by which compliance is assured. In his analysis, Hobson drew a parallel between international law and English criminal law. This is an overly narrow conception of law, firstly, because it neglects civil law in the English legal system. It is, furthermore, ethnocentric, because it ignores alternative approaches to law outside the Anglo-Saxon world. Finally, his critique of international law is tinged with idealism. He did not advance the argument, made by E. H. Carr, that international law might merely reflect the interests of the Great Powers.[16] He optimistically believed that the weakness of international law was a greater danger to small states and weaker peoples because it gave powerful states a free hand.

Diplomacy and foreign policy

In his political activity and journalism, Hobson had criticised British diplomacy leading to the Boer War. The experience of the First World War and his involvement in the UDC further reinforced his strong opinions on diplomacy and foreign policy. His critique relied heavily on nineteenth-century Radicals' attacks on traditional diplomacy and misguided British foreign policy resulting from aristocratic meddling and elitism. However, Hobson did not wish for the end of foreign policy as the Radicals did. Rather, he looked to the democratic representation of the true interests of society in foreign policy to replace aristocratic or other elite influence. Hobson's critique of diplomacy and foreign policy can be analysed into five elements: personnel, ideology, structure, process and substance. He summarized his approach as follows: 'Different men, different methods, different motives and ideals are required.'

The first problem with traditional diplomacy, according to Hobson, was the class bias of personnel. Diplomats were 'unrepresentative types of men, with ... false, antiquated conceptions of States and statecraft', drawn from the ranks of the rich and powerful, and propagating their self-interested viewpoints. These men's conceptions of their country's interests were opposed to the interests of society as a whole and to the interests of the international society, he argued. Instead, Hobson claimed, modern diplomacy required 'able, broad-minded men of large personal experience of the people and the popular activities of the people, experience amplified by contact with the peoples and activities of other countries, men accustomed in large, free intercourse to test and assimilate new facts and valuations and to practise arts of mediation and of arrangements'.[17] If the old diplomatic and foreign ministry officials could be removed and replaced by people who more truly represented the interests of society, then the relations of states would cease to be competitive and the relations of peoples, thus freed up, would be a harmonious pursuit of national and human welfare.[18]

Beyond the matter of personnel, the ideology of diplomats was reinforced by the structure of traditional diplomacy that also bred international antagonism. The cult of secrecy, distrust of foreigners, calculations of your rival's power and unprincipled compromise, multiplied the problems of class bias in the embassies and foreign ministries.

> Drawn from this narrow section of society, they [recruits to the diplomatic corps] enter a calling strongly stamped with the traditions of an even less enlightened and more autocratically ordered past, in which the normal relations of States and Governments are envisaged in terms of suspicion, hostility, and jealousy.[19]

Diplomacy reflected and reinforced the militarist attitude engendered by the competition of sovereign states with one another. Hobson also thought that multilateral diplomacy was preferable to bilateral negotiation[20] and he criticised the entire process of formulation and evaluation of foreign policy. If, Hobson claimed, the whole process of foreign policy making were public and open to debate, different, more pacific, foreign policies would emerge, as the pacific nature of the people gained expression.[21]

In short, the necessary reforms were, first, opening the Foreign Office and Diplomatic Corps to all qualified people; second, public discussion and parliamentary sanction of treaties, including the establishment of a Standing Committee on Foreign Affairs; third, representatives to the International Council that Hobson had proposed should be directly elected rather than be appointed diplomats.[22] On diplomatic negotiations, Hobson's view was similar to the Wilsonian call for 'open covenants, openly arrived at'.

Hobson countered the suggestion that the people could not be trusted with diplomacy and foreign policy because they were too ignorant of international affairs or as bellicose as their representatives. Hobson retorted that the ignorance and bellicosity of peoples was a function of their being kept in the dark about international affairs. Publicity and openness would at least mitigate the effects of these factors, if not end them altogether.

Hobson's ideas deviate from mainstream international relations literature that says little about the personnel of diplomacy, other than to suggest that skill and tact are useful personal characteristics. The structure of diplomacy, as the formal communication of states, is accepted as a reflection of the structure of international society, within which diplomacy is beneficial insofar as it is an alternative mode of communication between states to physical force.[23] Hobson claimed that democratic formulation, execution and evaluation of foreign policy would significantly alter international relations. Kenneth Waltz's realist retort to this liberal critique is that all states in the international system face constraints imposed by that system and that changes to the domestic formulation are insufficient to change international relations.[24] Hobson would have agreed with this, however, suggesting that democratic control was just one aspect of his reform of international relations that also included social reform and an international government.

During the inter-war period, Hobson's involvement in the UDC and discussions of how democratic control should be implemented tempered his radical views, though only marginally. By the end of his life, he was admitting that it was difficult to be specific about the precise meaning of 'democratic control' or its implementation.[25]

The use of force and the balance of power

As we saw in the last chapter, Hobson's opinions on the use of force by states followed his general views on the role of force in social life. Special problems appeared in international relations, however, because of the lack of a central enforcement agency. International relations was subject, therefore, to the balance of power where military force was central. For Hobson, by contrast, the legitimate use of force entailed its use by the right authority, only insofar as it achieved some definite just end, and only as a last resort. The use of force by states violated all these criteria. States used force indiscriminately or universally in the pursuance of sectionalist or separatist interests in order to 'settle' disputes or to (re)create social order.[26] War was the classic instance of the misuse of force. Wars resulted from states pursuing their own ends; the results were frequently inconclusive but always bloody.

Hobson believed that the development of civilisation meant that reason increasingly supplanted force as the method of settling disputes. Co-operation replaced conflict at the 'lower' levels of existence. Conflict over resources and for survival was transposed into beneficial competition at 'higher', e.g., intellectual and cultural, levels. His proposals for international government, as we saw in chapter 6, were attempts to economise on this use of force as well as making it more just.

More than anything else, international government was designed to replace the balance-of-power system. International force as articulated by an international authority was legitimate for Hobson, even to the point of using force to compel the backward nations to participate in the international economy on the basis of an argument that drew parallels between backward nations and the education of children.[27] The balance of power did not, Hobson argued, result in a sensible or civilised ratio of force to reason in the relations of states. Instead, the balance of power was really just the balance of force; international relations was an arena where force was the ultimate arbiter. The prevalence of the idea that force was central to international relations was redoubled with the outbreak of the First World War. 'What we are now confronted with is force as a gospel and a mission, force as the supreme arbiter within the nation and among the nations that constitute humanity', he gloomily proclaimed.[28] The machinations of the balance of power were the central cause of the Great War for Hobson. He argued that the War had, as a further consequence, the 'celebration' of force in all forms of human relations as well as a derationalising effect on personal and social life in general. This celebration and derationalisation further contributed to the increased possibility of war in the future, argued Hobson, through fatalism and even theories to the effect that war was beneficial.

The legitimacy or otherwise of the use of force by states in the pursuit of their interests is conceived to be at the centre of the differences between liberals and realists – hence Michael Howard's title, *War and the Liberal Conscience.* Realists, on the whole, sanction such national use of physical force. The centrality of the use of force as the ultimate arbiter of the relations of states is accepted in realist scholarship in international relations. But even outside of realism, contrary to Hobson's view, though there may be concern to limit the use of force by states, there is little love among international relations specialists for the idea of centralising force in an international government in order to eradicate state-sponsored conflict or as a route to disarmament. This has seemed an unlikely prospect in practice. There are also doubts as to the validity of the theory that centralised force would be just or would lead to a less armed world. For Hobson, on the other hand, so long as an international government was democratic, that is, federal in structure with the rights of all nations fairly represented and the due process followed, then, by definition, its use of force could not be arbitrary or unjust, but rather must represent the will of the international community or the expression of the views of humanity at large.

CONTINUITY AND CHANGE IN LIBERAL INTERNATIONALISM

Hobson's criticisms of contemporary international relations were inspired by his liberal reforming spirit. His prescriptions contrast markedly with the arrangements of the day and with various realist rationalisations of those arrangements. Yet while Hobson's is a liberal internationalist perspective, it is a distinctive one. While his ideas cohere around certain guiding liberal principles – such as a belief in progress and a defence of the importance of individual liberty within the context of a community (national or international) guided by the rule of law – his modification of liberal internationalism through his use of the organic analogy and his theories of surplus value make for a number of differences between him and those in the liberal internationalist tradition who either preceded him or followed him. Hobson can be placed in the liberal internationalist tradition through a comparison of his work with that of three other liberals, Richard Cobden, Norman Angell and David Mitrany.

Nineteenth-century liberal internationalism: J. S. Mill and Richard Cobden

The most important liberal predecessors of Hobson were John Stuart Mill and, particularly, Richard Cobden. Mill provided the liberal line on nationalism and internationalism; Cobden supplied the radical liberal position on peace, internationalism, free trade and foreign policy.[29] Cobden is best known to international relations as the campaigner for free trade and for non-intervention in foreign policy. His approach to international affairs mirrored his approach to domestic affairs. He was concerned with the liberty of all to go about their business without hindrance from governments and claimed that personal liberty in economic intercourse would lead to peace as well as prosperity. Cobden's position on international affairs followed this analysis: government should stay out of people's business as much as possible. According to Cobden, trade free of governmental restrictions permitted international specialisation of industry and increased commerce, thus creating the greatest good both for individuals and national societies. Prosperity was not the only result of free trade, however. Commercial intercourse encouraged sympathy and friendship between mutually dependent traders in different localities, countries, or national areas. For Cobden, peace and prosperity were mutually reinforcing. Prosperity would lead to peace, because peace was easier to come by in a prosperous world than in a desperately poor one. Peace would in turn enhance prosperity because prosperity is more readily maintained or created in periods of peace than in war-stricken times. Both, however, are dependent on arrangements to safeguard economic liberty and encourage commercial intercourse. As such, Cobden was a strident critic of current international affairs: he was anti-protection; against the policy and the idea of the balance of power, which he held was merely a justification for intervention in the affairs of other nations; and strongly criticised British imperial policy and empire-building in general. As we saw in chapter 4, the second of Hobson's four international systems was Cobdenism.

Hobson maintained but updated the liberal vision propounded by Mill and Cobden of peace, democracy and internationalism. He queried the easy relationship of nationalism and internationalism, evident in Mill's analysis that he had at one point accepted, especially when nationalism issued in aggressive imperialism. He also added a conception of positive liberty to liberal internationalism in the shape of equality of opportunity in international relations.[30] He modified Cobdenite doctrine by bringing interventionism into liberal internationalist thought, justifying a role for the growing numbers of international organisations and proposing a central international government to co-ordinate them.

In his theory of imperialism, Hobson altered the radical liberal critique of foreign policy. Relying on the concepts of surplus and organism, Hobson articulated a theory that saw governments intervene in the international economy in the interests of individual states and the elites which dominated them. In short, in his critique of the current conditions of international relations and in his prescription for a better future, the underlying premise was that governmental or social intervention was here to stay. The theory of imperialism also left a major mark on liberal internationalism in two related ways. First, economics and politics could no longer be regarded as independent of each other. Hobson conceived of economic power in a way that would have been meaningless to Cobden. Second, capitalism was no longer a force for peace, but was an incitement to war, because of the influence of sectional interests.[31] The centrality of economic issues in Hobson's analysis is not just a result of his being an economist; the theory of imperialism and the transformation of liberal internationalism is actually about the opposite, the undermining of the classical liberal idea of the independence of the economy from political pressure or social concern. Hobson believed that powerful political interests in the economic system had been neglected by previous liberal analysis, and particularly by Cobden. The powerful industrial and financial combines not only disproved aspects of liberal economic thought through their economic power, they constituted a site of significant political power also.[32] Thus, Hobson moved beyond the tenets of nineteenth-century liberalism in international relations as he had in liberalism at home.

The transformation of liberal internationalism: Angell, Mitrany and Hobson

The most important of Hobson's contemporaries in liberal internationalism was Norman Angell. Hobson and Angell were long-time associates in the UDC.[33] Despite being a Labour MP, Angell was something of an unreconstructed Cobdenite, a defender of the pacific tendencies of international financial capitalism. His major contribution to liberal internationalism was to expand the Cobdenite doctrine to apply the connection of free trade, peace and prosperity to international finance. In the advanced industrial countries, international interdependence was made up of not only the trade of goods but also flows of investment across national boundaries and a network of international, or perhaps better, cosmopolitan, finance. Angell was also concerned with the psychology of public opinion that apparently irrationally refused to accept his propositions about international affairs and particularly the futility of war.[34]

Hobson's opinions of Angell's arguments are something of a barometer for the changes in his own opinions. In the decade before the Great War, Hobson was almost an Angellite and lauded Angell's *The Great Illusion.*[35] After the War, and particularly in the later thirties, he criticised Angell's insistence that capitalism could not gain by war. Hobson pointed out that this was debatable for the capitalist system as a whole. More importantly, Hobson argued, capitalism did not operate as a whole; individual capitalists pursued their own interests at the expense of others. Sectional interests led capitalism to be a cause of war, contrary to Angell's beliefs.[36]

In developing his functional approach to international organisation, David Mitrany focused his attention on the economic and social welfare issues that were increasingly issues for government policy. The nature of the relationship of people to their governments was changing. The role of the state could no longer be limited to constitutional prohibitions of the restriction of liberty. Rather it now needed to be concerned with developing the bases for effective liberty to be exercised by all, through measures to ensure social and economic equality – the state in short was becoming a service state. Following this line of argument, Mitrany suggested that the national basis of government was inadequate to fulfil people's welfare needs. Satisfying these needs required international co-operation because it was impossible for national governments to achieve them on their own. Mitrany argued that in specific technical areas, nation-state institutions would be superseded by functional international organisations, and that people's loyalties would turn to the international organisations that fulfil their needs. He claimed that administrators of these functional organisations would provide for the needs of humanity more efficiently and justly than national politicians or political institutions. Mitrany further argued that the shape of international organisation would be along the lines of functional requirements rather than reflecting the aggregation of political authorities of sovereign states, as had been the common shape of reformism in international relations to that time.[37]

Cobdenite internationalism and Mitrany's functionalism are usually presented as categorically different forms of liberalism in international relations.[38] However, the changes wrought in liberal international theory by Hobson (and Angell) constitute an institutionalist 'turn' in liberal internationalism at the end of the last century. The transformation in liberal international theory can be highlighted by comparing the liberal internationalisms of Cobden and Mitrany. To begin with, they shared liberal aims, assumptions and a certain amount of analysis. Both Cobden's and Mitrany's proposals for improving international relations were welfare-oriented and broadly utilitarian. Mitrany's conception of welfare resolved to economic criteria. Control of economic criteria to provide for welfare needs required the setting up of specialised functional international institutions.[39] Cobden hoped that the removal of legal and political hindrances would enable people to increase their prosperity. Both had a negative attitude to national governments rooted in a disapproval of politics. In both cases national political government was seen as outmoded and detrimental to the improvement of the human lot. Mitrany's division of the high political and low political issues, so much attacked by his critics, mirrored the distinction made by Cobden. For Cobden and Mitrany, and indeed also for Norman Angell, peace and prosperity flowed from the correct functional arrangements.

The primary difference between Cobden and Mitrany was the stress on some form of intervention, not by government, to be sure, but by social and economic actors, as well as the importance of institutions as routes to satisfying needs. This difference resulted from their different attitudes to individual liberty: Cobden argued for a negative concept of liberty, the right of non-interference, though he did believe in treaties to facilitate free trade and to provide for arbitration of international conflicts; Angell, though he did not go as far as Mitrany with respect to institutionalism, has recently been plausibly labelled a functionalist, because of his search for guarantees for international financial stability in international political institutions;[40] Mitrany by contrast believed that international institutions were required to provide for certain welfare needs to guarantee positive liberty.

Hobson can be seen as an intermediate stage in the evolution of liberal internationalism between Cobdenism and functionalism from the nineteenth to the twentieth centuries. Hobson certainly saw himself as a social reformer and a reformer of liberalism. He consciously advanced beyond previous formulations of liberalism to incorporate the implications of recent events and social phenomena. His writings were a deliberate and frequently practical attempt to forge a new liberalism, specifically a socialised liberalism.

Mitrany drew on diverse influences in his functional approach to international organisation.[41] While the so-called 'Red Professors', G. D. H. Cole and R. H. Tawney, as well as Fabians such as Leonard Woolf, have been cited as prominent influences on and forerunners of functionalism, Mitrany's connection to Hobson has until now been largely overlooked.[42] Mitrany remarked on his days as an undergraduate at the LSE and particularly the formative influence of Leonard Hobhouse and Graham Wallas, two of Hobson's good friends with a similar outlook to his own.[43] Both Hobson and Mitrany wrote for the *Manchester Guardian*, though at different times. Mitrany's personal connection to Hobson is confirmed in his friendship with Ted Scott, the son of the editor of the *Guardian*, who was Hobson's son-in-law. Mitrany later commented that he had been surprised at the apparent exclusion of Hobson, someone who he considered a knowledgeable writer on international issues, from the newly created Royal Institute for International Affairs after the First World War.[44]

The influence of these personal connections and the liberal milieu in which they both moved are reflected in the consonance of Mitrany's functionalism and Hobson's new liberal internationalism. Both stress the importance of welfare in international relations and especially in moulding the new international organisations. Both approaches are institutionalist and evolutionist.[45] Hobson's federalism is driven by functionalist logic and, as such, is not as vulnerable to the anticonstitutional critique that Mitrany advanced of other international federalist schemes.[46] Both saw international co-operation initially being conducted privately by individuals and groups, and then proceeding to the establishment of functional institutions and the institutional direction of economic internationalism.[47]

Where Hobson differed from Mitrany was in his emphasis on, and belief in, beneficent and neutral government intervention at the international level as well as domestically. While Hobson believed in international government, Mitrany was more sceptical.[48] Indeed, Mitrany deviated from a number of Hobson's new liberal internationalist ideas. For instance, he jettisoned Hobson's emphasis on the necessity of a central international government, rejected any faith in federalism as a way of combining states in an international government, and tended to play down the radical notion of democratic reform as manifested in the call for industrial democracy. Mitrany inherited a decentralist emphasis from the guild socialist tradition of G. D. H. Cole and R. H. Tawney. Hobson, on the other hand, envisaged a much larger role for the political state and saw no problem with advancing political and legal reform as well as economic reform.[49] Hobson's use of the organic analogy highlighted the benefits from organisation in international relations. While both emphasise welfare and organisation to satisfy welfare needs, Hobson was led through the organic analogy to stress the need for central control, in contrast to the diffuse links that Mitrany felt would be most beneficial. In addition, the holism of Hobson's organic analogy led him to deny the narrowly economic meaning of welfare that appeared in Mitrany's formulation of functionalism.

When Hobson is placed in the context of the liberal tradition of international thought, it is evident that arguments that suggest that the changes in liberal internationalism are simply domestic liberalism writ large are incorrect.[50] In Hobson's work, institutionalisation and internationalisation go hand in hand theoretically, though there may be cases as we saw in the last chapter where this dialectical relationship might be disrupted in practice. Changes in liberal internationalism were the result of crises in, and subsequent modifications of, the logic of liberalism itself. Thus, while Cobden's and Hobson's domestically focused proposals had international implications, the internationally oriented proposals of Angell and Mitrany were integral parts of a liberal social and political philosophy in transition.

THE IMPACT OF THE FIRST WORLD WAR ON HOBSON'S LIBERAL INTERNATIONALISM

A large amount of scholarly attention has been devoted to the First World War as a marker of the end of the liberal century said to have begun in 1815. However, the Great War is not as neat a marker of the end of a liberal phase in international relations because the international experiment with the new League of Nations that began in the twenties is often perceived to have been inspired by liberalism.[51] Yet the War is taken to have begun the crisis of liberal internationalism even if it did not finish it. A consideration of Hobson's reactions to the First World War and to other wars demonstrates that the implications of the War for liberal internationalism may have been both overstated and misunderstood.

Hobson lived just long enough to see the final collapse of his hopes for an international government and peaceable international relations. Appropriately enough for a writer who has been identified as an idealist as well as a liberal international theorist, Hobson died on April Fools' Day in the first year of the Second World War.[52] Two earlier wars, the Boer War and the Great War, were turning points in Hobson's life and work. The First World War was a cataclysmic event for European politics, society, economics and culture.[53] Indeed, to those looking back now, the days before 1914 now appear unnaturally distant. Even in understanding the work of authors like Hobson, there has been a tendency to expect a sharp break in writings before and after the War. The Great War was certainly a watershed in a number of respects. In regard to politics, it is now believed that the War catapulted socialism and Fascism to the fore and drove a nail into the coffin of liberalism as a party political force and to some extent as an ideology. The British Liberal Party faltered after the War and was in ideological crisis from this point forward.[54] Unfortunately the very drama of the Great War has meant that it has been used as casual excuse for the many drastic changes in society, politics and international relations that occurred in the early part of this century, whose actual cause lay elsewhere, in processes taking place gradually since the second half of the nineteenth century.

Hobson was certainly shaken by the coming of war and by its protracted horrors. 1914 was a surprise and Hobson later claimed that the war had halved the percentage of rationality that he ascribed to humanity.[55] However, he was not like other liberals, such as David Mitrany, for whom the First World War required almost the equivalent of a paradigm shift.[56] Prior to 1914, Hobson and other liberals had been swept along on a wave of optimism, though the gathering crises of the decade after the turn of the century – the arms races and the crises in North Africa and the Balkans – cast a cloud over the rosy assessment of advancing internationalism.[57] Nevertheless, the War's impact on his theoretical approach to social life, including his international theory, can easily be exaggerated. The changes in international relations caused Hobson to alter his estimations of the potential for progress but not his explanation of progress or lack of it. The War simply led Hobson to revise his estimation of the international realm downwards, as we saw in the last chapter. His theoretical analyses of politics, economy and society were sufficient by themselves to explain the collapse into war, though. For instance, he refined and elaborated on his theory of imperialism and his analysis of militarism and protectionism, as well as expanding the application of his theory of unproductive surplus to explain the global scope and depth of the Great Depression.

For Hobson, the War had created problems and exacerbated others, but it had also revealed the potential for co-operation in societies, the resultant increases in productivity and the benefits (on the economic side) of state organisation of the economy. He hoped that, should the correct policies be implemented, recovery after the War would be swift. This was not to be. But, according to Hobson, the economic and political catastrophes of the inter-war years were not primarily the result of the dislocation of the War. Hobson ascribed the maladies affecting the economies of the world not to the Great War but to the underlying structure of capitalist distribution. In terms of economic relations, both nationally and internationally, the War created few new special problems; rather, it had worsened some, while temporarily solving others, e.g., respectively, the rise of protection and the stimulation of aggregate demand.

Much of Hobson's analysis during the First World War bears a striking resemblance to his writing during the Boer War. This is because his arguments during the World War are premised on arguments developed during the earlier war. In both cases Hobson argued that the underlying cause of war was the nature of capitalism and the economic relations of the Great Powers to each other and to the rest of the world, especially the backward peoples. He denied the simple explanations of inflamed nationalism and diplomatic failure, or that the war was an unintended accident.[58]

Hobson was particularly concerned with the economic costs of war. Indeed, the scale of the First World War contributed to one of the few novel aspects of Hobson's analysis compared to his examination of the Boer War, that is, an assessment of the long-term economic consequences of war to the British nation and to the various classes of British society. He analysed the costs of the War in terms of lost trade and the growth of protection. He scrutinised the financing of the War. Hobson noted that indirect taxation and borrowing were the favoured means of raising funds for the war effort. This allowed the War to be pursued at relatively little cost at the time, thus lengthening the conflict, Hobson believed. This was because people in general and particularly those who should have paid dearly, i.e., the governments that bought weapons on credit, did not feel the true cost of their actions and continued to support war.[59] Financing the War through indirect taxation meant that the working classes would pay for it. The wealthy, who had made war-gains in terms of contracts and lending to government at high rates of interest, escaped taxation that would reduce their benefits.[60] Hobson therefore proposed a war-gains tax and a progressive income tax as a way of paying for the War so that those that had gained, armaments makers and so on, as well as those most able to pay in any case, would pay for the costs of war.

In both wars, Hobson criticised the reduction in civil liberties. Though some restrictions might be justified, he argued that wholesale suspension of democratic rights would depress rather than enhance the war effort.[61] He attacked the propaganda of atrocities and the demonisation of the enemy, as well as the increasing secrecy of government activities. Finally, his social psychology of the brutality and credulity of the mob mind is echoed from the Boer War to the First World War.[62] He called for a negotiated peace and attacked those who looked for absolute victory over the enemy, calling them 'Never Endians'.[63]

Hobson's repetition and refinement of his previous arguments demonstrates that he was not thrown off balance by the First World War, though its scale and its intra-European character made it considerably worse than the Boer War. The difference in the severity of the conflict and the greater hostility to Germany did lead Hobson to be distanced from some of his good friends during the Great

War, however. Hobson's anti-war stance was highly unpopular in both cases but the First World War split the circle of radical liberal intellectuals of which Hobson was a part, with Hobhouse and Murray, for instance, strongly disagreeing with his position.[64] Hobson's consistent opposition to war as a solution to conflict is a tribute to the continuity of his international theory and contrasts with the many of his friends who were transformed by the First World War from peace activists to supporters of the 'war to end all wars'. Given the continuity, it has been argued that Hobson's analysis of war is already complete by around 1900, and is not actually generated by his experience of the First World War. This is not the case. Although the fundamentals were similar, the actual arguments themselves are generally more developed during and after the First World War. In his later writing Hobson integrated his economic and social-psychological analyses with his political message, and fitted them into his theories of surplus value, in the process producing some of his more acerbic and acute writings on the dire state of international political relations.

Hobson's reaction to the fact of war demonstrates some of the difficulties that war created for liberals. To liberals, war was both derationalising and demoralising. It split liberal internationalism in more than one way. It demolished the Cobdenite vision of international relations. It provided stark evidence that the march of civilisation was neither inexorable nor inevitable. It revealed that the major differences between the so-called advanced nations of the world could not be glossed over with phrases such as 'the common interest'. The creation of the League marked a shift in liberal internationalism away from arguments for the importance of law and public opinion as alternative peaceful routes to the settlement of disputes towards debates about ensuring the efficacy of collective security and the use of sanctions and force by the international community. By contrast, the changes in liberal internationalism that Hobson initiated were already in motion by the end of the nineteenth century. The First World War merely hastened the process and accelerated recognition of the changes in the international system – such as imperial rivalry and arms races – which had been prompted by the global processes associated with capitalism, primarily underconsumption resulting in regular general trade depression and economic crises. By the same token, the War had highlighted the benefits to be obtained from social organisation and central planning and direction of the economy.

NEW LIBERAL INTERNATIONALISM AND NEO-LIBERAL INSTITUTIONALISM

While it is useful to place Hobson in the immediate context of liberal internationalism, another comparison is worthwhile. Liberal internationalism has taken on many different guises since Hobson's formulation. It has, for instance, been profoundly influenced by the institutionalisation of international relations as an academic discipline. Liberal academic theories and approaches have ranged from functionalism, neo-functionalism and (regional) integration theory to studies of transnational relations, interdependence and, most recently, the neo-realist synthesis of regimes and co-operation theory.[65] The changes wrought in liberal international theory since Hobson's time can be illustrated by a comparison of Hobson's new liberal internationalism with Robert Keohane's neo-liberal institutionalism, which has been described as the 'newest liberal institutionalism' and for which Keohane self-consciously adopts the mantle of the liberal tradition.[66] This allows a comparison of two explicit attempts to develop new liberal international theory. Finally, the comparison also suggests the potential contribution of Hobson's new liberal internationalism to current international theory.

Keohane deploys game theory and rational choice in an attempt to transcend the anarchy *problematique* in international relations. Keohane argues that co-operation and the creation and maintenance of international institutions are a rational and predictable part of the behaviour of states. Keohane uses this insight to deny the realist assertion of international anarchy and consequent potentiality of war of all against all.[67]

While Keohane's analysis has undoubted merits, its contrast to Hobson's new liberal internationalism could hardly be greater. Keohane adopts a narrow utilitarian economic liberalism that posits rational actors seeking their own interests.[68] Indeed, Keohane defends international institutions on exactly the sort of utilitarian grounds that Hobson had criticised in his attacks on classical and neo-classical political economy. Keohane's approach depends on competition and rational selection among individuals. Hobson's conception of evolution, while involving aspects of competition, was much broader, including the idea that learning was not only part of co-operation in international relations (as it is for Keohane) but that culture, civilisation and reason also evolve. Hobson denied the atomistic rational egoism of Keohane's approach and sought to defend the growth of sociability and institutions in evolution as part of the realisation of the common good and a result of the operation of his theory of social surplus. Hobson sought the common good and believed in a collective social will, both apparently alien to Keohane's approach.[69] Finally, Keohane restricts his attention to the behaviour of states, playing down the importance of other actors. Hobson was emphatic that liberal internationalism consisted in the actions of nations rather than states; people as well as peoples are important for Hobson normatively and analytically.

The comparison with Keohane demonstrates that though Hobson is recognisably in the liberal tradition of international thought, he is also in some important respects an outsider to contemporary liberal international theory. His radicalism and his emphasis on the priority of social co-operation and the common good place him outside the current understanding of the classical tradition of liberalism concentrating on individual rights or utility. He does not fit into the modern utilitarianism of co-operation theory either. His approach is less economic-determinist than many variants of liberal internationalism. For instance, his proposals for international government went further than Mitrany's interventionism towards transcending the independence of politics and economics at the core of the liberal tradition. The economistic methodological orientation of much of the co-operation theory and regime literature is still further from Hobson's concerns and his approach.

HOBSON'S CONTRIBUTION TO INTERNATIONAL THEORY

J. A. Hobson is an anomaly in international theory because he does not fit comfortably into any of the established paradigms and is an outsider to the current understanding of the liberal internationalism to which he contributed so much. Yet he is a figure of critical importance to an understanding of the development of thinking on international relations, both liberal and non-liberal. He also has a limited but significant contribution to make to current theory.

As a liberal and a journalist, Hobson modified his theories and his ideological orientation with the current of events, yet interpreted those events in terms of his liberal ideological and theoretical framework. In terms of his new liberalism, an important problematic for Hobson was what he described as the social problem, the requirement for social solutions to the problems of poverty and unemployment. In his early writings, international relations appeared briefly as aspects of these issues. They were not seen so much as a problem in and of themselves but more as a context to a specific domestic social problem. After the Great War, the 'Bad Peace' and the disruption of inter-war international relations, however, Hobson began to concentrate more on international relations as a problem in itself. There was, in other words, an international problem, parallel to the social problem, associated with the development of the society of all humankind. This was the beginning of his development of a new liberal internationalism that was left incomplete by Hobson himself but was augmented in different guises (such as functionalism) by later writers.

A central feature of Hobson's contribution to international relations was his modification of liberalism and liberal internationalism towards what was described at the start of this book as new liberalism. While he was concerned with contemporary issues and events, Hobson also paid attention to liberal principles as they applied, or did not, or needed to be modified in response to developments. It is the near unique combination of theoretical insight and practical thinking that mark Hobson off as an important thinker in international relations.

Hobson is important to international theory as much for the type of theorist he was as for any specific theoretical contribution to the discipline of international relations. Hobson was one of an all too rare breed of journalists and political commentators whose work demonstrates an overall coherence derived from some theoretical rigour and attention to conceptual consistency. As we have seen, Hobson did not always obtain such lofty goals as conceptual or theoretical clarity. Yet these can be overstated as problems in his theory-building. Variations in tone and perspective are manifestations of the maturing of Hobson's writing on international relations. At the outset, his relative inexperience and lack of knowledge of international relations is quite obvious. Later, while he would still be categorised as one of the 'troublemakers', as A. J. P. Taylor has called the radical critics of foreign policy in Britain, he grew in stature as an expert on economic matters, including the international aspects in imperialism especially. Changes in outlook are surely to be expected, too, from someone who lived as long as Hobson did. International relations did not just change in Hobson's lifetime, they were altered drastically to the extent of being utterly transformed. Hobson responded to the various changes in the international environment: the growing internationalisation of the economy before 1914 and the subsequent advent of economic nationalism; the First World War and all it entailed; the Russian Revolution; the creation of the League of Nations; the collapse of three empires and the liberation of the nations of Eastern Europe; the Great Depression; the rise of dictatorship and parallel decline of democracy in the thirties; and, finally, the Second World War. It is a strength rather than a weakness of his writing that Hobson accommodated and reacted to these factors. He modified his perspective while maintaining its core characteristics; not to have done so would have indicated unbending dogmatism and idealism.

Yet it is important to recognise that, beyond the influence of changing times, Hobson's writings on international relations do not always constitute as coherent and clear a new liberal internationalism as I have presented. For instance, three contending visions of the ideal for future world order appear in Hobson's work and are reflected in this book: a Hobbesian idealist vision of a collective security organisation resting on the idea of the centralisation of force (in chapter 8); a Cobdenite free-trading economic internationalism (in chapter 7); and what I have called new liberal internationalism (set out in chapter 4 and reiterated in chapters 7 and 8).[70] These differ on fundamental propositions about international relations as well as in their prescriptions for a reformed world order. They differ on the fundamental goal of the international polity, whether it should be world order or global welfare, and on whether or not it is necessary to establish some form of international government to attain the goal.

The smooth progress from Cobdenism to constructive internationalism projected in the framework outlined in chapter 4 was disrupted by the First World War. During the chaotic interludes in international relations that he witnessed, Hobson clearly believed that coercive measures, inappropriate to a developed society, were required in international relations so that civilisation, let alone the nations of the world, would survive. Nevertheless, the problems and complexities of Hobson's writings on international relations remain those of a liberal facing the rapidly changing and challenging events and trends of the twentieth century.

This chapter has shown that in many cases Hobson's proposals appear to have been dead-ends in the history of ideas in international relations. Hobson's opinion on the need for an international government to maximise human welfare has been lost to current liberal theory, as we saw in the comparison with Keohane's neo-liberal institutionalism. To contemporary liberals in international relations,

Hobson's contribution is for the most part limited to the theory of imperialism. In the previous chapters it has been argued, on the contrary, that while Hobson's theory of imperialism is one of his key contributions to international theory it has wider ramifications than simply being an explanation of war or a precursor of the structuralist paradigm in international relations.[71]

Through the theories of surplus value and the use of the organic analogy, Hobson modified his liberalism and his liberal internationalism away from the classical non-interventionist free-trade formulation favoured in the nineteenth century. His new liberal internationalism was the predecessor of, and formed a theoretical basis for, Mitrany's functional approach to international organisation. In the context of liberal internationalism, Hobson reflects the turn from Cobdenism towards welfare internationalism and functionalist integration theory; his work is in a sense a microcosm of the transition that took place in liberal internationalism at the beginning of this century.

Hobson's emphasis on the organic nature in social life underpinned a holistic approach to the study of international relations and the theoretical orientation towards organisation in his new liberal internationalism. His work on welfare economics and the priority he gave to economic issues in international affairs made for a unique political economy of international relations.[72]

To conclude, Hobson's new liberal internationalism was an institutionalist challenge to classical liberalism in international relations and remains a challenge to current liberal international theorists. His writings on international relations range from imperialism to the League of Nations, from tariff legislation to the global control of population. However, Hobson's contribution to liberal internationalism consists less in the details of specific theories than in the transformation he effected in liberal social, political, economic and international theory. It is in this light that J. A. Hobson, far from being a figure from a distant historical past, continues to be influential in international relations.

Notes

1 INTRODUCTION

1 Though his stature was higher in the early years of the discipline of international relations, Hobson was one of only three twentieth-century figures allocated a place in Arnold Wolfers and Lawrence Martin's collection representing *The Anglo-American Tradition in Foreign Affairs* (New Haven: Yale University Press, 1986), ch. 19 – the others were Alfred Mahan and Woodrow Wilson.

2 Throughout the study, I refer to Hobson's books without naming him. When I refer to *Imperialism*, it is to the third edition, reprinted with a new introduction in 1988, and to *The Evolution of Modern Capitalism*, it is to the fourth edition, unless indicated otherwise.

3 See Hidemi Suganami, *Domestic Analogy and World Order Proposals* (Cambridge: Cambridge University Press, 1989), pp. 100–11; R. D. McKinlay and R. Little, *Global Problems and World Order* (London: Pinter, 1986), pp. 36–41; and John Gerard Ruggie, 'International Regimes, Transactions, and Change: Embedded Liberalism in the Post-War Economic Order', *International Organization* (Vol. 36, No. 2, 1982), and 'Political Structure and Change in the International Economy' in J. G. Ruggie (ed.), *The Antinomies of Interdependence: National Welfare and the International Division of Labour* (New York: Columbia University Press, 1983), p. 433.

4 For a discussion of liberalism in international relations, see Christopher Brewin, 'Liberal States and International Obligations', *Millennium: Journal of International Studies* (Vol. 17, No. 2, 1988), pp. 322–3. Other writers in this tradition include John Stuart Mill and John Maynard Keynes.

5 Accounts of Hobson's life and work can be found in Hobson's autobiography, *Confessions of an Economic Heretic*; A. J. F. Lee, 'The Social and Economic Thought of J. A. Hobson', unpublished Ph.D. thesis, University of London, 1970, ch. 1, and 'Hobson, John Atkinson (1858–1940), Economist and Journalist', in J. M. Bellamy and J. Saville (eds.), *Dictionary of Labour Biography* (London: Macmillan, 1972), pp. 176–81; Julian Townshend, 'J. A. Hobson and the Crisis of Liberalism', unpublished Ph.D. thesis, University of Southampton, 1973, pp. 7–13,

'Introduction', *Imperialism: A Study*, reprint of 3rd edn (London: Unwin Hyman, 1988 [1938]), pp. [11]–[14], and *J. A. Hobson* (Manchester: Manchester University Press, 1990); John Allett, *New Liberalism: The Political Economy of J. A. Hobson* (Toronto: University of Toronto Press, 1981), ch. 1; R. H. Tawney, 'Hobson, John Atkinson', in L. G. Wickham Legg (ed.), *Dictionary of National Biography, 1931–40* (London: Oxford University Press, 1949), pp. 435–6; Michael Freeden, 'Introduction', in M. Freeden (ed.), *J. A. Hobson: A Reader* (London: Unwin Hyman, 1988), pp. 2–4, 'Introduction', in M. Freeden (ed.), *Reappraising J. A. Hobson: Humanism and Welfare* (London: Unwin Hyman, 1990), pp. 1–10, and 'Introduction', to Hobson's *Confessions of an Economic Heretic*, reprint (Brighton: Harvester, 1974 [1938]), pp. v–xiv; P. F. Clarke, 'Introduction', to Hobson's *The Crisis of Liberalism*, reprint (Brighton: Harvester, 1974, [1909]), pp. ix–xxxviii; and H. N. Brailsford, *The Life-work of J. A. Hobson*, L. T. Hobhouse Memorial Lecture, 15 May 1947 (London: London School of Economics, 1948). One personal note: while in Exeter, Hobson taught at the author's old school!

6 Michael Freeden (ed.), *The Minutes of the Rainbow Circle, 1894–1924* (London: Royal Historical Society, 1989) lists Hobson's talks to this group from its inception to 1923.

7 *Confessions*, pp. 59–61.

8 For the most comprehensive list of articles Hobson contributed to journals and newspapers, see Lee, 'The Social and Economic Thought of J. A. Hobson', pp. 676–713. There are far too many to list here, but notable among them are the *Ethical World*, the *Progressive Review*, the *Contemporary Review*, the *Manchester Guardian*, the *Tribune*, the *New Leader*, the New York *Nation* and the *New Republic*.

9 Reputedly, this was in part because of the unfortunate impact of Hobson's first book, *The Physiology of Industry* (London: Murray, 1889). See *Confessions*, pp. 29–31. For an alternative interpretation of this episode, see Alon Kadish, 'The Non-canonical Context of *The Physiology of Industry*', in John Pheby (ed.), *J. A. Hobson After Fifty Years* (London: Macmillan, 1994), ch. 4; and 'Rewriting the Confessions', in Michael Freeden (ed.), *Reappraising J. A. Hobson*, ch. 8.

10 See the various incarnations of the journal of the South Place Ethical Society for reports of Hobson's talks there. A couple of Hobson's speeches appeared as pamphlets, for instance, 'Poverty', a speech given at the South Sectional Conference, and a speech given to the National Union of Gasworkers; 'Industrial Unrest', speech given at the National Liberal Club; and *Rationalism and Humanism*, a Conway Memorial Lecture (London: Watts, 1933).

11 See Peter Clarke, *Liberals and Social Democrats* (Cambridge: Cambridge University Press, 1978), pp. 164–9.

12 See his four-part series on 'The War and British Liberties', *Nation* (Vol. 19), pp. 68–9, 123–5, 307–8, 524–5.

13 On the UDC, see Marvin Swartz, *The Union of Democratic Control in British Politics During the First World War* (Oxford: Oxford University Press, 1971).

14 *Confessions*, pp. 123–6.

15 Compare his *The Economics of Reparation* (London: Allen and Unwin, 1921) and *The Obstacles to Economic Recovery in Europe* (London: Fight the Famine Council, 1920) with J. M. Keynes, *The Economic Consequences of the Peace* (New York: Harcourt, Brace, and Howe, 1920).

16 David Mitrany is mistaken when he claims that Hobson was excluded from the new international relations institute at Chatham House. Hobson did attend a number of meetings and there is a record of his comments on one talk in *International Affairs* (Vol. 10, No. 3, 1931), p. 303. See David Mitrany, 'The Making of the Functional Theory: A Memoir' in *A Functional Theory of Politics* (London: Martin Robertson, 1975), p. 39.

17 Hobson was a member of the Advisory Committee of the Labour Party on International Questions, the Whitley Committee, and the Reconstruction Sub-committee on Trusts. He was a witness to the Sankey Coal Commission.

18 See the prefaces to *Democracy and a Changing Civilisation* (London: Lane, 1934) and *Property and Improperty* (London: Gollancz, 1937).

19 'America in the War?', *South Place Monthly Record* (December 1939), pp. 3–4.

20 See the obituaries by G. D. H. Cole, 'J. A. Hobson, 1858–1940', *Economic Journal* (Vol. 50, 1940), pp. 351–60; C. D. Burns, 'J. A. Hobson: The Humanist', *South Place Monthly Record* (May 1940), p. 3; C. Delisle Burns, 'J. A. Hobson', *New Statesman* (April 1940).

2 RATIONALITY, WELFARE AND THE ORGANIC ANALOGY

1 Clarke, 'Introduction' to *Crisis of Liberalism*, p. xvii; Bernard Porter, *Critics of Empire* (London: Macmillan, 1968), p. 174; William Liu, *A Study of Hobson's Welfare Economics* (Peiping: Kwang Yuen Press, 1934), pp. 82–6, 92. Hobson's use of organic terminology is also examined in Michael Freeden, 'Introduction' to *Confessions*, pp. vii–viii; and 'Introduction', *J. A. Hobson: A Reader*, pp. 6–8. For a commentary on Freeden's discussion of new liberalism including Hobson, see Stephan Collini, 'Political Theory and the "Science of Society" in Victorian Britain', *The Historical Journal* (Vol. 23, No. 1, 1980), pp. 226–31.

2 Greta Jones, *Social Darwinism and English Thought* (Brighton: Harvester, 1980). Economists had also adopted the language of natural selection through free competition in a market economy. See the Preface to Alfred Marshall, *Principles of Economics*, 8th edn (London: Macmillan, 1966). Hobson commented on the use and abuse of the terms organic and evolution in *Free Thought in the Social Sciences* (London: Allen and Unwin, 1926), pp. 24–30. Talcott Parsons, *The Structure of Social Action* (New York: Free Press, 1949), part 1.

3 Michael Freeden, *New Liberalism* (Oxford: Clarendon, 1986 [1978]), pp. 102–5.

4 *Free Thought*, p. 19. In common with many authors of his time, Hobson used the term 'man' to mean human being. This sexist usage puts those examining his thought in a difficult position – to ignore the sexist usage is to reinforce or at least replay the sexism; on the other hand, to excise or edit Hobson's original language may miss the authentic meaning, including its sexist bias. I have chosen the former with caveats, in the hope that the reader will understand, and maybe share, my hesitancy.

5 *The Social Problem: Life and Work* (London: Nisbet, 1901), p. 3.

6 For Hobson's confidence in human progress, see *John Ruskin: Social Reformer* (London: Nisbet, 1898), p. 208; 'Sociology To-day', in British Committee of the Institute of Sociology and the World Service, *The Social Sciences* (London: Le Play University Press, 1936), p. 22. For his shaken attitude see *Confessions*, p. 96; *Problems of a New World* (London: Allen and Unwin, 1921), ch. 2; *The Psychology of Jingoism* (London: Grant Richards, 1901), pp. 20, 31, 33. On the instrumental notion of rationality in Hobson's thought, see *Social Problem*, p. 105, 'Sociology', pp. 20–1; *The Crisis of Liberalism* (London: P. S. King, 1909), p. 176.

7 *Wealth and Life* (London: Allen and Unwin, 1929), p. 17.

8 Though Hobson took this as an axiomatic part of evolution; see *John Ruskin: Social Reformer*, p. 88; *Wealth and Life*, p. 131. Hobson here closely parallels his friend Hobhouse. See L. T. Hobhouse, *Mind in Evolution* (London: Macmillan, 1915 [1901]). This is the meeting point of Hobson's use of biology and his adaptation of the ideas of the Philosophical Idealists such as Green and Bosanquet. See Michael Freeden, 'J. A. Hobson as a New Liberal Theorist', *Journal of the History of Ideas* (Vol. 34, No. 3, 1973), pp. 422–6.

9 *The Modern State* (London: BBC Publications, 1931), p. 30; *Confessions*, pp. 96, 104; *Rationalism and Humanism*, p. 31.

10 *Rationalism and Humanism*, pp. 10, 34–46.

11 *Free Thought*, p. 61.

12 *Free Thought*, pp. 11, 19; *Social Problem*, p. 66; *Wealth and Life*, p. 19. For Hobson's description of science conceived as 'a solemn marshalling of the several orders of concrete phenomena', see *John Ruskin:Social Reformer*, pp. 313–14.

13 *Free Thought*, pp. 19, 235; *John Ruskin: Social Reformer*, p. 59.

14 *Wealth and Life*, pp. 95–6.

15 *John Ruskin: Social Reformer*, p. 69; *Free Thought*, p. 281; *Wealth and Life*, pp. xxxi, 95.

16 Quote from *Wealth and Life*, p. 95. See also *Work and Wealth* (New York: Macmillan, 1922 [1914]), p. viii; *Free Thought*, pp. 5–6, 17; 'Sociology', p. 21; *Wealth and Life*, p. 109.

17 *Wealth and Life*, p. 95.

18 *Free Thought*, p. 30. See also pp. 23, 25–6; *Crisis of Liberalism*, pp 185, 265.

Social Problem, pp. 59–61; *Free Thought*, pp. 123–4. This also played into the hands of conservatives who sought to rule out dramatic change of the social system. See *Free Thought*, p. 52.

19 *Social Problem*, p. 62. See Hobson's discussion on pp. 52–62.

20 *John Ruskin: Social Reformer*, p. 200; *Social Problem*, p. 235.

21 *Social Problem*, pp. 59–60; *Wealth and Life*, p. vii.

22 *John Ruskin: Social Reformer*, p. 314.

23 *Social Problem*, pp. 66, 281–2.

24 *John Ruskin: Social Reformer*, pp. 79, 314; *Social Problem*, pp. 66–8.

25 *Social Problem*, pp. 66–7.

26 *Crisis of Liberalism*, pp. 216, 273; *Free Thought*, pp. 17–18, 222–3.

27 'Sociology', pp. 23, 25; *Work and Wealth*, p. 2.

28 *Free Thought*, p. 5; *Wealth and Life*, p. x.

29 *Social Problem*, p. 264.

30 *Work and Wealth*, p. 15–16. See *Free Thought*, p. 5; *Crisis of Liberalism*, pp. 184–5, 263. Also see on the co-ordination role of sociology in the social sciences, *John Ruskin: Social Reformer*, pp. 87, 198; *Social Problem*, pp. 60–1, 254.

31 'Sociology', p. 28; *Social Problem*, p. 61.

32 *Social Problem*, p. 61.

33 *John Ruskin: Social Reformer*, pp. 18, 87.

34 *Crisis of Liberalism*, p. 132. See also *Social Problem*, p. 284.

35 *Social Problem*, pp. 4, 6, 31.

36 *Crisis of Liberalism*, pp. 272, 274; *Social Problem*, p. 4. He disliked the neo-Hegelian Idealist philosophy prevalent in Oxford at the turn of the century, because he felt that the Idealists' abstract ideals were fixed and distant from present realities of society. See *Crisis of Liberalism*, pp. 187, 272.

37 *Social Problem*, p. 262; *John Ruskin: Social Reformer*, p. 258.

38 *Rationalism and Humanism*, pp. 20–1; *Democracy and a Changing Civilisation*, pp. 17–18.

39 *The Recording Angel: A Report from Earth* (London: Allen and Unwin, 1932), p. 75.

40 Hobson substituted 'federalism' for 'organism' in *Wealth and Life*.

41 *Confessions*, p. 209. See also *Work and Wealth*, p. 308; *Crisis of Liberalism*, p. 116. Hobson referred on occasion to his preferred system of distribution according to needs as the 'organic law of distribution'.

42 However, see the contrast in terminology used to excoriate the forces of reaction, from the mechanistic tones of *Imperialism: A Study*, 1st edn (London: Nisbet, 1902) to the organic tones of *Democracy After the War* (London: Allen and Unwin, 1917), p. 146.

43 And is part of the particularly dire warning issued to Western civilisation at the end of *Imperialism*, pp. 365–8.

44 Article commemorating the one-hundredth anniversary of the birth of J. A. Hobson, *South Place Monthly Record* (No. 63, July 1958).

45 R. N. Berki, *On Political Realism* (London: Dent, 1981), pp. 193–4.

According to Berki's definition, Carr's dichotomy of realism and utopianism as the opposition of power, relativism and necessity on the one hand, and reason, universalism and choice on the other, is itself a product of idealism. E. H. Carr, *The Twenty Years' Crisis* (London: Macmillan, 1946), ch. 2. Thus, both Hobson and Carr are idealists in Berki's definition. The difference between Carr and Hobson is that, in *The Twenty Years' Crisis*, Carr placed himself on the realist side, while Hobson remains on the utopian, according to Carr's criteria.

46 *Democracy After the War*, part 2, ch. 1.

47 Talcott Parsons, *On Institutions and Social Evolution*, ed. and intro. Leon H. Mayhew (Chicago: University of Chicago Press, 1982), p. 191. Parsons saw Durkheim as a step in the move of sociology away from the positivism of the likes of Hobson's friend, Leonard Hobhouse.

48 Charles Manning, *The Nature of International Society* (London: LSE/Bell, 1962), p. 151.

49 See *Free Thought*, pp. 142, 168–9; *Social Problem*, pp. 39, 50, 69, 76, where it is called 'social utility'.

50 *Free Thought*, pp. 167–73; *Social Problem*, pp. v–vi, 5, 7.

51 *Wealth and Life*, p. 16. See also p. 47, and *Free Thought*, p. 170. Hobson advocated a standard to avoid the chaos of subjectivism, where each person's valuation is worth as much as another, a view he took to be incorrect.

52 *Wealth and Life*, p. 16. See also p. 21. Hobson acknowledged, however, that there may be a different selection mechanism for cultural compared to biological needs.

53 *Wealth and Life*, pp. 11, 14. See also *Social Problem*, pp. 156, 236; *Work and Wealth*, p. 16.

54 *Work and Wealth*, pp. 19–20. Hobson also referred to race and humanity as collectivities.

55 If this was not the case, then logically the individual or group would have perished. *Social Problem*, p. 221: 'an intelligent individual ... may be conceived as working out a perfect organic economy of production and consumption designed to support him in full physical health and satisfaction'. See also *Free Thought*, pp. 133–4.

56 The difference between work and labour was that the former was a wholesome activity, while the latter was toil or loss of life. *John Ruskin: Social Reformer*, pp. 76–7, 84, 98n; *Social Problem*, p. 47; *Wealth and Life*, p. xxi. An 'illth' as contrasted to wealth would be, for example, cigarettes.

57 *John Ruskin: Social Reformer*, p. 310; *Free Thought*, p. 94.

58 *Work and Wealth*, pp. 17, 309.

59 *Social Problem*, p. 69; *Free Thought*, pp. 142, 172. See also Hobson's belief that this standard could be decided on by the most cultured members of society, in parallel to Mill's claim on this subject, *Wealth and Life*, pp. 60–1.

60 *Social Problem*, pp. 39, 45–7. See the discussion on the translation of economic into ethical values in *Wealth and Life*, part 1.

61 *Social Problem*, p. 7.

62 *Work and Wealth*, p. 12. There is a problem here. If each individual's conscious satisfactions are the basis of welfare, how is it possible to get to the notion of social welfare from such divergent estimations of the standard of welfare? Hobson states the problem baldly in referring to the population question: 'Who shall say whether one Darwin or Mozart is worth as much as a hundred million happy negroes?' Hobson's introduction of distinctions of quality as opposed to quantity made this even more difficult. See *Wealth and Life*, p. xxvi; *Free Thought*, pp. 64, 135; *Wealth and Life*, p. 51.

63 *John Ruskin: Social Reformer*, p. 74; *Free Thought*, p. 90.

64 These steps are outlined in *Work and Wealth*, ch. 3; *Social Problem*, book 1, ch. 5; *Wealth and Life*, pp. vii–ix, part 2, ch. 3.

65 The idea that value is derived from the right use of a good by the right person comes from John Ruskin, see *John Ruskin: Social Reformer*, p. 79. On the objective human standard, see pp. 84–5.

66 *Work and Wealth*, p. 2. See also *John Ruskin: Social Reformer*, p. 239. On the insuperable nature of these problems, see *Wealth and Life*, p. viii. For a criticism of Hobson along these lines, see Wesley C. Mitchell, *Lecture Notes on Types of Economic Theory* (New York: Augustus M. Kelley, 1969), chs. 37–9.

67 *John Ruskin: Social Reformer*, pp. 84–5; *Social Problem*, p. 87; *Work and Wealth*, pp. v, 309; *Free Thought*, pp. 65, 141; *Wealth and Life*, p. 58.

68 J. J. C. Smart and Bernard Williams, *Utilitarianism: For and Against* (Cambridge: Cambridge University Press, 1973), pp. 108–18; A. K. Sen, *On Ethics and Economics* (Oxford; Basil Blackwell, 1987), pp. 40–6, 74–6; A. K. Sen and Bernard Williams (eds.), *Utilitarianism and Beyond* (Cambridge: Cambridge University Press, 1982), pp. 1–21.

69 For instance, see H. B. Acton, 'Introduction', to J. S. Mill, *Utilitarianism, On Liberty and Considerations on Representative Government* (London: Dent, 1984) pp. xiv, xvii, xx.

70 See the aims of the Rainbow Circle in Samuel Papers, A.10, quoted in Porter, *Critics of Empire*, p. 164.

71 See, among others, Freeden, *New Liberalism*, ch. 3; Allett, *New Liberalism*, chs. 6–7; Clarke, 'Introduction' to *Crisis of Liberalism*, pp. xiii–xv.

72 *Crisis of Liberalism*, p. 207. There is a parallel repudiation of economic calculus in *Free Thought*, pp. 122–3.

73 *Free Thought*, p. 130.

74 *Social Problem*, p. 67; *Work and Wealth*, p. 307; *Crisis of Liberalism*, p. 77. On individual rights, see *Social Problem*, pp. 88, 95, 101; *Crisis of Liberalism*, pp. 77, 79–80. Hobson does concede the primacy of the individual regarding welfare, *Social Problem*, p. 172. On this issue see Michael Freeden, 'J. A. Hobson as a Political Theorist', in Pheby (ed.), *J. A. Hobson After Fifty Years*, pp. 19–33.

75 *Work and Wealth*, p. 308. See also *Social Problem*, p. 146; *Wealth and Life*, p. 167.

76 *John Ruskin: Social Reformer*, pp. 247–8.
77 These terms are explained in greater depth in the next chapter.
78 *Crisis of Liberalism*, p. xi.
79 *Recording Angel*, p. 20.
80 *Imperialism*, p. 225.
81 *Crisis of Liberalism*, p. 116.
82 See 'The Re-statement of Democracy' and 'The Tasks of Reconstruction' in *Crisis of Liberalism*.
83 *Crisis of Liberalism*, p. 115; *Wealth and Life*, p. 84.
84 *Wealth and Life*, p. 134.
85 *Wealth and Life*, p. 117.
86 Clarke, *Liberals and Social Democrats*, p. 50. See also John Allett, 'The Conservative Aspect of Hobson's New Liberalism' in Michael Freeden (ed.) *Reappraising J. A. Hobson: Humanism and Welfare* (London: Unwin Hyman, 1990).
87 Early in his career Hobson was quite close to this position himself. For his critique, see 'The Social Philosophy of Charity Organisation', in *Crisis of Liberalism*, and especially pp. 184–5. He remained unimpressed by Hegelian dialectics, but the attack on Hegel's philosophy and its influence was conducted with more fervour by Hobson's friend L. T. Hobhouse. See the latter's *The Metaphysical Theory of the State* (London: Allen, 1918), a critique of Bernard Bosanquet's *The Philosophical Theory of the State*.
88 *John Ruskin: Social Reformer*, p. 207.
89 *Social Problem*, p. 224. See also *Crisis of Liberalism*, pp. 76, 82–3. For Hobson's rather less liberal views, see, for instance, *John Ruskin: Social Reformer*, p. 16 on marriage, *Crisis of Liberalism*, p. 85 on democracy, and *Social Problem*, p. 88 on the impossibility of self-regarding actions.
90 See Suganami, *Domestic Analogy and World Order Proposals*, ch. 2; Irving M. Copi, *Introduction to Logic*, 5th edn (London: Collier Macmillan, 1978), ch. 11; Duncan Snidal, 'The Game *Theory* of International Politics', in Kenneth Oye (ed.), *Cooperation Under Anarchy* (Princeton: Princeton University Press, 1986), pp. 29–32.
91 Cristina Bicchieri, 'Should a Scientist Abstain from Metaphor?', in Arjo Klamer, Donald N. McCloskey and Robert M. Solow (eds.), *The Consequences of Economic Rhetoric* (Cambridge: Cambridge University Press, 1988), pp. 100–14, esp. 104.
92 See particularly, Donald N. McCloskey, *The Rhetoric of Economics* (Madison University of Wisconsin Press, 1985). In international relations, see the intriguing analysis by Isabelle Grunberg, 'Exploring the "Myth" of Hegemonic Stability', *International Organization* (Vol. 44, No. 4, 1990).
93 See *Free Thought*, part 1, ch. 2.
94 See Anatol Rapoport, *Conflict in Man-Made Environment* (Harmondsworth: Penguin, 1974), pp. 17–24, for a persuasive argument concerning the transfer of human concepts onto the natural world. Rapoport's central examples are also relevant here: co-operation and conflict do not make

sense in the animal world, for instance, because it is not clear what animals are conflicting about. See also Collini, 'Political Theory and the "Science of Society" in Victorian Britain'.

95 *Social Problem*, p. 155.

96 See L. T. Hobhouse, *Liberalism* (London: Williams and Norgate, 1911), pp. 127–30.

97 See *Imperialism*, part 1, ch. 4.

98 For example, see *Incentives in the New Industrial Order* (London: Allen and Unwin, 1922).

99 *Work and Wealth*, pp. 17–18.

3 CO-OPERATION, THE SURPLUS AND THE THEORY OF UNDERCONSUMPTION

1 *Social Problem*, p. 147.

2 *Social Problem*, pp. 146–7. Note once again the generic use of the term man to mean person.

3 *Social Problem*, pp. 144, 159; *Free Thought*, p. 245; *Wealth and Life*, pp. 43, 152, 168. While the market might be a form for the social determination of value, it was criticised by Hobson as working inefficiently and inequitably, as we shall see in the next section.

4 *Wealth and Life*, pp. 24, 27, 29; *Work and Wealth*, pp. 162, 281.

5 *John Ruskin: Social Reformer*, pp. 134–5; *Free Thought*, p. 157; *Wealth and Life*, pp. 162, 201; *Work and Wealth*, p. 6.

6 For Marx's criticisms of arguments like Hobson's, see his *Theories of Surplus Value* (London: Lawrence and Wishart, 1969), pp. 387–8. See Robert Freeman (ed.), *Marx on Economics* (Harmondsworth: Penguin, 1962), pp. 70–93. See Lenin's review of Hobson's *Evolution of Modern Capitalism* in *Economica* (Vol. 5, Nov. 1925), pp. 362–4. For a conflation of the two positions, see James Der Derian, *On Diplomacy: A Genealogy of Western Estrangement* (Oxford: Basil Blackwell, 1987), p. 186. On Hobson's critique of Marxist economics, see *The Economics of Distribution* (New York: Macmillan, 1900), p. 353; *Free Thought*, pp. 147, 152–3, 163; *Wealth and Life*, pp. xvi, 192–3. For Hobson's other criticisms of Marx and Marxism, see 'Sociology', p. 22; *Free Thought*, pp. 29, 77–8; '*Crisis of Liberalism*, pp. 138, 237; *Free Thought*, p. 249; *Physiology of Industry*, pp. 76–7.

7 Peter Weiler, in his *New Liberalism* (New York: Garland, 1982), expresses this worry about Hobson's work in general.

8 According to Hobson, this is an organic law that applies to all organisms and organic systems, of which human society is one. For an example of Hobson's emphasis on the role of surplus in organic systems, see *Social Problem*, p. 108: 'Man is the owner of a recurrent fund of superfluous energy ...'. See the discussion of the organic analogy below.

9 Hobson referred to Spencer's 'novel conception that social organisation could be material for scientific study, and that laws of evolution could be

discovered in the history of human institutions'. See *Free Thought*, p. 5. See also Freeden (ed.) *J. A. Hobson: A Reader*, pp. 60–3.

10 *John Ruskin: Social Reformer*, p. 103; *Wealth and Life*, p. 131.

11 See, for example, *Social Problem*, pp. 142–5; *Free Thought*, pp. 133–4.

12 *Social Problem*, pp. 76, 81.

13 *Crisis of Liberalism*, pp. 191, 208; *John Ruskin: Social Reformer*, p. 102; *Social Problem*, p. 49.

14 Here, Hobson is following Mill's distinction of higher and lower values. The distinction of higher and lower values appears in Mill, *Utilitarianism*. For a further discussion of utilitarianism, see Smart and Williams, *Utilitarianism: For and Against*.

15 *Free Thought*, pp. 12, 228–9; *The Evolution of Modern Capitalism*, 4th edn (London: Allen and Unwin, 1926), p. 402; *Crisis of Liberalism*, pp. 265–6.

16 *Wealth and Life*, p. 218; *Social Problem*, pp. 255, 259–61; *Free Thought*, p. 31.

17 *Work and Wealth*, p. 307. See also *Free Thought*, p. 265; *Evolution of Modern Capitalism*, p. 402.

18 This phrase is borrowed from the title of a book by Peter Singer. See his *The Expanding Circle: Ethics and Sociobiology* (New York: Farrar, 1981).

19 *Work and Wealth*, p. 172.

20 *Social Problem*, pp. 175–7; *Evolution of Modern Capitalism*, p. 410; *Wealth and Life*, pp. 173, 219. This control might be through nationalisation, the enforcement of arbitration or fair wage legislation.

21 Though he entertained the idea of a general will, Hobson severely criticised the 'mob mind' of jingoism and war fever. See *Psychology of Jingoism*, 'Introductory', chs. 2–3, and *Democracy After the War*, part 2. The determining factors in Hobson's differing opinions appear to be the limited and sectional nature of the combination as well as the irrational, directionless and malleable state of mind of the masses.

22 *Problems of Poverty*, 2nd edn (London: Methuen, 1895), pp. 201–2, 207–11, 213; *Evolution of Modern Capitalism*, pp. 113–40; *Work and Wealth*, pp. 277–8; *Wealth and Life*, p. 9; *Social Problem*, p. 177.

23 *Crisis of Liberalism*, pp. 120–2; also on the impossibility and undesirability of complete central control, see *Wealth and Life*, pp. 30–40, 43, 235, 238; *John Ruskin: Social Reformer*, pp. 204–5.

24 *Wealth and Life*, pp. 33, 68; *Social Problem*, pp. 245–6.

25 *Evolution of Modern Capitalism*, pp. 418, 420; *Social Problem*, pp. 183–5.

26 This last is commonly labelled entrepreneurship in economics today. Ability and entrepreneurship are not exactly the same, however. For Hobson, ability meant particularly the ability to organise the other factors, the reward for which was a salary; for economic theorists today, entrepreneurship means risk-taking as well as organisation, the reward for which is profit.

27 'The Law of Three Rents', *Quarterly Journal of Economics* (Vol. 5, 1891). Hobson's discussion of costs and surpluses in *The Industrial System* (London:

Longmans, 1909) is presented in an abbreviated form in *The Science of Wealth* (London: Williams and Norgate, 1911).

28 He elsewhere calls the last element unearned income or improperty. See *The Industrial System* and *Property and Improperty*.

29 *Science of Wealth*, p. 68.

30 *Science of Wealth*, p. 69.

31 *Wealth and Life*, p. xviii; *Work and Wealth*, pp. 177, 276. And thus the costs of growth cannot be more than potential costs. Indeed, Hobson's vacillation on whether this factor is a cost or a surplus is revealing: the distinction between productive and unproductive surplus in Hobson's writing demonstrates that there are two meanings of surplus; the terminology of costs of growth, on the other hand, highlights the evolutionary dynamism of Hobson's view of the economy.

32 *Wealth and Life*, p. 213; *Work and Wealth*, p. 276.

33 *Wealth and Life*, pp. xviii, 190.

34 *Work and Wealth*, p. 276; *Wealth and Life*, pp. 190, 195–6; *Science of Wealth*, pp. 105–6, 111. For the vagueness of the distinction between costs and surplus, see *Wealth and Life*, p. 211.

35 *Science of Wealth*, pp. 80–1.

36 *Science of Wealth*, p. 82.

37 *John Ruskin: Social Reformer*, p. 104; *Work and Wealth*, pp. vii, 163; *Free Thought*, p. 131; *Wealth and Life*, p. xxx; *Social Problem*, p. 162; *Crisis of Liberalism*, pp. 80–1.

38 *Free Thought*, p. 131.

39 *Wealth and Life*, p. xxx.

40 *Social Problem*, p. 254.

41 *Wealth and Life*, p. 198.

42 The Oxford English Dictionary lists Hobson as the originator of the word 'marginalism'. For some of Hobson's more sustained treatments of marginalism as well as classical economic theory, see *Social Problem*, chs. 3–4; *Free Thought*, part 2; *Industrial System*, appendix to ch. 5. For assessments of his mathematical abilities and his understanding of marginalism, see E. E. Nemmers, *Hobson and Underconsumption* (Amsterdam: North-Holland, 1956), pp. 95ff.; J. M. Keynes, Review of Hobson's *Gold, Prices and Wages* in the *Economic Journal* (1913), reprinted in *Collected Works*, vol. XI (London: Macmillan, 1983) pp. 388–94; T. W. Hutchinson, *A Review of Economic Doctrines, 1870–1929* (Oxford: Clarendon, 1953), p. 123.

43 R. F. Harrod, 'Epilogue', in *Science of Wealth*, 4th edn (Oxford: Oxford University Press, 1950); Clarke, 'Introduction' to *Crisis of Liberalism*, p. xxviii; Hutchinson, *Review of Economic Doctrines*, p. 126.

44 Take away the organic analogy and Hobson's theories of surplus value are arguments for guild socialism rather than state socialism.

45 John Allett has defended Hobson against the charge that he held a 'bourgeois' conception of needs. See his *New Liberalism*, p. 69.

46 As argued famously by Friedrich Hayek, *The Road to Serfdom* (London: Ark Paperbacks, 1986).

47 See generally John Rawls, *A Theory of Justice* (Cambridge, MA: Harvard University Press, 1971); Robert Nozick, *Anarchy, State and Utopia* (New York: Basic Books, 1974); Brian Barry, *Theories of Justice* (Berkeley: University of California Press, 1988).

48 For Hobson's defence of the surplus as the basis for taxation policy, see *Poverty in Plenty* (London: Allen and Unwin, 1931), p. 55.

49 For criticisms of liberals and liberalism along these lines, see William Connolly, *Appearance and Reality in Politics* (Cambridge: Cambridge University Press, 1981), ch. 4; John Dunn, *Rethinking Modern Political Theory: Essays 1979–83* (Cambridge: Cambridge University Press, 1985), ch. 9; and B. Crick, *In Defence of Politics* (Harmondsworth: Penguin, 1964), pp. 127–34.

50 For accounts of Hobson's discussion of these matters, see Allett, *New Liberalism*, ch. 4; Nemmers, *Hobson and Underconsumption*; Michael Bleaney, *Underconsumption Theories* (New York: International Publishers, 1976), ch. 8.

51 *Recording Angel*, p. 33. He thought that modern productive techniques could provide enough to feed humanity. For the production processes increasing disproportionately to consumption, see, among many others, *Imperialism*, p. [45].

52 *Democracy and a Changing Civilisation*, p. 36. See also p. 123, and *Imperialism*, p. 80.

53 Or is dismissed entirely. See the Preface to *Poverty in Plenty*.

54 *Imperialism*, p. 81; see also p. [45]; *Property and Improperty*, p. 38; *Recording Angel*, p. 48. For brief and accessible explanations of Say's Law, see William J. Barber, *A History of Economic Thought* (Harmondsworth: Penguin, 1967), pp. 68–70; and Robert Heilbroner, *The Worldly Philosophers* (Harmondsworth: Penguin, 1983), p. 77 (see also pp. 148–9 on Hobson's underconsumption). On Hobson and Say's Law see P. J. Cain, 'J. A. Hobson, Cobdenism and the Radical Theory of Economic Imperialism, 1898–1914', *Economic History Review* (Vol. 31, No. 4, 1978), pp. 571–2, and 'International Trade and Economic Development in the Work of J. A. Hobson Before 1914', *History of Political Economy* (Vol. 11, No. 3, 1979), p. 410.

55 *Imperialism*, p. 81.

56 *Physiology of Industry*, p. 111.

57 *Physiology of Industry*, p. 105.

58 *Physiology of Industry*, pp. iv, 205.

59 *Physiology of Industry*, pp. 130–2.

60 *Physiology of Industry*, p. 162.

61 There are a number of anomalies about the *Physiology* as part of Hobson's work. For instance, on page 37, there is a distinction of the concerns of economics from ethical concerns. This, along with other textual indications and the violation of the alphabetical convention on the listing of the

authors' names, has led some scholars to wonder whether it was Mummery who had the larger influence on this book. For an example of a recurrence of the any/every paradox, see 'Underconsumption: An Exposition and a Reply', *Economica* (Vol. 13, November 1933), pp. 407–8. On the international relations of underconsumption, see chapter 6 below.

62 *Poverty in Plenty*, p. 85.

63 'Rejoinder' to 'Underconsumption: An Exposition and a Reply', p. 427.

64 *International Trade: An Application of Economic Theory* (London: Methuen, 1904), pp. 149, 150. See also *Imperialism*, p. 29.

65 *The Economics of Unemployment* (London: Allen and Unwin, 1922), p. 8.

66 *Property and Improperty*, p. 39.

67 *Economics of Unemployment*, p. 41. Note the close parallel of the two pairs of quotes above despite the fact that they are separated by over a quarter of a century.

68 *Economics of Unemployment*, p. 8. For further discussion of the 'automatic' nature of the saving of the wealthy, see pp. 35–7.

69 See *Rationalisation and Unemployment* (London: Allen and Unwin, 1930), p. 55; *Economics of Unemployment*, pp. 47–8.

70 *Poverty in Plenty*, pp. 63–4. See also *Economics of Unemployment*, pp. 47–8.

71 F. Y. Edgeworth's review of *Physiology* is cited in Hutchinson, *Review of Economic Doctrines*, pp. 118–19. For an alternative view, see Alon Kadish's chapter in Michael Freeden (ed.), *Reappraising J. A. Hobson.*

72 See Nemmers, *Hobson and Underconsumption*, p. 48. For Hobson's account of alternative explanations of trade depressions, see *Economics of Unemployment.*

73 Nemmers, *Hobson and Underconsumption*, p. 40.

74 J. M. Keynes, *The General Theory of Employment, Interest and Money* (London: Macmillan, 1967), pp. 367–70; Clarke, *Liberals and Social Democrats*, pp. 226–31, and 'Hobson and Keynes as Economic Heretics', in Freeden (ed.), *Reappraising J. A. Hobson*, ch. 6; Nemmers, *Hobson and Underconsumption.* Michael Bleaney's criticism in *Underconsumption Theories*, p. 180, that Hobson failed to identify the dual aspects of investment as both saving and consumption follows from the Keynesian distinction of saving and investment.

75 Clarke, 'Hobson and Keynes as Economic Heretics', pp. 100–1.

76 For instance, Michael Schneider, 'Modelling Hobson's Underconsumption Theory', mimeo, 1990, and Roger E. Backhouse, 'Mummery and Hobson's *The Physiology of Industry*: A Centennial Evaluation', in John Pheby (ed.), *J. A. Hobson After Fifty Years* (London: Macmillan, 1994), ch. 6; D. Hamilton, 'Hobson with a Keynesian Twist', *American Journal of Economics and Sociology* (Vol. 13, 1954).

77 See Michael Freeden, *Liberalism Divided* (Oxford: Clarendon, 1986), pp. 12–14. Hobson's emphasis on the moral aspect of economic problems will be discussed further in chapter 4 as a response to the charge of economic determinism in the theory of imperialism.

78 See, in the first case, *Economics of Unemployment* and *Problems of a New World*,

and in the second, *Rationalisation and Unemployment*, *Poverty in Plenty*, *From Capitalism to Socialism* (London: Hogarth, 1932), *Recording Angel*, *Democracy and a Changing Civilisation* and *Property and Improperty*.

79 See 'The Mystery of Dumping', in *International Trade*.

4 AN EVOLUTIONARY FRAMEWORK FOR INTERNATIONAL RELATIONS

1 Fred Halliday, 'Three Concepts of Internationalism', *International Affairs* (Vol. 64, No. 2, 1988), p. 187.

2 'The Ethics of Humanity', *South Place Monthly Record* (August 1939), p. 4.

3 Hobson's internationalism retains the meaning of national within it, unlike international (as in international relations) which has come to mean interstate. See Hidemi Suganami, 'A Note on the Origin of the Word International', *Review of International Studies* (Vol. 4, 1978), pp. 226–32, for a discussion of the meaning of international. Internationalism has deviated from this meaning, although lately it has also been used to refer to the building of state relations, that is, intergovernmentalism. See Samuel Huntingdon, 'Transnational Organizations in World Politics', *World Politics* (Vol. 25, No. 3, April 1973), p. 338.

4 *Poverty in Plenty*, p. 84.

5 *Wealth and Life*, pp. 36, 222. In *Work and Wealth* (p. 17), he also made a rather mystical reference to the 'dimmer outline ... [of] some larger cosmic organism'.

6 *Work and Wealth*, p. 16.

7 *Democracy and a Changing Civilisation*, p. 138. See also *Work and Wealth*, p. 17; *The Social Problem*, pp. 132, 261; *Wealth and Life*, pp. 23–4. For Hobson's criticism of the Victorian complacency of the Cobdenite version of this argument, see *Rationalism and Humanism*, p. 20.

8 *Work and Wealth*, p. 358.

9 *Crisis of Liberalism*, p. 254.

10 'Nationalism and Imperialism', in *Imperialism*. It is worth noting that the connection between nationhood and civilisation is close for Hobson. How close is indicated by the fact that he never refers to backward nations, but only backward peoples. As we shall see, this has further implications for his ideas on the participation of backward peoples in an international government.

11 *Imperialism*, pp. 10–11.

12 See for instance the discussion of international finance in *Economic Interpretation of Investment* (London: Financial Review of Reviews, 1911), p. 112; *The Case for Arbitration* (London: International Arbitration League, 1911), p. 4; and *Problems of Poverty*, pp. 202–6. The second was a spiritual cosmopolitanism, a belief in the unity of all people as human beings, regardless of race, sex, age, etc. in *Imperialism*, pp. 5, 10. In *Imperialism*, internationalism is also the third alternative between imperialism and nationalism.

13 See, for example, *Recording Angel*, pp. 43, 101.
14 Compare his opinions in *Imperialism*, p. 169, with *From Capitalism to Socialism*, p. 49.
15 *Confessions*, p. 113; *Property and Improperty*, p. 106.
16 *Social Problem*, pp. 284–5; *Free Thought*, pp. 158, 259–60; *Recording Angel*, p. 112.
17 *Problems of a New World*, p. 142.
18 *Wealth and Life*, p. 36. But see p. 43.
19 *Wealth and Life*, p. 222; *Social Problem*, pp. 284–5; *Democracy and a Changing Civilisation*, p. 163; *The Importance of Instruction in the Facts of Internationalism* (London: National Peace Council, 1912).
20 See *Free Thought*, pp. 50–1, 234, 259; *Incentives in the New Industrial Order*, pp. 150–1. For a recent example of this argument, see Roy E. Jones, 'The English School of International Relations', *Review of International Studies* (Vol. 7, No. 1, 1981), and 'The Myth of the Special Problem in International Relations', *Review of International Studies* (Vol. 14, No. 4, 1988).
21 *Free Thought*, p. 257.
22 *Towards International Government* (London: Allen and Unwin, 1915), pp. 81, 86–7, 178.
23 *Wealth and Life*, p. 69. See also *Problems of a New World*, p. 151.
24 *Poverty in Plenty*, p. 84; *Problems of a New World*, p. 253.
25 *Towards International Government*, pp. 23, 126, 134.
26 On international law limiting sovereignty, see *Case for Arbitration*, p. 7; *Towards International Government*, pp. 33, 124–5.
27 *Democracy and a Changing Civilisation*, pp. 134–5; *Towards International Government*, p. 180.
28 Suganami, *Domestic Analogy and World Order Proposals*, p. 1, and 'Reflections on the Domestic Analogy', *Review of International Studies* (Vol. 12, No. 2, 1986), p. 155.
29 *Problems of a New World*, p. 253; see also *Towards International Government*, pp. 85, 153.
30 *The Morals of Economic Internationalism* (New York: Houghton, 1920), pp. 62–3; see also *Problems of a New World*, p. 251.
31 For a classic statement of the difference between international relations and domestic society, see Thomas Hobbes, *Leviathan*, ed. and intro. C. B. Macpherson (Harmondsworth: Penguin, 1968), ch. 13. For further analysis, see Hedley Bull, 'Society and Anarchy in International Relations', in Herbert Butterfield and Martin Wight (eds.), *Diplomatic Investigations* (London: Allen and Unwin, 1967) and *The Anarchical Society* (London: Macmillan, 1977); and on the dual nature of political obligation, see Andrew Linklater, *Men and Citizens in the Theory of International Relations* (London: Macmillan, 1982).
32 *The Conditions of Industrial Peace* (London: Allen and Unwin, 1927), p. 22. Also pp. 13, 30.
33 See Suganami, *Domestic Analogy and World Order Proposals*, pp. 29–33.
34 *Towards International Government*, p. 193; *League of Nations*, pp. 4ff.

35 *Case for Arbitration*, pp. 1–2; *League of Nations*, pp. 4, 7.
36 *Problems of a New World*, p. 253.
37 These four international systems differ in a number of ways from Giovanni Arrighi's four co-ordinates set out in *The Geometry of Imperialism*, revised edn (London: Verso, 1983), ch. 1.
38 Hobson's reference to Hobbes and Machiavelli tended to show that *realpolitik* had roots in European countries other than Germany. See for instance, *Free Thought*, p. 187; 'The Morality of Nations', in *Crisis of Liberalism*, p. 249; *Morals of Economic Internationalism*, pp. 5–6; *Problems of a New World*, p. 77; *Democracy After the War*, pp. 113, 188; *Towards International Government*, p. 179.
39 *Towards International Government*, p. 180. See chapter 7 for Hobson's condemnation of traditional diplomacy.
40 For an example, see *Traffic in Treason* (London: Unwin, 1914), pp. 9, 61.
41 *Towards International Government*, p. 181.
42 *Incentives in the New Industrial Order*, pp. 147–8.
43 As can be seen in Hobson's criticisms of *ad hoc* resolution in industrial disputes. See, *Incentives in the New Industrial Order*, pp. 147–8; see also *Democracy After the War*, pp. 175–6. Hobson also denied that there would be equilibrium, see *Towards International Government*, p. 182.
44 *Towards International Government*, p. 182.
45 'The Morality of Nations', in *Crisis of Liberalism*, pp. 248–9; *Democracy After the War*, p. 114.
46 *Free Thought*, p. 182. See also pp. 22–5, 30n; *Towards International Government*, pp. 181–2; *Modern State*, p. 32; and *Problems of a New World*, pp. 33–4.
47 *Democracy After the War*, p. 22.
48 'The Morality of Nations', in *Crisis of Liberalism*, p. 254
49 'The Morality of Nations', in *Crisis of Liberalism*, p. 260.
50 *Free Thought*, p. 199.
51 *Modern State*, p. 31.
52 On the impossibility of splendid isolation, see *Towards International Government*, p. 23, 90; *Morals of Economic Internationalism*, p. 4; and *Democracy After the War*, pp. 85–6. On America as a possible exception to this rule, see *Morals of Economic Internationalism*, pp. 28–9. On *realpolitik* and unreason, see *Towards International Government*, p. 99.
53 *Richard Cobden: The International Man* (London: Unwin, 1918), p. 34.
54 'The Political Basis of a World State', in F. S. Marvin (ed.), *The Unity of Western Civilisation*, 2nd edn (London: Oxford University Press, 1922), pp. 260–1. Hobson examines Cobdenism in his biography, *Richard Cobden*, though it is also implicit in his critique of imperialism in *Imperialism*.
55 *Richard Cobden*, pp. 388–9.
56 *Richard Cobden*, p. 21. See also pp. 9–10.
57 *Richard Cobden*, pp. 390–1. See also p. 35.
58 Richard Cobden, *The Political Writings of Richard Cobden* (New York: Garland, 1973), vol. 1, p. 36.

59 *The New Protectionism* (London: Unwin, 1916), p. 115. See also *Democracy After the War*, p. 198; *Property and Improperty*, p. 205; *International Government*, p. 95; *The Case for Arbitration*, p. 3. See also 'Free Trade as a Factor in Civilisation', *South Place Monthly List* (June 1915), pp. 6–7. The arguments put forward by Hobson for free trade are considered in greater depth in chapter 5.
60 *Modern State*, p. 33.
61 *Economic Interpretation of Investment*, p. 121.
62 *Democracy and a Changing Civilisation*, pp. 138–9; *Problems of a New World*, pp. 17–18, 32.
63 *Imperialism*, p. [42].
64 But see *Imperialism*, p. 19, where Hobson prefers 1884 over 1870.
65 *Imperialism*, p. 281. For further examples of Hobson's discussion of imperialism as the subjugation of national to sectional interests, see *Property and Improperty*, p. 105; *Problems of a New World*, pp. 269–72; *Democracy After the War*, pp. 85–6; *Imperialism*, pp. 106, 127, 168.
66 For the supersession of the premises of Cobdenism, both in terms of the growth of imperialism and constructive internationalism, see *Richard Cobden*, pp. 406–8; *Problems of a New World*, pp. 19–21, 23–9, 190; *Democracy After the War*, p. 28; *Imperialism*, p. 225.
67 For more detail on this argument, see the following chapter.
68 *Richard Cobden*, pp. 400–1.
69 *Imperialism*, pp. 135, 167, 181.
70 See 'For Whom Are We Fighting?', in *The War in South Africa* (London: Nisbet, 1900).
71 See *Imperialism*, part 2, for Hobson's discussion of these ideologies.
72 For examples of Hobson's use of 'parasitism', see *Democracy After the War*, pp. 145, 172; *Imperialism*, p. 59, 107, 151, 313–14, 364–8, especially pp. 367–8.
73 *Imperialism*, p. 59. For concentration and control being one of the facets of the new imperialism, see p. 356.
74 *Richard Cobden*, p. 406.
75 *Recording Angel*, p. 111.
76 *Problems of a New World*, p. 139. See also *Work and Wealth*, pp. 350–1, 355.
77 He also referred to it as real or positive internationalism. See *Modern State*, p. 36; *Richard Cobden*, ch. 13.
78 *Democracy After the War*, pp. 85–6.
79 *Evolution of Modern Capitalism*, pp. 458–60; *Economic Interpretation of Investment*, pp. 17ff; 'A World Economy', *New Statesman and Nation* (Vol. 1, 18 April 1931), pp. 274–5.
80 *Wealth and Life*, p. 390; *Modern State*, p. 36.
81 I use the term functional in the context of functionalism in the international relations literature. See Paul Taylor, 'Functionalism: The Theory of David Mitrany', in Paul Taylor and A. J. R. Groom (eds.), *International Organisation: A Conceptual Approach* (London: Pinter, 1978); Ernst Haas,

Beyond the Nation-State: Functionalism and International Organization (Stanford: Stanford University Press, 1964); Mitrany, *Functional Theory of Politics*; James A. Caporaso, *Functionalism and Regional Integration: A Logical and Empirical Assessment* (London: Sage, 1972); R. J. Vincent, 'The Functions of Functionalism in International Relations', *The Yearbook of World Affairs* (Vol. 26, 1973).

82 *Case for Arbitration*, pp. 1–2; *League of Nations*, pp. 4ff; *International Government*, pp. 193–4. See also 'Political Basis of a World State', p. 268, and 'The Origins of the I.L.O.', *Contemporary Review* (Vol. 147, No. 403, August 1935).

83 *Morals of Economic Internationalism*, pp. 31ff.

84 *Imperialism*, pp. 191–3, 232–9.

85 *Rationalisation and Unemployment*, pp. 124–5; *Modern State*, p. 36; *Wealth and Life*, p. 390.

86 *Problems of a New World*, p. 266; *Poverty in Plenty*, p. 81; *Rationalism and Humanism*, p. 20; *The Moral Challenge to the Economic System* (London: Ethical Union's Ethical and Economics Trust Fund, 1933), p. 19.

87 'Free Trade as a Factor in Civilisation'.

88 *Evolution of Modern Capitalism*, ch. 3.

89 From a British perspective, at least, see *Imperialism*, part 1, chs. 1 and 5.

90 Compare his prognosis in *Democracy and a Changing Civilisation* or *Property and Impropery* with *Towards International Government.*

91 Note there is no place here for Marxist internationalism, an idea Hobson rarely considered.

92 Richard K. Ashley, 'Three Modes of Economism', *International Studies Quarterly* (Vol. 27, No. 4, 1983), p. 463. Economism entails, first, the division of the various elements of social life into economic, cultural, personal, political, and so on. Second, it entails the privileging of economic factors over the rest, and usually the determination of the other factors by economic factors.

93 *Property and Impropery*, p. 205. The context of this quotation is not, however, Hobson defending a Cobdenite or Angellite position.

94 For a discussion of Hobson's defence of free-trade doctrine, see chapter 7. For a consideration of the charge of economic determinism in Hobson's theory of imperialism, see chapter 5.

95 By extension from Hobson's comments in *Social Problem*, pp. 61, 261, 271.

5 THE DOMESTIC DETERMINANTS OF AN IMPERIALISTIC FOREIGN POLICY

1 *Imperialism*, p. 3. On the changing senses of imperialism, see Richard Koebner and Helmut Dan Schmidt, *Imperialism: The Story and Significance of a Political Word, 1840–1960* (Cambridge: Cambridge University Press, 1964), p. 221. On the contradictory nature of some of the more recent

meanings, see Roger Owen, 'Introduction', in Roger Owen and Bob Sutcliffe (eds.), *Studies in the Theory of Imperialism* (London: Longman, 1972).

2 While Hobson's discussion is often in the context of the British Empire and foreign policy, he meant his propositions to apply generally, and I will discuss them in this way.

3 These distinctions are made in 'Nationalism and Imperialism' in *Imperialism*. Giovanni Arrighi has also used this chapter as the basis of his analysis of Hobson's theory of imperialism. However, Arrighi's aim of clarifying the Leninist theory of imperialism through an analysis of the 'scientific treatment' of Hobson leads him into error, specifically his understanding of empire and internationalism, which he conceives as formal and informal empire respectively, far from Hobson's meanings. See Arrighi, *Geometry of Imperialism*, ch. 1. On Hobson's use of the term colonialism, see *Imperialism*, p. 6.

4 *Imperialism*, p. 12. Mill's definition of nationality is cited on p. 5. As we have seen in chapter 4, Hobson's opinions of nationalism subsequently changed.

5 *Imperialism*, p. 227.

6 See generally, 'Imperialism in Asia', *Imperialism*, part 2, ch. 5.

7 *Imperialism*, p. 8.

8 *Imperialism*, p. 8. See also pp. 19, 304

9 *Imperialism*, part 1, chs. 2–3.

10 *Imperialism*, pp. 49–50; *Democracy After the War*, pp. 44–8.

11 *Imperialism*, pp. 46, 49.

12 *Imperialism*, p. 53.

13 The theory of underconsumption was discussed in greater depth in chapter 3. For divergent opinions on the role of underconsumption and trustification in Hobson's theory of imperialism, see Cain, 'J. A. Hobson, Cobdenism, and the Radical Theory of Economic Imperialism'; Norman Etherington, *Theories of Imperialism: War, Conquest and Capital* (London: Croom Helm, 1984), ch. 3; Trevor Lloyd, 'Africa and Hobson's Imperialism', *Past and Present* (No. 55, 1972), p. 134; Nemmers, *Hobson and Underconsumption*, ch. 4. Some have insisted on the necessity of trustification for Hobson's theory (Norman Etherington, 'The Capitalist Theory of Capitalist Imperialism', *History of Political Economy* (Vol. 15, No. 1, 1983)); others who have claimed that underconsumption produces trusts which are therefore merely the conduits of surplus capital (P. J. Cain's reply to Etherington, 'Hobson, Wilshire, and the Capitalist Theory of Capitalist Imperialism', *History of Political Economy* (Vol. 17, No. 3, 1985)). As we shall see, there is also an international context to underconsumption that contributes to imperialism proper rather than merely to the pressure to export capital.

14 *Democracy After the War*, p. 34.

15 Hobson's main example of the trusts and trust-makers in *Imperialism* is America. It was here that the processes of industrialisation and mono-

polisation in capitalism were most clearly played out without the obstacles of tradition. *Imperialism*, pp. 73ff.

16 For Hobson's discussion of trusts, under which head he included all similar combinations, associations, agreements, monopolies and cartels, see *Evolution of Modern Capitalism*, chs. 7–9.

17 While they could be the product of a healthy economic system, they were also powerful sectional interests. See chapter 3.

18 *Imperialism*, p. 85.

19 *Imperialism*, pp. 74, 76.

20 *Evolution of Modern Capitalism*, pp. 257, 261.

21 *Evolution of Modern Capitalism*, pp. 262–3. My emphasis. See also *Imperialism*, pp. 77–8.

22 *Evolution of Modern Capitalism*, p. 263. See also the example of South Africa on pp. 265–72.

23 *Imperialism*, pp. [58]–[59].

24 *Imperialism*, pp. 55, 56.

25 *Democracy After the War*, pp. 81, 203; *Imperialism*, p. 57; *Evolution of Modern Capitalism*, pp. 241–2.

26 *Imperialism*, pp. 57–8. Hobson believed that financiers were not interested in the actual operations of industry but merely the paper value of assets. They were interested in the gambling aspect of finance in order to make their gains. Hobson described the financiers as analogous to the owners of gambling halls, and the ordinary investor as the gamblers. *Evolution of Modern Capitalism*, pp. 250–1. This gambling was the reason that financiers benefited from a policy that might lead to war. See also 'The Ethics of Gambling', in B. S. Rowntree (ed.), *Betting and Gambling: A National Evil* (London: Macmillan, 1905).

27 He appreciated that this view could be refuted by evidence from diplomatic records, but argued that theories based simply on biography of leaders were superficial historical explanations. See *Problems of a New World*, p. 150.

28 *Imperialism*, pp. 124–39. For a view of Hobson's theory along these lines, see P. J. Cain, 'J. A. Hobson, Financial Capitalism and Imperialism in Late Victorian and Edwardian England', *Journal of Imperial and Commonwealth History* (Vol. 13, 1985), pp. 1–27, and 'J. A. Hobson, Cobdenism and the Radical Theory of Economic Imperialism', p. 565.

29 *Democracy After the War*, pp. 9, 36; *Imperialism*, p. [47].

30 *Imperialism*, p. 127; see also pp. 46, [48]–[49].

31 *Democracy After the War*, pp. 145–6.

32 On the press, see *Imperialism*, pp. 60, 216; *The Psychology of Jingoism*, part 2, ch. 1. On conservative forces using other institutions in general, see *Imperialism*, pp. 214–17. On the role of the church see, in particular, *Psychology of Jingoism*, part 1, ch. 3. Also *Democracy After the War*, part 1, chs. 6–7.

33 See *Psychology of Jingoism*, part 1, chs. 1–4; *Imperialism*, p. [51]; 'Militarism

and the Will to Power' in *Democracy After the War*; 'The Spirit of the Herd' and 'The Submergence of Personality' in *Problems of a New World*. Also see *Property and Improperty*, p. 121, and Hobson's satire of government policy during the First World War in *1920: Dips into the Near Future* (London: Headley, 1918).

34 *Imperialism*, p. 161. See also p. 155.

35 These arguments appear in *Imperialism*. On social Darwinism, pp. 153–65; on the civilising mission, pp. 285–306, 325–6; on the British genius for government, pp. 114–24; on the outlet for population, pp. 41–5.

36 *Imperialism*, p. 88.

37 *Imperialism*, pp. [59]–[60]. This is one of the differences between Hobson and Lenin often remarked upon. For Hobson, imperialism was a policy pursued by capitalists which could be remedied by a change in governmental policy. Lenin suggested that it was the system of capitalism that was to blame and that nothing short of its overthrow would rid the world of the scourge of imperialism. See V. I. Lenin, *Imperialism: The Highest Stage of Capitalism* (Moscow: Progress, 1982 [1916]), p. 105. Though they have been described as reformist, Hobson's proposals were nothing short of revolutionary in their implications, involving the restructuring of the entire system of distribution in the economic system. On attitudes to reformism, Hobson's and others, see Clarke, *Liberals and Social Democrats*.

38 *Imperialism*, p. 71.

39 *Imperialism*, p. 86.

40 Unlike Keynes he was not a proponent of deficit financing. See Allett, *New Liberalism*, p. 128. Hobson attached his hopes not to the creation of credit, nor to the taking out of loans in order artificially to stimulate demand, but purely to redistribution of income.

41 For example, *Property and Improperty*, p. 106; 'The Close State vs. Internationalism', in *Democracy After the War*; 'The Closed State', in *Democracy and a Changing Civilisation*.

42 There has been much work developing neo-Marxist theories of imperialism and dependency theory. For example, see Owen and Sutcliffe, *Studies in the Theory of Imperialism*; Johan Galtung, 'A Structural Theory of Imperialism', *Journal of Peace Research* (Vol. 8, 1971); Samir Amin, *Unequal Development* (New York: Monthly Review Press, 1976); Paul Baran and Paul Sweezy, *Monopoly Capital* (Harmondsworth: Penguin, 1968); Andre Gunder Frank, *Capitalism and Underdevelopment in Latin America* (New York: Monthly Review Press, 1969). For a collection of writings on imperialism, see Kenneth Boulding and Tapan Mukherjee (eds.), *Economic Imperialism* (Ann Arbor: University of Michigan Press, 1972). There are even different names for the theory: the theory of economic imperialism, the economic theory of imperialism, and the theory of capitalist imperialism. See Charles Reynolds, *Modes of Imperialism* (Oxford: Martin Robertson, 1981), ch. 3; Kenneth N. Waltz, *Theory of International Politics* (Reading, MA:

Addison-Wesley, 1979), p. 19; and D. K. Fieldhouse (ed.), *The Theory of Capitalist Imperialism* (London: Longmans, 1967).

43 Kenneth N. Waltz, *Man, the State, and War: A Theoretical Analysis* (New York: Columbia University Press, 1959), pp. 145–55, and *Theory of International Politics*, pp. 19–27. The discussion is also a contribution to the restoration of the reputations of scholars criticised by Waltz. For counter-critiques of Waltz's interpretations of Rousseau and Kant, see Michael Williams, 'Rousseau, Realism and *Realpolitik*', *Millennium: Journal of International Studies* (Vol. 18, No. 2, 1989), and Andrew Hurrell, 'Kant and the Kantian Paradigm in International Relations', *Review of International Studies* (Vol. 16, No. 3, 1990).

44 Waltz makes other less serious errors of interpretation. For instance, Hobson was a liberal in 1902 and cannot in any case be regarded a Marxist revisionist (*Man, the State, and War*, p. 149).

Waltz makes a number of points against the general theory of imperialism he attributes to Hobson. For instance, if Hobson is pointing to a condition of capitalist countries causing imperialism, there are the problems that imperialism, the effect, as in the Roman Empire, is older than the cause, capitalism; that not all imperialist countries were capitalist or surplus-producing for the time Hobson discussed; and that not all capitalist countries were imperialist. Waltz attempts to soften this test of Hobson's theory by stressing that only *most* (not all) capitalist states must be imperialist, and only *most* imperialist states must be capitalist. Waltz, *Theory of International Politics*, pp. 24–5. These are well-worn criticisms derived from the economic history literature cataloguing the deficiencies of Hobson's empirical analysis. See note 40, above. Waltz fails to specify what he means by 'capitalism', 'socialism', 'imperialism' and 'surplus', and whether these are Hobson's meanings. For instance, Hobson's notion of surplus differs from the Marxian notion that Lenin used and Hobson's economic theory lacks the monetary aspects so central to Keynesian economics (*Theory of International Politics*, p. 21n). Waltz conflates Hobson's and Lenin's theories of imperialism (*Theory of International Politics*, p. 20). Waltz misunderstands the importance of the distinction between ancient empire and new imperialism. As we have seen, Hobson extended the meaning of imperialism beyond the basic meaning of control of foreign territory to incorporate the competition of empires in the new imperialism (*Theory of International Politics*, p. 25).

45 Waltz, *Man, the State, and War*, pp. 81, 146; *Theory of International Politics*, pp. 18, 20.

46 Waltz, *Theory of International Politics*, p. 36

47 Waltz, *Man, the State, and War*, p. 145. See also *Theory of International Politics*, pp. 20–1.

48 *Confessions*, p. 63.

49 See *Confessions*, ch. 16. Hobson's humanist welfare economics is developed in, for example, *Work and Wealth* and *Wealth and Life*.

50 *Free Thought*, pp. 77–8.
51 Indeed, Waltz recognises this rationale. See *Theory of International Politics*, pp. 21–2, in particular the question 'If one government supports its businessmen abroad, can other governments do less?'.
52 Waltz, *Theory of International Politics*, p. 20, advises students wishing to understand Hobson's theory of imperialism to read only chapter 6 of the wide-ranging *Imperialism*. For a criticism of Waltz's tendency to reduce an argument and then accuse the author of reductionism, see Ashley, 'Three Modes of Economism', p. 467.
53 Waltz, *Theory of International Politics*, p. 25, even compares the theory to Newtonian physics.
54 Construed as a general theory applying across time and space, Hobson's theory is easy to falsify. However, the most significant doubt concerns the credibility of any general theory as an explanation of history. Any such theory must inevitably overlook other important factors in specific imperial expansions, and thereby be compromised.
55 Parts of *Imperialism* were published as articles in *The Speaker*, *The British Friend*, *Political Science Quarterly* and *Contemporary Review*. *Imperialism* was preceded by *The War in South Africa*, *The Psychology of Jingoism*, and a number of articles and letters written to newspapers and journals during the Boer War. There were a number of extremely hostile reviews of *Imperialism* in the press of the time. See Hobson's papers for cuttings of these reviews. For another controversy, see Hobson's critique of the Fabian support for imperialism in 'Socialistic Imperialism', *International Journal of Ethics* (Vol. 12, No. 1, October 1901).
56 See Waltz, *Man, the State, and War*, p. 145, and J. D. B. Miller, *The World of States* (London: Croom Helm, 1981), p. 116n.
57 It appeared first in the *Contemporary Review* in the summer of 1902. For alternative estimations of the significance of this article/chapter, see Porter, *Critics of Empire*, pp. 176–7, 190, and Clarke, *Liberals and Social Democrats*, p. 96, on the historical context of the development of Hobson's theory.
58 See Cain, 'J. A. Hobson, Cobdenism and the Radical Theory of Economic Imperialism'; Clarke, 'Hobson, Free Trade, and Imperialism', and P. J. Cain, 'Hobson's Developing Theory of Imperialism', *Economic History Review* (Vol. 34, No. 2, 1981).
59 *Psychology of Jingoism*, part 1, ch. 6.
60 *Imperialism*, p. [43].
61 See chapter 2.
62 This necessitarian perspective and strict bifurcation into imperialism and social reform is redolent of idealism as identified by R. N. Berki. See his *On Political Realism*, pp. 194–5.
63 Lance E. Davis and Robert A. Huttenback, *Mammon and the Pursuit of Empire: The Political Economy of British Imperialism, 1860–1912* (Cambridge: Cambridge University Press, 1986); A. K. Cairncross, *Home and Foreign*

Investment (Cambridge: Cambridge University Press, 1953); John R. Oneal and Frances H. Oneal, 'Hegemony, Imperialism and the Profitability of Foreign Investments', *International Organization* (Vol. 42, No. 2, Spring 1988). Though Hobson's discussion is specifically concerned with nations, some have investigated the effects on governments/states, e.g., Phillip Darby, *Three Faces of Imperialism* (New Haven: Yale University Press, 1987) and D. K. Fieldhouse, *The Colonial Empires* (London: Weidenfeld and Nicolson, 1965), ch. 16. See also Fieldhouse (ed.), *Theory of Capitalist Imperialism*, where it is acknowledged by the editor that there was no gain to the nation in imperialism, while some of the contributions, by A. K. Cairncross and by R. Nuske, use data based on states. As Julian Townshend points out in his 'Introduction' to *Imperialism*, many have criticised Hobson's theory as simply not fitting the facts. Purported factual errors of Hobson's theory include the lack of consonance of imperial expansion with the flow of foreign investment, the small amount of capital exported to the new colonies, the small to non-existent differential gains for investment in the new colonies compared to other parts of the world, the absence of economic surpluses in the imperial states, and the relatively low level of development of trusts and cartels in the imperial states, including Britain.

64 Compare Hobson's discussion of the growth of foreign and colonial trade in 'The Commercial Value of Imperialism' with his discussion of foreign investments on pp. 51–2 of *Imperialism*. Cf. D. K. Fieldhouse, '"Imperialism": An Historiographical Revision', in Boulding and Mukherjee (eds.), *Economic Imperialism*, p. 110.

65 See Lloyd, 'Africa and Hobson's Imperialism', pp. 141, 152; Clarke, *Liberals and Social Democrats*, pp. 97–8, and 'Hobson, Free Trade, and Imperialism'; Porter, *Critics of Empire*, pp. 216–18.

66 See 'The Mystery of Dumping', in *International Trade*. For an examination of the significance of this paper, see W. P. Culbertson, Jr, and R. B. Ekelund, Jr, 'John A. Hobson and the Theory of Discriminating Monopoly', *History of Political Economy* (Vol. 9, No. 2, 1977), pp. 273–82. For the argument that backward countries are inadequate markets for surplus goods, see Bleaney, *Underconsumption Theories*, p. 167.

67 Richard Koebner, 'The Concept of Economic Imperialism', *Economic History Review* (Vol. 2, No. 1, 1949), pp. 3, 6; Reynolds, *Theory and Explanation in International Politics*, pp. 219–20.

68 Reynolds, *Modes of Imperialism*, pp. 108–9, 113–14.

69 See *The War in South Africa*; 'Capitalism and Imperialism in South Africa', *Contemporary Review* (Vol. 77, January 1900); *Evolution of Modern Capitalism*, pp. 266, 268–72. On Hobson's anti-semitism, see Hannah Arendt, *The Origins of Totalitarianism*, 2nd edn (London: George Allen and Unwin, 1958), p. 135; Harvey Mitchell, 'Hobson Revisited', *Journal of the History of Ideas* (Vol. 26, No. 3, 1965), pp. 398–405. For further examples of Hobson's pursuit of the conspirators, see 'The Proconsulate of Milner', *Contemporary*

Review (Vol. 78, October 1900), 'The Testimony From Johannesburg', *Contemporary Review* (Vol. 77, May 1900), and 'Mr. Rhodes on the Future of South Africa', *The New Age* (Vol. 13, No. 359, 15 August 1901).

70 *Democracy After the War*, p. 85.

71 For instance, in *Imperialism* and in *Democracy After the War*.

72 *Imperialism*, p. [49]; *Democracy After the War*, pp. 131–2.

73 As argued by Porter, *Critics of Empire*, p. 215.

74 *Imperialism*, pp. 357–8.

75 Porter, *Critics of Empire*, p. 225.

76 Porter, *Critics of Empire*, p. 229.

77 *Imperialism*, p. 359. As Hobson conceded (*Wealth and Life*, p. 402), '[w]hile for some purposes [big business] may disregard tariff barriers, its general interests are definitely opposed to such interferences with free trade and the commercial division of labour that it serves.'

78 See Allett, *New Liberalism*, p. 150; Townshend, 'Introduction', *Imperialism*, p. [39], for criticisms of Porter.

79 *Science of Wealth*, p. 240. Foreign investment was thus a department of export trade, according to Hobson.

80 *Economic Interpretation of Investment*, preface.

81 I discuss the distinction of national and international finance further in chapter 7.

82 See Arrighi, *Geometry of Imperialism*, ch. 4, for a critique of Hobson along these lines.

83 *Imperialism*, pp. 56–7, 59, 84–5.

84 John Gallagher and Ronald Robinson, 'The Imperialism of Free Trade', *Economic History Review* (Vol. 6, No. 1, 1953). Also see their *Africa and the Victorians* (London: Macmillan, 1961); and Bernard Semmel, *The Rise of Free Trade Imperialism* (Cambridge: Cambridge University Press, 1970).

85 In this context, Hobson's work is a possible avenue for critics of the anti-democratic tendency of theorists of hegemony. Hobson also provides arguments that suggest that any hegemony is chronically unstable. While the debt to Lenin in hegemonic stability theory is well known, Hobson's liberal democratic critique of imperial policy, paradoxically perhaps, provides more room for criticism of recent international theory. For the acceptance of Hobson's claim about the increase of imperial activity, see Waltz, *Theory of International Politics*, p. 26. The classics of the hegemonic stability theory literature are Robert Gilpin, *War and Change in World Politics* (New York: Cambridge University Press, 1981); Robert O. Keohane, *After Hegemony* (Princeton: Princeton University Press, 1984); Paul Kennedy, *The Rise and Fall of the Great Powers* (New York: Random House, 1987).

86 *Imperialism*, p. [43]. This is Hobson's description of the book in the preface to the first edition. Note that Hobson claimed this was a scientific treatment in the sense of diagnosing an ill and providing a remedy, a distinctively normative aim.

6 THE INTERNATIONAL RELATIONS OF IMPERIALISM

1 *Democracy and a Changing Civilisation*, pp. 160–1.
2 *Imperialism*, p. 11.
3 This is the basis for Hannah Arendt's incisive analysis of imperialism in *Origins of Totalitarianism*. On the lack of control in international economic relations, see *Poverty in Plenty*, pp. 17–19.
4 *Confessions*, pp. 59, 185. This is similarly Lenin's meaning of monopoly as applied to the relations of states. Lenin acknowledged the dual meaning of monopoly in Hobson's analysis and criticised Kautsky for neglecting this insight. See Lenin, *Imperialism*, pp. 83–7.
5 *Imperialism*, pp. [51]–[52].
6 *From Capitalism to Socialism*, pp. 11–12. See also *Recording Angel*, p. 50.
7 *Imperialism*, p. 139. See also p. 72; *Recording Angel*, p. 53. This argument is redolent of Robert Gilpin's in *War and Change in World Politics*.
8 'Underconsumption: An Exposition and Reply', 'Reactions of National Policy on Trade and Unemployment', *Political Quarterly* (Vol. 2, No. 4, October 1931) and 'The World's Economic Crisis', *Nation* [New York] (Vol. 135, No. 3498, 20 July 1932).
9 *Economics of Unemployment*, p. 132.
10 *Rationalisation and Unemployment*, pp. 124–5; *Democracy and a Changing Civilisation*, p. 162.
11 *Evolution of Modern Capitalism*, chs. 3–5.
12 *International Trade*, p. 173.
13 *International Trade*, p. 174.
14 *International Trade*, p. 179. See generally 'Imperialism and Protectionism' in *Imperialism*; *New Protectionism*; *Democracy After the War*.
15 Hobson's discussion of free trade and refutation of economic nationalism is discussed in depth in chapter 7.
16 'Free Trade and Foreign Policy'. This is the first formulation of the imperialism theory and the influence of Cobdenite principles is clearer here than in some of the later formulations. See Cain, 'J. A. Hobson, Cobdenism and the Radical Theory of Economic Imperialism'.
17 *Imperialism*, pp. 65–6.
18 *Imperialism*, p. 15; *International Trade*, p. 171.
19 *New Protectionism*, p. 16. For Hobson such a division was also a crime against civilisation. See also pp. 58, 113. Hobson applied this analysis to the proposals for a protective system around the allied powers after the First World War. The result of this proposal, claimed Hobson, would be a reinforcement of the war battle-lines and the breaking of Europe into hostile camps. See *New Protectionism*, p. xvi, 58. Hobson also opposed the idea of imperial federations or preference. Such closure to trade and investment would further stimulate the rivalry of other states. See *Imperialism*, pp. 340ff., and 'Colonial Preference' and 'Canada's Fiscal Future' in *Canada Today* (London: Unwin, 1906).

20 *Imperialism*, part 1, ch. 5.
21 *Imperialism*, p. 138.
22 *Democracy After the War*, p. 21.
23 *Democracy After the War*, part 2, ch. 5; *From Capitalism to Socialism*, p. 12; *Democracy and a Changing Civilisation*, p. 125.
24 *Democracy and a Changing Civilisation*, pp. 55–6.
25 *Democracy After the War*, p. 101. See also *Imperialism*, p. 128.
26 *Imperialism*, pp. 13, 186, 325; *Democracy And a Changing Civilisation*, pp. 16, 129; *Problems of a New World*, pp. 245, 251–2, 272. This was reflected in the adoption by politicians and academics of *realpolitik* and various other nationalist-imperialist theories. See *Imperialism*, pp. 12–13, 167.
27 *Imperialism*, p. 138. See also p. 126.
28 *Problems of a New World*, pp. 269–70; *Imperialism*, p. [55].
29 *Problems of a New World*, p. 177; *Confessions*, p. 109. *Property and Improperty*, p. 113, and *Imperialism*, pp. [49]–[50], [62]. Hobson had predicted a re-emergence of the balance of power and imperial competition if there was no just solution to imperialism in *Problems of a New World*, pp. 269–70.
30 *Democracy and a Changing Civilisation*, p. 54.
31 *Democracy and a Changing Civilisation*, p. 54. This is very close to the situation Hobson claims that Veblen is describing. See *Veblen* (London: Chapman and Hall, 1936), p. 146; *Imperialism*, p. [53]. Hobson argues a similar case regarding the effects of the Franco-Prussian War in *Physiology of Industry*, pp. 161–2, 176–7.
32 *Imperialism*, p. [53].
33 *Democracy After the War*, p. 48. See also p. 50.
34 The domestic impact of the foreign policy and international relations of imperialism was one of Hobson's prime concerns in *Imperialism*. In this sense, at least, Hobson's theory of imperialism is as much a theory of British society as a theory of international relations.
35 *Property and Improperty*, p. 143; *Traffic in Treason*, p. 9. See also *Property and Improperty*, pp. 107–8. *Imperialism*, pp. 58, 127; *Democracy After the War*, pp. 181–2; *Imperialism*, pp. 141–2.
36 *Imperialism*, pp. 151–2. Also p. 150, *Democracy and a Changing Civilisation*, pp. 108–9.
37 *Imperialism*, pp. 145–7.
38 *Poverty in Plenty*, pp. 75–6.
39 *Evolution of Modern Capitalism*, pp. 195–6; *International Trade*, p. 181; *New Protectionism*, p. 12.
40 *Imperialism*, pp. 124–35.
41 *Problems of a New World*, pp. 246, 267–8; *Free Thought*, p. 267; *Modern State*, p. 6.
42 *From Capitalism to Socialism*, p. 28.
43 *Democracy After the War*, p. 161; *Problems of a New World*, p. 49. For discussions of this issue during the inter-war period, see Lionel Robbins,

Economic Planning and International Order (London: Macmillan, 1937) and E. H. Carr, *Conditions of Peace* (London: Macmillan, 1943).

44 *Democracy and a Changing Civilisation*, p. 18; *The Modern State*, p. 6. See also *Democracy and a Changing Civilisation*, pp. 129–30; *Imperialism*, p. 135.

45 *Democracy After the War*, pp. 202–3.

46 *Problems of a New World*, p. 83. See also *Wealth and Life*, p. 221.

47 For a general discussion of the atmosphere in pre-war Europe, see 'The Surprise of 1914' in *Problems of a New World*. On economic matters, see *Economics of Unemployment*, chs. 1, 8.

48 *Imperialism*, p. 152.

49 *Imperialism*, p. 360.

50 *Imperialism*, pp. 164, 186, 193.

51 See H. N. Brailsford, *The Life-work of J. A. Hobson*, p. 25, who claims that Hobson was a forerunner of the mandate policy. See *Imperialism*, p. 232.

52 As did Lenin in his critique of Karl Kautsky's parallel concept, ultra-imperialism.

53 *Rationalisation and Unemployment*, p. 115.

54 *Problems of a New World*, p. 183.

55 Hobson had previously been sceptical of the prospects of international cartels. See *The Fruits of American Protection* (New York: Cassell, 1906), p. 34.

56 *Wealth and Life*, p. 402.

57 *Wealth and Life*, p. 402.

58 *League of Nations*, p. 20; *Democracy After the War*, p. 191. See also *Problems of a New World*, pp. 183, 186.

59 *League of Nations*, p. 20.

60 *Poverty in Plenty*, pp. 79–80.

61 *Poverty in Plenty*, p. 80. See also *Democracy After the War*, p. 195. Hobson withdrew the comment 'final' from this passage in *Problems of a New World*, p. 185.

62 *Problems of a New World*, pp. 28–9.

63 *Conditions of Industrial Peace*, pp. 111, 116; *Wealth and Life*, p. 403, *Poverty in Plenty*, pp. 80–1.

64 *Wealth and Life*, pp. xxvii–xxviii.

65 Cain, 'J. A. Hobson, Cobdenism, and the Radical Theory of Economic Imperialism', pp. 569–76. See also Nemmers, *Hobson and Underconsumption*, p. 22; Mitchell, 'Hobson Revisited', p. 415.

66 Cain, 'J. A. Hobson, Cobdenism, and the Radical Theory of Economic Imperialism', pp. 570–6.

67 Clarke, *Liberals and Social Democrats*, pp. 177–8; Porter, *Critics of Empire*, p. 197; and also Cain, 'J. A. Hobson, Cobdenism, and the Radical Theory of Economic Imperialism', p. 581, and Clarke, 'Hobson, Free Trade, and Imperialism', p. 308.

68 *Imperialism*, pp. 56–8.

69 *Imperialism*, p. 59.

70 *Science of Wealth*, pp. 241–2.

71 *Imperialism*, pp. 85, 87–8.
72 *Evolution of Modern Capitalism*, p. 237. See also *Economic Interpretation of Investment*, p. 104.
73 On Say's Law, see Heilbroner, *Worldly Philosophers*, p. 77, and Barber, *History of Economic Thought*, pp. 68–9, 187–8.
74 *Economic Interpretation of Investment*, p. 132.
75 *Evolution of Modern Capitalism*, p. 236.
76 *Economic Interpretation of Investment*, pp. 112–13.
77 *Economic Interpretation of Investment*, pp. 104–5.
78 *Evolution of Modern Capitalism*, pp. 248–9.
79 *Imperialism*, pp. 56–7.
80 *Imperialism*, p. 57.
81 *Evolution of Modern Capitalism*, pp. 242ff.
82 See, for instance, *Economic Interpretation of Investment*, pp. 119–20. There were simultaneous concerns with the international political situation and the accelerating arms race, but these only heightened the emphasis of writers such as Hobson on the benefits (and constraints) of the new economic interdependence.
83 Townshend, *J. A. Hobson.*
84 *Crisis of Liberalism*, p. 256; *Democracy and a Changing Civilisation*, pp. 141–2.
85 *New Protectionism*, p. 128.
86 *Crisis of Liberalism*, p. 257; *International Government*, pp. 139–40; *Economic Interpretation of Investment*, p. 77; *Wealth and Life*, p. 394.
87 *Imperialism*, p. 232; *Recording Angel*, p. 77.
88 *Imperialism*, p. 232.
89 *New Protectionism*, pp. 131–2. See also *International Government*, p. 141; *Wealth and Life*, p. 393; *Recording Angel*, p. 78; *Democracy and a Changing Civilisation*, p. 142.
90 *New Protectionism*, p. 130; *Wealth and Life*, p. 393; *Recording Angel*, p. 78; *Imperialism*, p. 232.
91 *Wealth and Life*, p. 393; *Recording Angel*, p. 79; *Imperialism*, p. 232.
92 *Crisis of Liberalism*, p. 259.
93 *Democracy and a Changing Civilisation*, p. 143.
94 *Wealth and Life*, p. 391.
95 *Problems of a New World*, p. 186; *Modern State*, p. 35.
96 *Economic Interpretation of Investment*, pp. 100–1; *Social Problem*, p. 278.
97 On Lenin and uneven development, see Robert Gilpin, *The Political Economy of International Relations* (Princeton: Princeton University Press, 1987), pp. 39–41.
98 Accepting Waltz's characterisation would mean that Hobson's theory would break down before we reached Waltz's criticisms regarding a domestic condition causing an international outcome. Hobson's theory of underconsumption has been challenged by economists, including Keynes. Indeed, every link in the chain of causation has been challenged. Waltz's is only one, and not the most significant, criticism of Hobson's theory.

99 Peter Gourevitch, 'The Second Image Reversed', *International Organization* (Vol. 32, No. 4, 1978).

7 ECONOMIC INTERNATIONALISM, FREE TRADE AND INTERNATIONAL GOVERNMENT

1 There are at least two other ways that a chapter on Hobson's ideas on international economic relations could be written; by concentrating on his successive critiques of the variety of tariff proposals and schemes for imperial preference, or by looking at his treatment of the population question as it impacted on his economic internationalist ideas on labour mobility and his conception of human welfare.

2 *Morals of Economic Internationalism*, p. 29.

3 *International Trade*, p. 13.

4 *International Trade*, pp. 14–22; *Science of Wealth*, ch. 13.

5 *International Trade*, p. 20.

6 In *International Trade*, chs. 1–4, esp. p. 53, Hobson refuted the argument that nations were non-competing groups, the argument he believed to be the basis of the separation of theories of national and international trade.

7 *Work and Wealth*, p. 273.

8 'The Inner Meaning of Protectionism', *Contemporary Review* (Vol. 84, 1903), p. 374. See also 'Free Trade and Foreign Policy', *Contemporary Review* (Vol. 74, 1898), p. 170; 'Foreign Competition and Its Influence on Home Industries', *Co-operative Societies Annual* (1899), p. 197.

9 *The New Protectionism*, p. 115; *Morals of Economic Internationalism*, p. 20.

10 'Free Trade and Foreign Policy', p. 168.

11 *International Trade*, p. 165.

12 That a nation was not an economic unit was a common theme for Hobson. See *Problem of the Unemployed*, p. 86; *International Trade*, p. 21; *Case for Arbitration*, p. 3; *Economic Interpretation of Investment*, p. 95; *The German Panic* (London: Cobden Club, 1913), pp. 25–6; *Work and Wealth*, p. viii; *New Protectionism*, pp. 2–5; *Democracy After the War*, p. 75; *Morals of Economic Internationalism*, pp. 9–10.

13 *Work and Wealth*, pp. 348–9; *Democracy After the War*, p. 76; *Economics of Unemployment*, pp. 20–1; *Imperialism*, p. [50].

14 For examples of Hobson's examination of the economics of tariffs, see *Fruits of American Protection*; *Canada Today*, part 2; *The Industrial System*, ch. 15; *New Protectionism*, ch. 3; *Taxation in the New State* (London: Methuen, 1919), part 1, ch. 8. Hobson was also concerned by the potential impact of an economic boycott imposed by the League of Nations. See *Towards International Government*, ch. 7.

15 'Can Protection Cure Unemployment?', *National Review* (Vol. 53, 1909); 'The Open Door', in C. R. Buxton (ed.), *Towards a Lasting Settlement* (London: Allen and Unwin, 1915).

16 *International Trade*, p. 21. See Semmel, *Rise of Free Trade Imperialism*, for a discussion of attempts to reconcile imperialism and free trade.

17 See *New Protectionism*, p. xiii. For Hobson's discussions of the prospects for systems of imperial preference and the more extensive suggestions for an imperial federation, see *War in South Africa*, part 3, ch. 5; *Canada Today*, part 2; 'The British Imperial Conference', *Nation* [New York] (Vol. 131, 1930), pp. 342–4; 'The British Empire in Conference', *Nation* [New York], (Vol. 131, 1930), p. 662; and 'Britain's Protective Budget', *Nation* [New York] (Vol. 134, 1932). On zollvereins, and particularly the suggestion for an economically united Europe, see 'The Economic Union of Europe', *Contemporary Review*, (Vol. 130, 1926), pp. 290–7; 'The Economic Organization of Europe', *Foreign Affairs* (Vol. 8, 1927), pp. 238–9; and 'The United States of Europe', *Nation* [New York] (Vol. 129, 1929), pp. 484–5.

18 See, for instance, 'Protection as a Working Class Policy', in H. W. Massingham (ed.), *Labour and Protection* (London: T. Fisher Unwin, 1903).

19 *Fruits of American Protection*, p. 29; *New Protectionism*, p. 11; *Poverty in Plenty*, p. 65.

20 *Imperialism*, part 1, ch. 5; *New Protectionism*, ch. 4.

21 *New Protectionism*, pp. 24, 103–5, 112.

22 'Free Trade and Foreign Policy', pp. 167–80; 'The Approaching Abandonment of Free Trade', *Fortnightly Review*, (Vol. 71, 1902), pp. 434–44; and *New Protectionism*, ch. 3.

23 *New Protectionism*, *passim*.

24 In these criticisms of the post-war settlement Hobson differed little from Keynes' *The Economic Consequences of the Peace*, in that he also attributed many of the political and economic woes to the artificial division of Europe into separate small states.

25 See Jagdish Bhagwati, *Protectionism* (Cambridge, MA: MIT Press, 1988).

26 *Science of Wealth*, p. 192.

27 *Imperialism*, pp. 308–9; *International Trade*, p. 174.

28 *Economics of Unemployment*, pp. 149–50; *Science of Wealth*, pp. 190–1.

29 *Science of Wealth*, p. 192; *Economics of Unemployment*, p. 147. See Adam Smith, *The Wealth of Nations* (Harmondsworth: Penguin, 1982), pp. 469–72. Note that Hobson does not reflect on the fact that this says nothing of the global impact of this reasoning. Whether traders are nationals or not is, in global terms, irrelevant to free-traders and Hobson here plays into the hands of the protectionists.

30 *Property and Improperty*, pp. 128–30; *Science of Wealth*, p. 193; *International Trade*, pp. 155–8.

31 *International Trade*, p. 163.

32 See McKinlay and Little, *Global Problems and World Order*, pp. 29–36.

33 *Democracy After the War*, pp. 73–5; *Veblen*, pp. 144–5; *International Trade*, p. 22; *Property and Improperty*, pp. 175–6. Hobson was aware of this even at the turn of the century, see 'The Approaching Abandonment of Free Trade', *Fortnightly Review* (Vol. 71, 1902), p. 436.

34 However, his opinions on the implications of this trend varied over his lifetime. Compare his belief, in *Evolution of Modern Capitalism*, that a world market would establish true prices and, in *Fruits of American Protection*, that there could be no international cartels, with his worries about inter-imperialism and capitalist collusion in *Wealth and Life* as well as his changing opinions on international finance discussed below.

35 *Science of Wealth*, pp. 186–8; *Democracy After the War*, p. 178; *Richard Cobden*, p. 402; *Physiology of Industry*, pp. 205–6.

36 *Democracy After the War*, p. 78; *Democracy and a Changing Civilisation*, p. 161.

37 *Richard Cobden*, ch. 13; *Problems of a New World*, p. 20.

38 *Property and Improperty*, pp. 56–7; *Confessions*, pp. 186–7; *Imperialism*, p. [50].

39 'Inner Meaning of Protectionism', p. 372.

40 *New Protectionism*, pp. 122–3; *Richard Cobden*, pp. 398–9; *Imperialism*, pp. 230–1.

41 'Free Trade and "Free Labour" ', *Free Trader* (Vol. 1, 1903).

42 *Property and Improperty*, pp. 106–7. Similarly Hobson denied the right of intervention in national economic government, e.g., with regard to the setting of tariffs. See *International Trade*, pp. 184–90; *International Government*, p. 136. For a discussion of the conflicting logic being employed by Hobson here, see Cain, 'J. A. Hobson, Cobdenism and the Radical Theory of Economic Imperialism'.

43 *Property and Improperty*, pp. 200–5. See the discussions of the problems of national economic planning and international relations in Robbins, *Economic Planning and International Order*.

44 Hobson acknowledged the monopolistic tendencies of such an arrangement in *Property and Improperty*, p. 205.

45 *International Government*, pp. 134–5; *New Protectionism*, p. 137.

46 *New Protectionism*, pp. 132–4.

47 *Imperialism*, p. 185.

48 *The Modern State*, p. 33; *From Capitalism to Socialism*, pp. 50–1; *Democracy and a Changing Civilisation*, pp. 145–6; *Economics of Unemployment*, p. 138; *Conditions of Industrial Peace*, pp. 110, 115.

49 *Richard Cobden*, p. 408.

50 *Richard Cobden*, p. 21

51 *International Government*, p. 137. See Freeden, *Liberalism Divided*, pp. 148–50, on Hobson's ideas on equality of opportunity.

52 *Morals of Economic Internationalism*, p. 67.

53 *Wealth and Life*, pp. 399–400.

54 *Richard Cobden*, pp. 408–9; *Morals of Economic Internationalism*, pp. 35, 44–5.

55 *Conditions of Industrial Peace*, p. 114

56 *Economic Interpretation of Investment*, pp. 137–9; *Work and Wealth*, pp. 274–5; *Poverty in Plenty*, p. 73.

57 *Rationalisation and Unemployment*, p. 119; *Physiology of Industry*, p. 212; *Social Problem*, p. 207; *Problems of Poverty*, pp. 59–62, 125.

58 *Problems of Poverty*, p. 136; *Economics of Distribution*, p. 161; *Economic Interpretation of Investment*, pp. 138–9; *Rationalisation and Unemployment*, pp. 119–20.

59 The products of cheap labour imported from abroad had a similar effect of course.

60 *Economic Interpretation of Investment*, p. 139; *International Government*, pp. 143–4; *Economics of Unemployment*, p. 135; *Recording Angel*, pp. 76–7.

61 *Wealth and Life*, pp. 356–7; *International Government*, p. 143; *Physiology of Industry*, p. 214.

62 *Recording Angel*, pp. 79–80.

63 *John Ruskin: Social Reformer*, pp. 116–18; *Problems of Poverty*, p. 125; *Social Problem*, pp. 11–12.

64 *John Ruskin: Social Reformer*, pp. 230–1; *Social Problem*, pp. 17–20, 229–30; 'Can England Keep Her Free Trade?', *National Review* (Vol. 17, 1891), p. 8.

65 *Social Problem*, p. 9.

66 *Wealth and Life*, pp. 7–8, has a four-point critique of industrialism.

67 See *Wealth and Life*, p. 353; *Social Problem*, p. 275.

68 *Crisis of Liberalism*, p. 265.

69 The extreme conclusion of his views on labour mobility and the international direction of labour to satisfy global welfare needs is found in some of his writings on population. Hobson was often highly illiberal in his discussion of the international implications of, and need for, an international policy of population control. While he acknowledged rational planning of population intruded upon 'the most highly valued of the self-determining functions of nations', and that it was a distant ideal, Hobson embraced the idea as one of his four conditions for civilised humanity. (See *Wealth and Life*, p. 453.) Hobson argued that ideally internationalism would be guided by 'the right of mankind as a whole to determine what numbers and kinds of men shall occupy the different areas of the earth'. (*Wealth and Life*, p. 357.)

70 The paradigm for international trade theory has, until recently, been the Heckscher–Ohlin modification of Ricardo's theory of comparative advantage. See Paul Krugman and Maurice Obstfeld, *International Economics: Theory and Policy* (Glenview, IL: Scott, Foresman, 1988), ch. 4. This paradigm was challenged by radical development economists. For recent approaches to international trade theory, see Paul Krugman, *Rethinking International Trade* (Cambridge, MA: MIT Press, 1982).

71 *Richard Cobden*, p. 401.

72 Susan Strange, 'Protectionism and World Politics', *International Organization* (Vol. 39, No. 2, 1985).

73 *Imperialism*, pp. 30–1. See also, *International Trade*, p. 7 – though he had changed his opinion by 1911; see *Science of Wealth*, p. 241.

74 *Evolution of Modern Capitalism*, p. 493. *International Government*, p. 196; *Democracy After the War*, pp. 175–6.

75 For instance, Ruggie, 'International Regimes, Transactions, and Change; Robert O. Keohane and Joseph S. Nye, Jr. (eds.), *Transnational Relations*

and World Politics (Cambridge, MA: Harvard University Press, 1972); as well as the more radical perspective put forward in the Independent Commission on International Development Issues, *North–South* (Cambridge, MA: MIT Press, 1980).

8 INTERNATIONAL GOVERNMENT AND THE MAINTENANCE OF PEACE

1 Hobson was not alone in making such proposals. See, for instance, Leonard Woolf, *International Government* (New York: Bretano's, 1916); Viscount Bryce and others, *Proposals for the Prevention of Future Wars* (London: George Allen and Unwin, 1917). See the collection of schemes and proposals in Leonard Woolf (ed.), *The Framework of a Lasting Peace* (London: George Allen and Unwin, 1917) and in Lord Phillimore, *Schemes for Maintaining General Peace* (London: H.M. S.O., 1920).

2 For a summary statement of Hobson's version of what a League treaty should look like, see *Towards International Government*, p. 27; 'Political Basis of a World State', p. 263.

3 *Towards International Government*, preface.

4 See *Towards International Government*, ch. 3; *League of Nations*, p. 8; and 'Political Basis of a World State', p. 272.

5 *Towards International Government*, pp. 34–40; *League of Nations*, p. 8

6 *Towards International Government*, p. 34; *League of Nations*, p. 10; 'Political Basis of a World State', p. 269.

7 *League of Nations*, p. 11; *Towards International Government*, pp. 47–8.

8 Or an alternative resolution agreed to by both disputants.

9 *Towards International Government*, pp. 55–6.

10 He cited as examples the treaties made in 1914 between the United States and a number of other countries that established a 'cooling off' period and set up Permanent International Commissions to examine any disputes between the signatories. See *Towards International Government*, pp. 51–2.

11 *Problems of a New World*, pp. 134, 136. See also *Towards International Government*, pp. 50–3; 'Political Basis of a World State', pp. 270–2.

12 *Towards International Government*, pp. 47–8; *League of Nations*, p. 11.

13 *Towards International Government*, p. 56.

14 *Towards International Government*, pp. 99–100.

15 The turn to force was not uncommon in international relations writing at the time. See Suganami, *Domestic Analogy and World Order Proposals*, ch. 5; F. S. Northedge and M. D. Donelan, *International Disputes: The Political Aspects* (London: Europa, 1971), p. 21.

16 *Towards International Government*, pp. 84, 96; cf. 'Political Basis of a World State', p. 269.

17 Kenneth Waltz is thus in error when he claims that Hobson emphasises the force of public opinion as a sanction for the international government.

This is a misreading of Hobson's ideas of the long-term nature of democratic international government. See Waltz, *Man, the State, and War*, p. 150. For the context of Hobson's remarks, see *Towards International Government*, ch. 12.

18 *Towards International Government*, p. 21. See also pp. 22–3. Hobson believed that the treaty would be so effective that member states would have to be bound to 'maintain a proper quota of military and naval forces for common purposes of defence' (p. 58).

19 *Towards International Government*, p. 84.

20 *Towards International Government*, pp. 76–9, 96–100. Collective security is not a term used by Hobson but his proposals are equivalent to such a system.

21 *Towards International Government*, pp. 90–5.

22 *Towards International Government*, pp. 55–6, 101–9; *League of Nations*, p. 12.

23 *Towards International Government*, p. 109. See also pp. 110–11, and 'Political Basis of a World State', pp. 272–5.

24 'Political Basis of a World State', p. 260.

25 Michael Freeden mistakenly argues that Hobson used 'Society of Nations' as a replacement for the flawed League of Nations during the thirties. See his Introduction to *J. A. Hobson: A Reader*, p. 21. In fact, Hobson used the term, inconsistently. However, he used the term both before and during the First World War, usually to mean the collectivity of nations. Occasionally, using capitals, Hobson referred to the Society of Nations to mean the government of the collectivity of nations. For Hobson's early uses of the term, see 'The Morality of Nations', in *Crisis of Liberalism*, p. 248; *Case for Arbitration*, p. 2; and *Towards International Government*, p. 192.

26 *Towards International Government*, ch. 2.

27 *Towards International Government*, pp. 114–19.

28 The quotes are from *League of Nations*, p. 19 and *Towards International Government*, p. 157. For more extensive discussion, see *Towards International Government*, pp. 24–5, 154–61; *League of Nations*, pp. 17–19.

29 *Towards International Government*, p. 165. See also pp. 162–6, and *League of Nations*, p. 19, though he was to contradict this argument later. See *Democracy and a Changing Civilisation*, pp. 147–50; *The Modern State*, p. 35.

30 *Towards International Government*, pp. 64–71. No doubt intending this remark also to apply to women, Hobson maintained the convention throughout his writing of using 'men' to mean all people.

31 *Towards International Government*, pp. 62–4, 67–70, 104–9; *League of Nations*, pp. 15–16. 'International Mind' was a phrase first coined before the First World War by Nicholas Murray Butler in *The International Mind: An Argument for the Judicial Settlement of International Disputes* (New York: Scribner's, 1913).

32 *Confessions*, p. 104; *Towards International Government*, pp. 200–11; on British policy, see *League of Nations*, p. 20, but compare to point 2 in *The New Holy*

Alliance (London: Union of Democratic Control, 1919), p. 8. Also see *Democracy After the War*, p. 210.

33 'Political Basis of a World State', pp. 268–9. See also pp. 261–2; *League of Nations*, pp. 3–4.

34 *Towards International Government*, p. 117. See also pp. 112–18; *League of Nations*, p. 7. Such private intercourse could also benefit from the central direction of the international government.

35 *Towards International Government*, pp. 147–8, 170–2.

36 *Democracy and a Changing Civilisation*, p. viii.

37 Education in internationalism would be required for the effective operation of an informed and reasonable public opinion, counteracting the effects of capitalist and nationalist media, Hobson thought. Part of this education would be through experience in internationalism; a working international government would teach the benefits of international co-operation. See *Towards International Government*, chs. 12–13.

38 *Democracy and a Changing Civilisation*, p. 138. See also *Problems of a New World*, pp. 253, 260.

39 *Towards International Government*, pp. 117, 148, 191–2; *Democracy and a Changing Civilisation*, pp. 143–7, 150–2, 173.

40 *New Holy Alliance*, pp. 1, 7; *Problems of a New World*, pp. 119–20, 186, 228, 235; *Democracy After the War*, p. 196.

41 Cf. *Democracy After the War*, p. 209; *New Holy Alliance*, p. 1.

42 See *Problems of a New World*, part 3, particularly chs. 1–2.

43 Hobson's opinions on the outcome of the Great War, its effects on national and international relations, along with some of his reactions to the Peace at Versailles, can be found in *Problems of a New World*, part 5.

44 Cf. *Towards International Government*, p. 120; *Problems of a New World*, pp. 111, 117, 234, 252; *Democracy and a Changing Civilisation*, pp. 121–2.

45 *Democracy After the War*, p. 208.

46 *Problems of a New World*, p. 229.

47 *Towards International Government*, p. 173; *Democracy After the War*, p. 208; *New Holy Alliance*, pp. 3–5; *Problems of a New World*, pp. 113, 124, 228–9, 269–70; *Modern State*, p. 32.

48 *New Holy Alliance*, p. 5.

49 *New Holy Alliance*, p. 8; *Problems of a New World*, p. 229.

50 *New Holy Alliance*, p. 6.

51 *Modern State*, p. 36; *Democracy and a Changing Civilisation*, p. 171; *Problems of a New World*, p. 227. Cf. *League of Nations*, p. 6.

52 *New Holy Alliance*, p. 6.

53 *Democracy After the War*, p. 193.

54 *New Holy Alliance*, pp. 6–7; *Democracy After the War*, pp. 191–3; *Problems of a New World*, pp. 106, 186, 219, 226, 230–2; *Modern State*, p. 35; *Democracy and a Changing Civilisation*, pp. 141–3.

55 *Modern State*, p. 32; *Democracy and a Changing Civilisation*, p. 140.

56 *Case for Arbitration*, p. 6.

57 *Democracy After the War*, p. 208; *Democracy and a Changing Civilisation*, p. 160. Cf. *Towards International Government*, p. 5.
58 *Democracy and a Changing Civilisation*, pp. 135–6; see also p. 144.
59 *Towards International Government*, pp. 192–3; 'Political Basis of a World State', pp. 260–1.
60 *Problems of a New World*, p. 234; *Modern State*, pp. 32–4; *Democracy and a Changing Civilisation*, p. 140. Hobson had hoped that the post-war world would not be so disrupted; see *League of Nations*, p. 2. This, however, does call into question Hobson's optimistic belief in the transformative capacities of the populations in the wake of the War.
61 *New Holy Alliance*, p. 8; *Problems of a New World*, p. 233. The International Labour Office did come into existence. For an example of Hobson's later thoughts on constructive internationalism, see 'Origins of the I.L.O.'.
62 Compare the tone of *Towards International Government*, preface and p. 127, with *New Holy Alliance*.
63 This question exercised a good many left-leaning liberals at this time. The culmination of this angst can be found in the rejecting attitude of Harold Laski's essay on *The Decline of Liberalism* (Oxford: Oxford University Press, 1940).
64 *Property and Improperty*, foreword, pp. 132ff.; 'Thoughts on our Present Discontents', *Political Quarterly* (Vol. 9, No. 1, January 1938), p. 48.
65 For another instance where Hobson appears rather Victorian, see *Problems of a New World*, p. 42. A note of caution should be added to this criticism. After all, the structure of the suggestion of an international air force is not too dissimilar from the proposal that all nuclear weapons and knowledge concerning such weapons be collected in the United Nations. This latter proposal has been, and continues to be in some quarters, considered seriously. See also Northedge and Donelan, *International Disputes*, p. 20.
66 'Force Necessary to Government', *Hibbert Journal* (Vol. 33, No. 3, April 1935), p. 342.
67 *Confessions*, p. 113. See also *Property and Improperty*, p. 106; and 'Ethics of Humanity'.
68 Cf., Waltz, *Man, the State, and War*, p. 146; Townshend, 'Introduction', *Imperialism*, p. [32].
69 'Nationalism, Economic and Political', *South Place Monthly Record* (June 1939), p. 4.
70 'America in the War?', p. 4.
71 'Political Basis of a World State', pp. 276–8. Cf. *League of Nations*, p. 2; *Towards International Government*, pp. 100, 153, 196–9. For the quotes, see p. 212 and *Modern State*, p. 36.
72 *Towards International Government*, p. 89.
73 *Towards International Government*, pp. 86–9.
74 *Towards International Government*, p. 96. See also pp. 74–7, 87–9.
75 'Political Basis of a World State', pp. 276–8.

76 *Towards International Government*, pp. 109, 153, 212.
77 Later he even attacked the use of the term 'power' in international relations in *Towards International Government*! See pp. 180–1.
78 *League of Nations*, p. 6; *Towards International Government*, p. 116.
79 *Towards International Government*, p. 161.
80 For a classic statement on collective security, comparing it as an international system to the balance of power and world government, and a survey of some of the criticisms of each system, see Inis Claude, *Power in International Relations* (New York: Random House, 1962).
81 *Towards International Government*, p. 39.
82 *Towards International Government*, pp. 81–5; *League of Nations*, pp. 9, 13–14; 'Political Basis of a World State', p. 275.
83 *Crisis of Liberalism*, p. 110.
84 'Political Basis of a World State', pp. 273–5; *League of Nations*, p. 9; pp. 13–14; *Towards International Government*, pp. 42–3, 81–5.
85 *International Government*, pp. 70, 125, 176; *League of Nations*, p. 19; *Free Thought*, p. 259; *Wealth and Life*, p. 395; *Democracy and a Changing Civilisation*, pp. 115–16, 121.
86 *League of Nations*, p. 19.
87 *Towards International Government*, pp. 175–6; *League of Nations*, p. 13. Dickinson's criticism is quoted in Clarke, *Liberals and Social Democrats*, pp. 178–9. See also the debate between Hobson and Leonard Woolf, *Nation* (Vol. 17, August 1915), pp. 615, 639; J. M. Keynes, *The Collected Writings of J. M. Keynes*, Vol. XXVIII, (London: Macmillan, 1982) p. 11; and Alfred Zimmern, 'Nationality and Government', in his *Nationality and Government* (London: Chatto and Windus, 1918).
88 *International Government*, ch. 2.
89 *International Government*, pp. 204–5.
90 He was accused by his friend H. N. Brailsford, of attempting to build an international government before the democratic basis of domestic governments was laid. The implication is that Hobson unwittingly supported a capitalist project. See Brailsford, *Life-work of J.A. Hobson*. Also Townshend's Introduction to *Imperialism*, p. [31]. Hobson proposes but dismisses this problem in *Democracy After the War*, pp. 191–6, 209. But he takes a rather different view in *Democracy and a Changing Civilisation*, p. 133, and his reference to Kant in *Towards International Government*, along with his reversion to putting your own house in order, qualifies this assessment.
91 Compare *Imperialism* with *League of Nations*, p. 3. Also the qualification in *Towards International Government*, p. 139.
92 With the exception of the detachment from any Peace Treaty. Hobson stated in *Towards International Government* that the constitution of the League should not be part of any peace treaty at the end of the war; see p. 173. See also *Towards International Government*, p. 166; similarly his views on mandates and the possibility of inter-imperialism on pp. 144–6. Also see *Democracy and a Changing Civilisation*, pp. 141–3.

93 Compare *Towards International Government*, pp. 164–6 with *Democracy and Changing Civilisation*, p. 148.

94 *Towards International Government*, pp. 165–6.

95 For example, see Hans J. Morgenthau, *Politics Among Nations*, 3rd edn (Chicago: University of Chicago Press, 1965).

96 *From Capitalism to Socialism*, p. 36; *Democracy and a Changing Civilisation*, p. 140; *Imperialism*, p. [62].

9 J. A. HOBSON AND LIBERAL INTERNATIONALISM

1 *Rationalism and Humanism*, pp. 9–11.

2 See, for example, Clarke, *Liberals and Social Democrats*, p. 177; and also Townshend, 'Introduction', *Imperialism*, pp. 20–2.

3 The only exception to this rule is the interest in the relationship of Hobson and Keynes. Yet, Keynes's perspective on society, economy and politics is at best a cousin of Hobson's.

4 David Long, 'Hobson and Idealism in International Relations', *Review of International Studies* (Vol. 17, No. 3, 1991) and David Long and Peter Wilson (eds.), *Thinkers of the Twenty Years' Crisis* (Oxford: Clarendon, 1995).

5 Michael Banks, 'The Inter-Paradigm Debate', in M. Light and A. J. R. Groom (eds.), *International Relations* (London: Pinter, 1985); *Imperialism*, p. 167.

6 Michael Banks (ed.), *Conflict in World Society* (Brighton: Wheatsheaf, 1984).

7 M. Howard, *War and the Liberal Conscience* (Oxford: Oxford University Press, 1981).

8 *Free Thought*, p. 257.

9 On international law limiting sovereignty, see *Case for Arbitration*, p. 7; *Towards International Government*, pp. 33, 124–5.

10 *Towards International Government*, pp. 81, 86–7, 178.

11 *Democracy and a Changing Civilisation*, p. 139.

12 *Democracy and a Changing Civilisation*, pp. 139, 145; *Case for Arbitration*, p. 4.

13 *Notes on Law and Order* (London: Hogarth Press, 1926), pp. 24–5; *Case for Arbitration*, p. 7; on functional co-operation, see *League of Nations*, p. 2; *Towards International Government*, p. 177; *Imperialism*, p. 167. For a discussion of this view of international law, see Hidemi Suganami, 'The "Peace Through Law" Approach', in Trevor Taylor (ed.), *Approaches and Theory in International Relations* (London: Longman, 1978).

14 See Alan James, *Sovereign Statehood: The Basis of International Society* (London: Allen and Unwin, 1986).

15 See Michael Akehurst, *A Modern Introduction to International Law* (London: George Allen and Unwin, 1982), ch. 1.

16 Carr, *Twenty Years' Crisis*, p. 182.

17 *Towards International Government*, pp. 65, 67–8. See also pp. 7, 70, 169; *League of Nations*, pp. 15, 20. One wonders if this was a rather immodest self-description by Hobson!

18 *Free Thought*, p. 217; *Richard Cobden*, pp. 10, 408; *Democracy After the War*, p. 210; *Case for Arbitration*, p. 1; *The German Panic*, p. 23.
19 *Towards International Government*, pp. 67–8.
20 *Richard Cobden*, p. 388; *Democracy After the War*, p. 210; *German Panic*, p. 27; *League of Nations*, pp. 15–16; *Towards International Government*, pp. 66–8, 70.
21 *Free Thought*, p. 259; *Crisis of Liberalism*, p. 9; *Towards International Government*, pp. 184–6, 203–6, 211; *Confessions*, p. 104.
22 *League of Nations*, p. 20. See also *Towards International Government*, pp. 200–1, 209.
23 For an example, see K. J. Holsti, *International Politics: A Framework for Analysis*, 3rd edn (Englewood Cliffs: Prentice-Hall, 1977), ch. 7.
24 See Waltz, *Man, the State, and War*, p. 150.
25 *Confessions*, pp. 104–5.
26 *Rationalism and Humanism*, p. 31.
27 *Democracy and a Changing Civilisation*, p. 72. See chapter 7 above.
28 *Democracy and a Changing Civilisation*, p. 72.
29 'Free Trade and Foreign Policy'; *Richard Cobden*, esp. ch. 13.
30 Compare Hobson's discussion of the domestic implication of equality of opportunity in *Crisis of Liberalism*, pp. 96–113, with *Towards International Government*, pp. 134, 137–40, where it is discussed in an international context.
31 On the influence of sectional interests, see *Imperialism*, part 1, chs. 4 and 6. For the connection of imperialism and tyranny, see part 2, ch. 1.
32 Hobson calls them economic interests, see *Imperialism*, part 1, ch. 4. See also his discussion of the political interests in the development of political economy in *Free Thought*, part 2.
33 See the letter appealing for funds on behalf of the UDC from Angell and Hobson in *New Statesman and Nation* (2 October 1937), p. 483.
34 Angell's works include: *The Great Illusion* (London: Heinemann, 1912); *Foreign Policy and Our Daily Bread* (London: Collins, 1925); *The Great Illusion 1933* (London: Heinemann, 1933); *Preface to Peace* (London: Hamish Hamilton, 1935). See J. D. B. Miller, *Norman Angell and the Futility of War* (London: Macmillan, 1986) for a discussion of Angell's international theory.
35 *Economic Interpretation of Investment*, pp. 118–23; see also Miller, *Norman Angell and the Futility of War*.
36 *Imperialism*, p. [59].
37 For example, David Mitrany, 'A Functional Approach to World Organization', *International Affairs* (Vol. 24, No. 3, July 1948).
38 As in McKinlay and Little, *Global Problems and World Order*, ch. 2; and Joseph M. Grieco, 'Anarchy and the Limits of Cooperation: A Realist Critique of the Newest Liberal Internationalism', *International Organization* (Vol. 42, No. 3, 1988).
39 Roger Tooze, 'The Progress of International Functionalism', *British Journal of International Studies* (Vol. 3, No. 2, 1977), p. 212–13.

40 Cornelia Navari, 'The Great Illusion Revisited: The International Theory of Norman Angell', *Review of International Studies* (Vol. 15, No. 4, 1989), p. 343.

41 Mitrany is the first liberal international theorist discussed so far to be an academic, albeit a roving one. For an autobiographical account, see Mitrany's 'Memoir', in *Functional Theory of Politics*. By contrast, Cobden was a politician, a campaigner for free trade and peace and a pamphleteer. Angell was a politician and publicist, and Hobson a journalist and public campaigner.

42 Taylor, 'Functionalism: The Theory of David Mitrany', p. 237; and Paul Taylor, 'Introduction' to Mitrany's *Functional Theory of Politics*.

43 Mitrany, 'Memoir', in *Functional Theory of Politics*, pp. 16–17. Mitrany notes also the influence of James Shotwell at a slighter later stage in his career.

44 Hobson's exclusion from membership of the Royal Institute for International Affairs is noted by Mitrany in *Functional Theory of Politics*, p. 39. Mitrany's personal connection to Hobson is remarked upon on pp. 53–4.

45 Unlike structural functionalism in sociology; see Parsons, *Structure of Social Action*. For the mistaken view that Mitrany's functionalism and structural functional sociology can be simply equated or cross fertilised, see Vincent, 'Functions of Functionalism in International Relations' and Haas, *Beyond the Nation-State*, p. 6.

46 Notably Clarence K. Streit's *Union Now* (London: Jonathan Cape, 1939). For a critical view, see Mitrany, *Working Peace System*, pp. 13–15.

47 *Work and Wealth*, p. 16; *Democracy and a Changing Civilisation*, p. 121; *International Government*, p. 196; *Free Thought*, p. 259.

48 See Mitrany, *Working Peace System*.

49 *Wealth and Life*, pp. 228–9.

50 Suganami quoting Hans Morgenthau in *Domestic Analogy and World Order Proposals*, p. 2.

51 See, for instance, Carr, *The Twenty Years' Crisis*, ch. 3.

52 A. J. P. Taylor uses Hobson's tumble down the stairs of the 1917 Club as a metaphor for the collapse of idealism in 1931. See *The Trouble-Makers*, pp. 145–6.

53 David Mitrany quoted in Suganami, *Domestic Analogy and World Order Proposals*, p. 79.

54 Freeden, *Liberalism Divided*.

55 For Hobson's claims of surprise and his reduced faith in the rationality of humanity, see *Problems of a New World*, part 1, and *Confessions*, pp. 96, 104.

56 Mitrany, *Functional Theory of Politics*, pp. 4–5

57 For one of Hobson's less optimistic assessments, see his reaction to the treaty between Britain and Russia in 'England's Duty to the Russian People', *South Place Magazine* (Vol. 12, No. 10, July 1907).

58 *Democracy After the War* and *Problems of a New World*.

59 Compare the analysis of imperialist finance in *Imperialism*, part 1, ch. 7,

with *Labour and the Costs of War* (London: Union of Democratic Control, 1916), pp. 10, 16.

60 'The Coming Taxation', *Contemporary Review* (Vol. 108, September 1915); *Taxation in the New State*, part 2, ch. 2.

61 'The War and British Liberties', 4 parts, *The Nation* (Vol. 19, Nos. 3, 5, 11, 18, April–July 1916); *Forced Labour* (London: National Council for Civil Liberties, 1917).

62 As in *Psychology of Jingoism* during the Boer War; in his satirical First World War book, *1920: Dips Into the Near Future*; and in his post-war assessment, *Problems of a New World*.

63 *The War in South Africa*, part 3, ch. 6. Cf. *1920: Dips Into the Near Future*.

64 Clarke, *Liberals and Social Democrats*, p. 168.

65 Ernst Haas, *The Uniting of Europe* (Stanford: Stanford University Press, 1958) and *Beyond the Nation-State*; Keohane and Nye (eds.), *Transnational Relations and World Politics*; Robert O. Keohane and Joseph S. Nye, *Power and Interdependence* (Boston: Little, Brown, 1977); Joseph Nye, *Peace in Parts* (Boston: Little, Brown, 1971); Keohane, *After Hegemony*; Stephen Krasner (ed.), *International Regimes* (Ithaca: Cornell University Press, 1983); and Kenneth Oye (ed.), *Cooperation Under Anarchy* (Princeton: Princeton University Press, 1986).

66 Grieco, 'Anarchy and the Limits of Cooperation'. For Keohane's discussion of neo-liberal institutionalism, see his *International Institutions and State Power* (Boulder, CO: Westview, 1989), ch. 1.

67 Keohane, *After Hegemony*, ch. 5. Regrettably I cannot in this short space do justice to the subtleties of Keohane's approach but have to restrict discussion to the general parameters of neo-liberal institutionalism as he sets them out. For a discussion of the evolution of the approach, see Keohane, *International Institutions and State Power*, ch. 1. For further readings on neo-liberal institutionalism, see Robert Baldwin (ed.), *Neorealism and Neoliberalism: The Contemporary Debate* (New York: Columbia University Press, 1993); Robert Axelrod and R. O. Keohane, 'Achieving Cooperation Under Anarchy: Strategies and Institutions', in Oye (ed.), *Cooperation Under Anarchy*; and also Robert Axelrod, *The Evolution of Cooperation* (New York: Basic Books, 1984), esp. chs. 1, 4.

68 R. B. J. Walker, 'History and Structure in the Theory of International Relations', *Millennium: Journal of International Studies* (Vol. 18, No. 2, 1989). This approach, the application of the methodology of economics and game theory to the other social sciences, has been called 'economic imperialism'. See Gerard Radnitsky and Peter Bernholz (eds.), *Economic Imperialism: The Economic Approach Applied Outside the Field of Economics* (New York: Paragon House, 1987).

69 Robert Keohane, 'International Institutions: Two Approaches', *International Studies Quarterly* (Vol. 32, No. 4, December 1989).

70 Banks, 'The Inter-Paradigm Debate', p. 15. Traditional idealism is a phrase used by Michael Banks to refer to inter-war progressive thought in

international relations. Hobson also described Cobden's approach to international politics as non-interventionalism. See *Richard Cobden*, p. 406.

71 Banks, 'The Inter-Paradigm Debate', pp. 17–20.

72 This was the case for a number of other writers during the inter-war period in particular. I have examined the contribution of inter-war theorists to international political economy in my ' "Not at all Profound"? Reassessing Inter-War International Theory', paper presented at the Annual Meeting of the Canadian Political Science Association, Queen's University, Kingston, Ontario, Canada, 2–4 June 1991.

Bibliography

Hobson wrote for a living and his published work is extensive, ranging from reports of his lectures at Conway Hall, the home of the South Place Ethical Society, to his tomes on welfare economics, *Work and Wealth* and *Wealth and Life*, with a variety of articles in numerous periodicals in between. He wrote over thirty books on a wide range of topics. Often they were compiled from journal articles, lectures and talks, either at South Place or the Rainbow Circle, or as part of his political campaigning. Even his autobiography was first aired at South Place. Sometimes these collections had a strong theme, as with *The Social Problem*, *Imperialism* and *The Crisis of Liberalism*. Other books were selections of Hobson's newspaper reports from abroad, some were on Hobson's travels, like *The War in South Africa* and *Canada Today*, and others were on current issues, such as *A Modern Outlook*. Suggestions for writing books occasionally came from friends or through connections in the Ethical Movement, the origins of both *The Evolution of Modern Capitalism* and *John Ruskin: Social Reformer*. Hobson wrote biographies on or edited collections of work by some of those who had had the greatest intellectual impact on him, such as John Ruskin, Richard Cobden, Thorstein Veblen, L. T. Hobhouse and William Clarke.

My perspective on Hobson's writing is influenced to a great extent by academic training in the discipline of international relations. Nonetheless, understanding Hobson's international relations is not possible without a consideration of the major tenets of his social philosophy and political economy, as I show in chapters 2 and 3. There are a number of other studies of Hobson and his work from a variety of different perspectives that provide context on Hobson and his writings. Until recently, though, it was true to say that Hobson was both neglected and well-known. (See P. J. Cain, 'J. A. Hobson, Cobdenism, and the Radical Theory of Economic Imperialism, 1898–1914', p. 565; A. J. F. Lee comments in 1970 on the lack of significant work on Hobson's writings as a whole in the Introduction to his 'The Social and Economic Thought of J. A. Hobson'.) There was a great deal of analysis, particularly by economic historians and Marxist scholars, of his theory of imperialism. There were, however, only a few analyses of Hobson's work as a whole; until 1968 there was only a brief account in a lecture given by Hobson's friend H. N. Brailsford called *The Life-work of J. A. Hobson*. Since the publication of Bernard Porter's ground-breaking study, *Critics of Empire*, however, there has been a burgeoning literature on Hobson, as well as on the turn-of-the-century new liberalism of which he was a key figure, mainly in the history of ideas and political theory. The most recent work has been Michael Freeden (ed.), *J. A. Hobson: A Reader* and *Reappraising J. A. Hobson: Humanism and Welfare*, Jules Townshend, *J. A. Hobson*, and John Pheby (ed.), *J. A. Hobson After Fifty Years: Free Thinker of the Social Sciences.*

Among those who have studied Hobson's life and work, there is agreement on two matters. First, generally, Hobson's corpus of work is best understood through an analysis of a couple of central ideas: the organic analogy and the theory of surplus value. Second, Hobson's theory of imperialism is a facet of his general social philosophy rather than a separate contribution to the theories of imperialism. All of the studies of his work in intellectual history/ political theory discuss Hobson's theory of imperialism and his writings on international affairs, such as free trade, the First World War and the League of Nations, but generally lump them together in a chapter at the end of the text (with the exception of Peter Weiler who explicitly excludes these issues from consideration). Hobson's arguments for internationalism, a predominant concern towards the end of his life, are a marginal concern for most Hobson scholars. These writers concentrate on Hobson's gloomy prognosis of contemporary international relations, exemplified by his writings on imperialism, which looms larger in his earlier writings where his theoretical approach is considered to have been forged. Lee ('The Social and Economic Thought of J. A. Hobson', ch. 8), Allett (*New Liberalism*, ch. 5), and Freeden (*J. A. Hobson: A Reader*, ch. 4), all collapse Hobson's international relations into one chapter towards the end of the study, with imperialism predominating. While Townshend devotes more space to imperialism and Hobson's international relations, he brings imperialism even more to the forefront; see 'J. A. Hobson and the Crisis of Liberalism', chs. 8–9, as well as his book *J. A. Hobson.*

There have been a number of studies of Hobson's underconsumption theory and his theory of imperialism. The problem with much of this work is that it tends to ignore the significance of Hobson's other work and the historical and ideological context in which he was writing. An exception to this rule is E. M. Winslow's account 'Hobson and the Theory of Economic Imperialism', chapter 5 in his *The Pattern of Imperialism.* J. M. Keynes's famed discussion of Hobson's underconsumption theory in his *General Theory of Employment, Interest and Money* was also something of a mixed blessing. While he applauded Mummery and Hobson's underconsumption theory as marking 'an epoch in economic thought', Keynes claimed that he had exposed the root of Hobson's mistake and transcended Hobson's analysis of unemployment, depression and trade cycles in economic theory. On the other hand, Mark Blaug has denied that there is a significant theoretical link between Hobson and Keynes. (See Blaug, *Economic Theory in Retrospect*, p. 665, and *Great Economists Before Keynes*, p. 94. See also John R. Commons review, 'Hobson's "Economics of Unemployment"'.)

Subsequent studies in economics have complained of Hobson's defective understandings of the role of the interest rate, of money and credit, his failure to distinguish between saving and investment, the vagueness of his concept of surplus, his neglect of the distinction between positive and normative economics, the 'theological terminology' of his discussion of the 'social organism', and his lack of academic rigour and anti-academic bias. These studies, while enlightening on the theoretical deficiencies of Hobson's economics, have treated his economic theories in isolation from his other work and from his social philosophy. They thus fail to appreciate Hobson's attempt to integrate economics, politics and sociology under an overarching 'science' of ethics. Unfortunately, Hobson nowadays attracts little attention from economists. The decline of interest can be accounted for by Hobson's opposition to the mathematisation of economics and the so-called marginal revolution as well as the decline in the institutionalist economics with which Hobson might have been most closely associated. Hobson's version of welfare economics has not taken root in the discipline and he is less likely to be considered an economist now than he was during his lifetime. Nevertheless, he does appear in Mark Blaug's *Great Economists Before Keynes*, pp. 93–5. Similar revision of status as an economist, it might be noted, has befallen Thorstein Veblen.

The studies of Hobson's contribution to the origin and structure of the theory of imperialism have come from almost every conceivable methodological, theoretical and ideological standpoint. Most of this work has been done by intellectual historians, economic historians and Marxist scholars. The major issues in the discussions of Hobson's contribution to the theory of imperialism have been: first, the shape and major components of the classical theory of imperialism originated by Hobson and refined by Lenin; second, the distinction or otherwise between Hobson and Lenin, or the extent of Hobson's influence on Lenin; third, the fit or lack thereof of the theory with the facts of the imperial expansion; and finally, the nature of the explanation in the theory.

Specialists in international relations, with the exception of Kenneth Waltz and Charles Reynolds, have been content to follow the conclusions of the work from other disciplines, adopting the Leninist version of the theory of imperialism via the interpretations of the economic historians. Hobson's theory of imperialism is briefly referred to or oftentimes caricatured in textbooks on international relations. Examples here are very numerous: Tony Thorndike, 'The Revolutionary Approach: the Marxist Perspective', in Trevor Taylor (ed.), *Approaches and Theory in International Relations*, p. 71; Martin Shaw (ed.), *War, State and Society*, p. 53; Geoffrey Blainey, *The Causes of War*, pp. 146–7; Keith L. Nelson and Spencer C. Ohlin, Jr, *Why War? Ideology, Theory, and History*, pp. 78–81; J. E. Dougherty and R. L. Pfaltzgraff, Jr, *Contending Theories of International Relations*, pp. 176–8; Charles Reynolds, *Theory and Explanation in International Politics*, ch. 7; Hans Morgenthau, *Power Among Nations*, 3rd edn, p. 48; Raymond Aron, *Peace and War*, ch. 9; Ian Clark, *The Hierarchy of Powers: Reform and Resistance in the International Order*, p. 136; J. D. B. Miller, *The World of States: Connected Essays*, p. 118, n. 8. These studies have contributed to Hobson's reduced status in the history of international theory, where he is credited merely with developing an economic determinist explanation of imperialism, while his wider contribution to international theory elsewhere is ignored. Other errors are of rather less consequence: Fred Parkinson, for instance, in his *The Philosophy of International Relations*, pp. 114–16, notes Hobson's contribution to the neo-Marxist theory of imperialism, but suggests that Hobson was working for the *Daily Telegraph* in South Africa; and James Der Derian refers to J. B. Hobson throughout his *On Diplomacy: A Genealogy of Western Estrangement.*

Reaction to imperialism theory has, however, lately generated a substantial challenge to the realist orthodoxy in international relations, in the shape of world systems analysis and the so-called structuralist paradigm. For a discussion of the different paradigms in international relations and the possible place of Hobson in them, see Michael Banks, 'The Inter-paradigm Debate', in M. Light and A. J. R. Groom (eds.), *International Relations: A Handbook of Current Theory*, p. 18. The major contribution to the discussion of Hobson's *Imperialism* in international relations remains that of Kenneth Waltz. As we saw in chapters 5 and 6, adopting the simple descriptions of the theory given by studies in economic history, Waltz accuses Hobson's theory of being a state-level explanation of war, that is, of ignoring the importance of the international system, and of being a simplistic monocausal explanation of imperialism.

Hobson's other writings on international relations remain under-researched. His writings on internationalism have earned scant acknowledgement in international relations, particularly his work on economic internationalism and on the League of Nations. In one of Hobson's rare appearances outside the theory of imperialism, F. H. Hinsley quotes a secondary source in his reference to Hobson proposing a world state. Hinsley's source is a Foreign Office report by one of the authors of the British proposals for the League of Nations – hardly a neutral observer. (See F. H. Hinsley, *Power and the Pursuit of Peace*, p. 143; and Lord Phillimore, *Schemes for Maintaining General Peace*, esp. pp. 10–11.) Martin Ceadel includes Hobson as one of the inter-war peace activists in his *Thinking About Peace and War*, pp. 96, 118. Ceadel reflects something of the schizophrenic attitude to Hobson's international writings. He notes both Hobson's social-democratic interest in an extensive League of Nations that would deal with socio-economic problems of the world, and also Hobson's updating of Cobden's international relations. Things might be on the mend, however, with a recent increase in interest in international theorists of the inter-war period of whom Hobson is a notable figure. For instance, there are now a number of papers in *Review of International Studies*, including Cornelia Navari, 'The Great Illusion Revisited: The International Theory of Norman Angell'; Don Markwell, 'Sir Alfred Zimmern Revisited: Fifty Years On'; Brian Porter 'David Davies: A Hunter After Peace'; David Long, 'J. A. Hobson and Idealism in International Relations'; and Christopher Brewin, 'Research in a Global Context: a Discussion of

Toynbee's Legacy'; as well as a collection of studies in David Long and Peter Wilson (eds.), *Thinkers of the Twenty Years' Crisis.*

The select bibliography is far from a comprehensive listing of Hobson's published work. It is also rather more than a catalogue of Hobson's writing on international relations. The selection of secondary sources is also tailored to the scope of this study, Hobson's theory of international relations. For a more comprehensive bibliography of Hobson's writings, see A. J. F. Lee, 'The Social and Economic Thought of J. A. Hobson' or the bibliography provided in John Pheby (ed.), *J. A. Hobson After Fifty Years.* Those interested in pursuing Hobson's unpublished work need to consult the rather slight collection of Hobson papers in the archives of the Brynmor Jones Library, University of Hull, though reference to the private papers of Hobson's friends and colleagues, L. T. Hobhouse, Graham Wallas, Norman Angell, and so on, is also recommended.

HOBSON'S PUBLISHED WORK

BOOKS AND PAMPHLETS

With A. F. Mummery, *The Physiology of Industry* (London: Murray, 1889).

Subjective and Objective Views of Distribution (New York: American Academy of Political Science, 1893).

Problems of Poverty, 2nd edn (London: Methuen, 1895).

John Ruskin: Social Reformer (London: Nisbet, 1898).

The War in South Africa (London: Nisbet, 1900).

The Economics of Distribution (New York: Macmillan, 1900).

The Psychology of Jingoism (London: Grant Richards, 1901).

The Social Problem (London: Nisbet, 1901).

International Trade: An Application of Economic Theory (London: Methuen, 1904)

The Problem of the Unemployed, 2nd edn (London: Methuen, 1906)

Canada Today (London: Unwin, 1906).

The Fruits of American Protection (New York: Cassell, 1906).

(Ed.) with William Burrows, *William Clarke: A Collection of His Writings* (London, Swan, Sonnenschein, 1908).

The Crisis of Liberalism (London: P. S. King, 1909).

The Industrial System (London: Longmans, 1909).

A Modern Outlook (London: Herbert and Daniel, 1910).

The Case for Arbitration (London: International Arbitration League Pamphlet no. 16, 1911).

The Science of Wealth (London: Williams and Norgate, 1911; 4th edn, Oxford University Press, 1950).

The Economic Interpretation of Investment (London: Financial Reviews of Reviews, 1911).

The Importance of Instruction in the Facts of Internationalism (London: National Peace Council Educational Series, 1912).

Industrial Unrest (London: Political Committee of the National Liberal Club, 1912).
Gold, Prices and Wages (London: Methuen, 1913).
The German Panic (London: Cobden Club, 1913).
Traffic in Treason (London: Unwin, 1914).
Towards International Government (London: Allen and Unwin, 1915).
A League of Nations (London: Union of Democratic Control, 1915).
Labour and the Costs of War (London: Union of Democratic Control, 1916).
The New Protectionism (London: Unwin, 1916).
The Fight for Democracy (Manchester: National Labour Press, 1917).
Democracy After the War (London: Allen and Unwin, 1917).
Forced Labour (London: National Council for Civil Liberties, 1917).
(As Lucian), *1920: Dips Into the Near Future* (London: Headley, 1918).
Richard Cobden: The International Man (London: Unwin, 1918).
The New Holy Alliance (London: Union of Democratic Control, 1919).
Taxation in the New State (London: Methuen, 1919).
The Morals of Economic Internationalism (New York: Houghton, 1920).
Taxation (London: Labour Party, 1920).
The Obstacles to Economic Recovery in Europe (London: Fight the Famine Council, 1920).
The Economics of Reparation (London: Allen and Unwin, 1921).
Problems of a New World (London: Allen and Unwin, 1921).
Work and Wealth (New York: Macmillan, 1922 [1914])
The Economics of Unemployment (London: Allen and Unwin, 1922).
Incentives in the New Industrial Order (London: Allen and Unwin, 1922).
With D. H. Macgregor and R. Lennard, *Some Aspects of Recent British Economics* (Chicago: Chicago University Press, 1923).
The Evolution of Modern Capitalism, 4th edn (London: Allen and Unwin, 1926)
Free Thought in the Social Sciences (London: Allen and Unwin, 1926).
Notes on Law and Order (London: Hogarth Press, 1926).
The Conditions of Industrial Peace (London: Allen and Unwin, 1927).
Wealth and Life (London: Allen and Unwin, 1929).
Rationalisation and Unemployment (London: Allen and Unwin, 1930).
With Morris Ginsberg, *L. T. Hobhouse: His Life and Work* (London: Allen and Unwin, 1931).
God and Mammon (London: Rationalist Press Association, 1931).
Towards Social Equality, L. T. Hobhouse Memorial Lecture, no. 1 (London: Oxford University Press, 1931).
The Modern State, The Changing World, No. 4 (London: BBC Publications, 1931).
Poverty in Plenty (London: Allen and Unwin, 1931).
From Capitalism to Socialism (London: Hogarth, 1932).
The Recording Angel: A Report from Earth (London: Allen and Unwin, 1932).
Rationalism and Humanism, Conway Memorial Lecture (London: Watts, 1933).

The Moral Challenge to the Economic System (London: Ethical Union's Ethical and Economics Trust Fund, 1933).
Democracy and a Changing Civilisation (London: Lane, 1934).
Veblen (London: Chapman and Hall, 1936).
Property and Improperty (London: Gollancz, 1937).
Confessions of an Economic Heretic (London: Allen and Unwin, 1938).
Imperialism: A Study, reprint of 3rd edn (London: Unwin Hyman, 1988 [1938])
With H. Finer and H. Meuter, *Le Sens de la Responsabilité* (Paris: Librairie du Recueil Surey, 1938).

CHAPTERS AND ARTICLES

'The Law of Three Rents', *Quarterly Journal of Economics* (Vol. 5, 1891), pp. 263–88.
'Can England Keep Her Free Trade?', *National Review* (Vol. 17, No. 97, March 1891), pp. 1–11.
'The Population Question I', *Commonwealth: A Social Magazine* (Vol. 2, No. 4, April 1897), pp. 105–6.
'The Population Question II', *Commonwealth: A Social Magazine* (Vol. 2, No. 6, June 1897), pp. 170–1.
'War or Peace in Industry?', *Reformer* (Vol. 1, No. 12, February 1898), pp. 335–8.
'Free Trade and Foreign Policy', *Contemporary Review* (Vol. 74, August 1898), pp. 167–80.
'Foreign Competition and Its Influence on Home Industries', *Co-operative Societies Annual* (1899), pp. 197–223.
'Of Labour' and 'On Capital', in J. E. Hand, *Good Citizenship* (London: George Allen, 1899).
'Capitalism and Imperialism in South Africa', *Contemporary Review* (Vol. 77, January 1900), pp. 1–17.
'The Testimony from Johannesburg: A Reply to Mr. Hosken', *Contemporary Review* (Vol. 77, May 1900), pp. 656–62.
'The Proconsulate of Milner', *Contemporary Review* (Vol. 78, October 1900), pp. 540–54.
'Facing the Bill', *Speaker* (New Series, Vol. 3, No. 61, 1 December 1900), pp. 223–4.
'The Ethics of Industrialism', in Stanton Coit (ed.), *Ethical Democracy* (London: Grant Richards, 1900).
'The Soul of Illiberalism', *The New Age* (Vol. 13, No. 354, 11 July 1901), pp. 440–1.
'Mr. Rhodes on the Future of South Africa', *The New Age* (Vol. 13, No. 359, 15 August 1901).
'Socialistic Imperialism', *International Journal of Ethics* (Vol. 12, No. 1, October 1901), pp. 44–58.
'The Approaching Abandonment of Free Trade', *Fortnightly Review* (Vol. 71, No. 423, 1 March 1902), pp. 434–44.

'The Inner Meaning of Protectionism', *Contemporary Review* (Vol. 84, September 1903), pp. 365–74.

'Free Trade and 'Free Labour'', *Free Trader* (Vol. 1, No. 12, 16 October 1903), pp. 94–5.

'Protection as a Working Class Policy', in H. W. Massingham (ed.), *Labour and Protection* (London: T. Fisher Unwin, 1903).

'The Ethics of Gambling', in B. S. Rowntree (ed.), *Betting and Gambling: A National Evil* (London: Macmillan, 1905).

'The Ethics of Internationalism', *International Journal of Ethics* (Vol. 17, No. 1, October 1906), pp. 16–28.

'Science in Industry', in J. E. Hand, *Science in Public Affairs* (London: George Allen, 1906).

'A Sovereign People', *South Place Magazine* (Vol. 12, No. 5, February 1907), pp. 64–6.

'The World We Make', *South Place Magazine* (Vol. 12, No. 6, March 1907), pp. 82–3.

'England's Duty to the Russian People', *South Place Magazine* (Vol. 12, No. 10, July 1907), pp. 147–8.

'State Interference', *South Place Magazine* (Vol. 13, No. 5, January 1908), pp. 78–9.

'Fiscal Fallacies: A Tariff as a Cure for Unemployment', *Nation* [London] (Vol. 2, No. 26, 28 March 1908), pp. 933–4.

'Fiscal Fallacies: The Single Trade Test', *Nation* [London] (Vol. 3, No. 2, 11 April 1908), p. 47.

'The Unpopularity of Peace Movements', *South Place Magazine* (Vol. 14, No. 2, November 1908), pp. 17–18.

'The Morality of Nations', *South Place Magazine* (Vol. 14, No. 4, January 1909), pp. 53–5.

'Thoughts about the Earthquake', *South Place Magazine* (Vol. 14, No. 6, March 1909), pp. 84–5.

'The Art of Panic-making', *South Place Magazine* (Vol. 14, No. 8, May 1909), pp. 118–20.

'Can Protection Cure Unemployment?', *National Review* (Vol. 53, No. 318, August 1909), pp. 1015–24.

'South Africa as an Imperial Asset', *English Review* (Vol. 3, September 1909), pp. 324–34.

'Social Parasitism', *English Review* (Vol. 4, January 1910), pp. 347–58.

'Opening of Markets and Countries', in G. Spiller (ed.), *Papers on Inter-Racial Problems* (London: P.S. King, 1911).

'The Contact of Higher and Lower Races', *South Place Monthly List* (May 1911), pp. 4–7.

'The Cost of War', *Nineteenth Century* (Vol. 78, No. 463, 1915), pp. 691–701.

'The War and Its Effects on Work and Wages', *Fortnightly Review* (Vol. 97, No. 577, 1915), pp. 144–54.

'Free Trade as a Factor in Civilisation', *South Place Monthly List* (June 1915), pp. 6–7.

'How Can England Pay the Bill?', *New Republic* (Vol. 3, No. 36, 10 July 1915), pp. 255–7.

'Reprisals', *South Place Monthly List* (August 1915), pp. 3–7.

'England's Changing War-Mind', *New Republic* (Vol. 4, No. 46, 18 September 1915), pp. 173–5.

'The Coming Taxation', *Contemporary Review* (Vol. 108, September 1915), pp. 284–95.

'Foreword' to Harold Picton, *Is it to be Hate? An Essay in War-time* (London: Allen and Unwin, 1915).

'The Open Door' in C. R. Buxton (ed.), *Towards A Lasting Settlement* (London: Allen and Unwin, 1915).

'The Open Door', *The U.D.C.* (Vol. 1, No. 6, April 1916), pp. 57–8.

'The War and British Liberties I: The Suppression of Free Speech', *The Nation* [London] (Vol. 19, No. 3, 15 April 1916), pp. 68–9.

'The War and British Liberties II: Secret Trial or No Trial', *The Nation* [London] (Vol. 19, No. 5, 29 April 1916), pp. 123–5.

'The War and British Liberties III: The Claims of the State upon the Individual', *The Nation* [London] (Vol. 19, No. 11, 10 June 1916), pp. 307–8.

'The War and British Liberties IV: Liberty as a True War Economy', *The Nation* [London] (Vol. 19, No. 18, 29 July 1916), pp. 524–5.

'Lord Grey and the League of Peace', *The U.D.C.* (Vol. 2, No. 1, November 1916), pp. 1–2.

'Shall We Be Poorer After the War?', *Contemporary Review* (Vol. 111, No. 613, January 1917), pp. 43–53.

'Is International Government Possible?', *Hibbert Journal* (Vol. 15, No. 2, January 1917), pp. 199–203.

'Economic War', *The U.D.C.* (Vol. 2, No. 13, November 1917), p. 154.

'Self-Determination', *The U.D.C.* (Vol. 3, No. 6, April 1918), pp. 209–10.

'A World Safe for Democracy', *Survey* (29 June 1918), pp. 366–7.

'Protection Versus A League of Nations', *The U.D.C.* (Vol. 3, No. 10, August 1918), p. 254.

'The Structure of a League of Nations', *The U.D.C.* (Vol. 3, No. 12, October 1918), p. 270.

Chapters 62 and 64 in J. Maurice Clark, Walton H. Hamilton and Harold G. Moulton (eds.), *Readings in the Economics of War* (Chicago: University of Chicago Press, 1918).

'Gen. Smuts on World Government', *Common Sense* (Vol.4, No. 3, 18 January 1919), p. 34.

'"The Big Five"', *The U.D.C.* (Vol. 4, No. 5, March 1919), p. 305.

'Introduction' to J. Bruce Glasier, *The Meaning of Socialism* (Manchester: National Labour Press, 1919).

'America's Place in the World', *Contemporary Review* (Vol. 118, No. 655, July 1920), pp. 13–21.

'The German Indemnity: A British View', *Nation* [New York] (Vol. 112, No. 2905, 9 March 1921), pp. 370–1.

'England's Plunge into Protection', *Nation* [New York] (Vol. 113, No. 2936, 12 October 1921), pp. 398–9.

'War Guilt: Prince Max of Baden Appeals for a "Moral Offensive"', *Foreign Affairs* (Vol. 3, No. 5, November 1921), p. 74.

'Britain's Economic Outlook on Europe', *Journal of Political Economy* (Vol. 30, No. 4, August 1922), pp. 469–93.

'The Political Basis of a World State', in F. S. Marvin (ed.), *The Unity of Western Civilisation*, 2nd edn (London: Oxford University Press, 1922).

'What Will Happen in January?', *Foreign Affairs* (Vol. 4, No. 7, January 1923), pp. 131–2.

'Is America Moving?', *Foreign Affairs* (Vol. 5, No. 1, July 1923), pp. 3–4

'The New Scheme for Reparations', *Foreign Affairs* (Vol. 5, No. 11, May 1924), pp. 219–20.

'America and Europe', *Foreign Affairs* (Vol. 5, No. 12, June 1924), p. 255

'What Outlawry of War Signifies', *Foreign Affairs* (Vol. 6, No. 4, October 1924), p. 79.

'The Limited Market', *Nation* [New York] (Vol. 120, No. 3117, 1 April 1925), pp. 350–2.

'The Gold Standard', *Nation* [New York] (Vol. 120, No. 3121, 29 April 1925), pp. 487–8.

'The Population Question', *Nation* [New York] (Vol. 120, No. 3123, 13 May 1925), pp. 540–2.

'America and Internationalism', *Nation* [New York] (Vol. 120, No. 3125, 27 May 1925), pp. 599–600.

'The Economic Urge Toward Free Trade', *Nation* [New York] (Vol. 121, No. 3130, 1 July 1925), pp. 24–5.

'Half-Century Progress in Social Ethics', *South Place Monthly Record* (May 1926), pp. 3–5.

'The Economic Union of Europe', *Contemporary Review* (Vol. 130, No. 729, September 1926), pp. 290–7.

'Introduction' to H. Abbati, *The Unclaimed Wealth: How Money Stops Production* (London: Allen and Unwin, 1926).

'The Economic Organization of Europe', *Foreign Affairs* (Vol. 8, No. 9, March 1927), pp. 238–9.

'Half the World in Political Subjection: The New Imperialism', *The New Leader* (11 March 1927).

'Free Trade and British Labor', *Nation* [New York] (Vol. 128, No. 3319, 13 February 1929), pp. 184–5.

'The Saving Faith of Internationalism', *Contemporary Review* (Vol. 135, No. 762, June 1929), pp. 668–94.

'"Nationalism"', *South Place Monthly Record* (October 1929), pp. 5–6.

'The United States of Europe', *Nation* [New York] (Vol. 129, No. 3356, 30 October 1929), pp. 484–5.

'The New Protectionists', *Nineteenth Century* (Vol. 108, No. 643, September 1930), pp. 310–12.
'The British Imperial Conference', *Nation* [New York] (Vol. 131, No. 3404, 1 October 1930), pp. 342–4.
'The British Empire in Conference', *Nation* [New York] (Vol. 131, No. 3414, 10 December 1930), p. 662.
'A World Economy', *New Statesman and Nation* (Vol. 1, No. 8, 18 April 1931), pp. 274–5.
'Reactions of National Policy on Trade and Unemployment', *Political Quarterly* (Vol. 2, No. 4, October 1931), pp. 463–6.
'The Tariff Victory in Britain', *Nation* [New York] (Vol. 134, No. 3483, 6 April 1932), pp. 393–4.
'Britain's Protective Budget', *Nation* [New York] (Vol. 134, No. 3489, 18 May 1932), pp. 568–9.
'The World's Economic Crisis', *Nation* [New York] (Vol. 135, No. 3498, 20 July 1932), pp. 53–4.
'Underconsumption: an Exposition and a Reply', *Economica* (Vol. 13, No. 42, November 1933), pp. 402–27.
'The High Road to Peace and Prosperity', *New Statesman and Nation* (Vol. 9, No. 204 (new series), 19 January 1935), pp. 67–8.
'Force Necessary to Government', *Hibbert Journal* (Vol. 33, No. 3, April 1935), pp. 331–42.
'The Origins of the I.L.O.', *Contemporary Review* (Vol. 147, No. 403, August 1935).
'Foreword' to A. G. Macgregor, *The Correct Economy for the Machine Age* (London: Pitman, 1935).
'Foreword' to G. P. Gooch, *Dictatorship in Theory and Practice* (London: Conway Memorial Lecture, 1935).
'Sociology To-day', in British Committee of the Institute of Sociology and the World University Service, *The Social Sciences* (London: Le Play University Press, 1936).
'A Dangerous World', *South Place Monthly Record* (April 1937), pp. 2–3.
'Tolerance and Intolerance', *South Place Monthly Record* (October 1937), pp. 2–3.
'Thoughts About Democracy', *South Place Monthly Record* (December 1937), pp. 2–3.
'Thoughts on our Present Discontents', *Political Quarterly* (Vol. 9, No. 1, January 1938), pp. 47–57.
'"A Cultural Lag"', *South Place Monthly Record* (February 1938), pp. 2–3.
'A World-Brain and a World-Heart', *South Place Monthly Record* (April 1938), pp. 2–3.
'Liberalism', *South Place Monthly Record* (June 1938), pp. 2–3.
'Ethics versus Politics', *South Place Monthly Record* (December 1938), pp. 2–3.
'Democracy, Its Internal and External Conflicts', *South Place Monthly Record* (February 1939), pp. 3–4.
'Rationalism and Ethics', *South Place Monthly Record* (April 1939), pp. 3–5.

'Nationalism, Economic and Political', *South Place Monthly Record* (June 1939), pp. 3–4.
'The Ethics of Humanity', *South Place Monthly Record* (August 1939), pp. 3–4.
'Will War Teach Peace?', *South Place Monthly Record* (October 1939), pp. 3–4.
'America in the War?', *South Place Monthly Record* (December 1939), pp. 3–4.

LETTERS AND REVIEWS

'Mr. Hobson and the Causes of War', letter, *Speaker* (New Series, Vol. 1, No. 23, 10 March 1900), pp. 620–1.
Review of John Ruskin, 'Praetoria', *Speaker* (New Series, Vol. 1, No. 27, 7 April 1900), p. 16.
Letter, *Speaker* (New Series, Vol. 1, No. 28, 14 April 1900).
Letter on 'Fiscal Fallacies', *Nation* [London] (Vol. 3, No. 2, 11 April 1908), p. 50.
Review of 'The Need of Nations', *Sociological Review* (Vol. 1, No. 4, October 1908), pp. 401–2.
Letter, *Nation* [London] (Vol. 7, No. 15, 9 July 1910), p. 529
Letter on review of 'Towards International Government', *New Statesman* (Vol. 5, 24 July 1915), pp. 379–80.
Letter on review of *Towards International Government*, *Nation* [London] (Vol. 17, No. 19, 7 August 1915), p. 615.
'Approaches to Peace', letter, *Nation* [London] (Vol. 18, 16 October 1915), pp. 115–16; with subsequent discussion: pp. 212–13, 243, 289–90, 355–6, 386–7.
'Peace that is Inconclusive', letter, *New Republic* (Vol. 5, No. 53, 6 November 1915), pp. 17–19.
'Approaches to Peace', letter, *New Statesman* (Vol. 6, No. 139, 4 December 1915), pp. 204–5.
'Liberty of Speech', letter, *Nation* [London] (Vol. 18, No. 10, 4 December 1915), p. 358.
'How Long and Why?', letter, *Nation* [London] (Vol. 20, No. 22, 3 March 1917), pp. 733–4.
'An American Victory in 1920?', letter, *Nation* [London] (Vol. 21, No. 12, 23 June 1917), pp. 298–9.
'One More Wilson', review of W. Dodd, 'Woodrow Wilson and his Work', *Nation* [New York] (Vol. 111, No. 2876, 14 August 1920), pp. 189–90.
Review of J. M. Keynes, 'A Revision of the Treaty', *Foreign Affairs* (Vol. 13, No. 8, February 1922), p. 126.
'The People and the Diplomats', review of P. Reinsch, 'Secret Diplomacy', *Nation* [New York] (Vol. 115, No. 2976, 19 July 1922), pp. 73–4.
'Lord Bryce and Economics', review, *Nation* [New York] (Vol. 115, No. 2988, 11 October 1922), pp. 380–1.
Review of S. and B. Webb, 'The Decay of Capitalist Civilization', *Nation* [New York] (Vol. 116, No. 3015, 18 April 1923), p. 472.

'The Stupidity of War', review of A. Ponsonby, 'Now is the Time', *Foreign Affairs* (Vol. 7, No. 4, October 1925), p. 112.
Review of H. Laski, 'A Grammar of Politics', *Foreign Affairs* (Vol. 7, No. 5, November 1925), p. 143.
'The Religion of the State', review of C. Hayes, 'Essays on Nationalism', *Nation* [New York] (Vol. 123, No. 3197, 13 October 1926), pp. 378–9.
'Oil, the Invisible King', review of L. Fischer, 'Oil Imperialism', *Foreign Affairs* (Vol. 8, No. 5, November 1926), pp. 132–3.
Review of P. T. Moon, 'Imperialism and World Politics', *Nation* [New York] (Vol. 124, No. 3211, 19 January 1927), pp. 69–70.
Review of F. W. Hirst, 'Safeguarding and Protection', *Foreign Affairs* (Vol. 9, No. 3, September 1927), p. 88.
'The National Myth', review of F. Delaisi, 'Political Myths and Economic Realities', *Nation* [New York] (Vol. 126, No. 3255, 23 November 1927), p. 575.
Review of Cobden biography, *Nation* [New York] (Vol. 126, No. 3272, 21 March 1928), pp. 324–5.
Review of N. Pfeffer, 'The White Man's Dilemma', *Nation* [New York] (Vol. 126, No. 3283, 6 June 1928), pp. 647–8.
Review of L. L. Lorwin, 'Labour and Internationalism', *Nation* [New York] (Vol. 129, No. 3346, 21 August 1929), p. 201.
Comment on T. E. Gregory, 'Economic Nationalism', *International Affairs* (Vol. 10, No. 3, May 1931), p. 303.
'Will America Stop Another War?', letter, *New Republic* (Vol. 91, No. 1178, 30 June 1937), pp. 209–10, 224.
Letter on 'Union of Democratic Control', *New Statesman and Nation* (Vol. 14, 2 October 1937), p. 483.
Review of R. G. Hawtrey, 'Capital and Employment', *International Affairs* (Vol. 17, No. 1, January–February 1938), pp. 102–3.

SECONDARY SOURCES

Acton, H.B., 'Introduction', to Mill, *Utilitarianism, On Liberty and Considerations on Representative Government.*
Akehurst, Michael, *A Modern Introduction to International Law*, 4th edn (London: George Allen and Unwin, 1982).
Alker, H.R., Jr and T. J. Biersteker, 'The Dialectics of World Order: Notes for a Future Archaeologist of International *Savoir Faire*', *International Studies Quarterly* (Vol. 28, No. 2, 1984).
Allett, John, *New Liberalism: The Political Economy of J. A. Hobson* (Toronto: University of Toronto Press, 1981).
'The Conservative Aspect of Hobson's New Liberalism', in Freeden (ed.), *Reappraising J. A. Hobson.*
Amin, Samir, *Unequal Development* (New York: Monthly Review Press, 1976).
Angell, Norman, *The Great Illusion* (London: Heinemann, 1912).

The Foundations of International Polity (Toronto: William Briggs, 1914).
Foreign Policy and Our Daily Bread (London: Collins, 1925).
The Great Illusion 1933 (London: Heinemann, 1933).
Preface to Peace: A Guide for the Plain Man (London: Hamish Hamilton, 1935).
Let the People Know (New York: Viking, 1943).
Arendt, Hannah, *The Origins of Totalitarianism*, 2nd edn (London: George Allen and Unwin, 1958).
Aron, Raymond, *Peace and War* (New York: Doubleday, 1960).
Arrighi, Giovanni, *The Geometry of Imperialism: The Limits of Hobson's Paradigm*, revised edn (London: Verso, 1983).
Ashley, Richard K., 'Three Modes of Economism', *International Studies Quarterly* (Vol. 27, No. 4, 1983).
Ashley, R.K., 'The Powers of Anarchy: The Domestic Analogy and the Anarchy Problematique', paper presented at the British International Studies Annual Meeting, December 1987.
Australian League of Nations Union, *The League and Its Critics* (Sydney: Australian League of Nations Union, 1920).
Axelrod, Robert, *The Evolution of Cooperation* (New York: Basic Books, 1984).
Backhouse, Roger E., 'Mummery and Hobson's *The Physiology of Industry*', in Pheby (ed.), *J. A. Hobson After Fifty Years*.
Baldwin, David A., 'Interdependence and Power: A Conceptual Analysis', *International Organization* (Vol. 34, No. 4, 1980).
Baldwin, Robert, (ed.), *Neorealism and Neoliberalism: The Contemporary Debate* (New York: Columbia University Press, 1993).
Banks, M.,'The Inter-Paradigm Debate', in M. Light and A. J. R. Groom (eds.), *International Relations: A Handbook of Current Theory* (London: Pinter, 1985).
(ed.), *Conflict in World Society* (Brighton: Wheatsheaf, 1984).
Baran, Paul, and Paul Sweezy, *Monopoly Capital* (Harmondsworth: Penguin, 1968).
Barber, B. R., *The Conquest of Politics* (Princeton: Princeton University Press, 1988).
Barber, William J., *A History of Economic Thought* (Harmondsworth: Penguin, 1967).
Barrat Brown, Michael, 'A Critique of Marxist Theories of Imperialism', in Owen and Sutcliffe (eds.), *Studies in the Theory of Imperialism*.
Barry, Brian, *Political Argument* (London: Routledge and Kegan Paul, 1965).
Theories of Justice (Berkeley: University of California Press, 1988).
Behrman, Cynthia F., 'Introduction' to Hobson's *The War in South Africa* (New York and London: Garland, 1972).
Beitz, Charles R., *Political Theory and International Relations* (Princeton: Princeton University Press, 1979).
Berki, R. N., *On Political Realism* (London: Dent, 1981).
Betts, Raymond F., *The False Dawn: European Imperialism in the Nineteenth Century* (Minneapolis: University of Minnesota Press, 1976).

Bhagwati, Jagdish, *Protectionism* (Cambridge, MA: MIT Press, 1988).
Bicchieri, Cristina, 'Should a Scientist Abstain From Metaphor?', in Arjo Klamer, Donald N. McCloskey and Robert M. Solow (eds.), *The Consequences of Economic Rhetoric* (Cambridge: Cambridge University Press, 1988).
Blaug, Mark, *Economic Theory in Retrospect*, 4th edn (Cambridge: Cambridge University Press, 1985).
Great Economists Before Keynes: An Introduction to the Lives and Works of One Hundred Great Economists of the Past (Cambridge: Cambridge University Press, 1986).
Bleaney, Michael, *Underconsumption Theories* (New York: International Publishers, 1976).
Boulding, Kenneth E., and Tapan Mukherjee (eds.), *Economic Imperialism: A Book of Readings* (Ann Arbor: University of Michigan Press, 1972).
Bowen, Ian, *Cobden* (London: Duckworth, 1935).
Brailsford, H. N., *The Life-work of J. A. Hobson*, L. T. Hobhouse Memorial Lecture, 15 May 1947 (London: London School of Economics, 1948).
Brewin, Christopher, 'Liberal States and International Obligations', *Millennium: Journal of International Studies* (Vol. 17, No. 2, 1988).
Bryce, Viscount and others, *Proposals for the Prevention of Future Wars* (London: George Allen and Unwin, 1917).
Bull, Hedley, 'Society and Anarchy in International Relations', in Butterfield and Wight (eds.), *Diplomatic Investigations*.
'The Theory of International Politics 1919–1969', in B. Porter (ed.), *The Aberystwyth Papers* (London: Oxford University Press, 1972).
The Anarchical Society (London: Macmillan, 1977).
Burns, C. Delisle, 'J. A. Hobson', *New Statesman* (April 1940).
'J. A. Hobson: The Humanist', *South Place Monthly Record* (May 1940).
Burrow, J. W., *Evolution and Society: A Study in Victorian Social Theory* (Cambridge: Cambridge University Press, 1968).
Butler, Nicholas Murray, *The International Mind: An Argument for the Judicial Settlement of International Disputes* (New York: Scribner's, 1912).
Butterfield, Herbert, and Martin Wight (eds.), *Diplomatic Investigations* (London: Allen and Unwin, 1966).
Cain, P. J., 'J. A. Hobson, Cobdenism, and the Radical Theory of Economic Imperialism, 1898–1914', *Economic History Review* (Vol. 31, No. 4, 1978).
'Capitalism, War and Internationalism in the Thought of Richard Cobden', *British Journal of International Studies* (Vol. 5, No. 3, 1979).
'International Trade and Economic Development in the Work of J. A. Hobson Before 1914', *History of Political Economy* (Vol. 11, No. 3, 1979).
'Hobson's Developing Theory of Imperialism', *Economic History Review* (Vol. 34, No. 2, 1981).
'Hobson, Wilshire, and the Capitalist Theory of Capitalist Imperialism', *History of Political Economy* (Vol. 17, No. 3, 1985).
'J. A. Hobson, Financial Capitalism and Imperialism in Late Victorian and

Edwardian England', *Journal of Imperial and Commonwealth History* (Vol. 13, No. 3, 1985).

'Variations on a Famous Theme: Hobson, International Trade and Imperialism, 1902–1938', in Freeden (ed.), *Reappraising J. A. Hobson.*

Cairncross, A. K., *Home and Foreign Investment* (Cambridge: Cambridge University Press, 1953).

Caitlin, G. E. G., Review of Hobson's 'Free Thought in the Social Sciences', *Political Science Quarterly* (Vol. 41, No. 4, 1926).

Caporaso, James A., *Functionalism and Regional Integration: A Logical and Empirical Assessment* (London: Sage, 1972).

Carr, E. H., *International Relations Since the Peace Treaties*, 2nd edn (London: Macmillan, 1940).

The Twenty Years' Crisis, 2nd edn (London: Macmillan, 1946).

Conditions of Peace (London: Macmillan, 1943).

The New Society, paperback edn (Boston: Beacon, 1957).

Ceadel, Martin, *Thinking About Peace and War* (Oxford: Oxford University Press, 1987).

Clark, Ian, *Reform and Resistance in the International Order* (Cambridge: Cambridge University Press, 1980).

Clarke, P. F., *Lancashire and the New Liberalism* (Cambridge: Cambridge University Press, 1971).

'Introduction' to Hobson's *The Crisis of Liberalism* (Brighton: Harvester, 1974).

Liberals and Social Democrats (Cambridge: Cambridge University Press, 1978).

'Hobson, Free Trade, and Imperialism', *Economic History Review* (Vol. 34, No. 2, 1981).

'Hobson and Keynes as Economic Heretics', in Freeden (ed.), *Reappraising J. A. Hobson.*

Claude, Inis, *Power in International Relations* (New York: Random House, 1962).

Cobden, Richard, *The Political Writings of Richard Cobden*, 2 vols. (New York: Garland, 1973).

Cohen, Benjamin J., *The Question of Imperialism: The Political Economy of Dominance and Dependence* (New York: Basic Books, 1973).

Cole, G. D. H., *Guild Socialism: A Plan for Economic Democracy* (New York: Stokes, 1920).

'J. A. Hobson, 1858–1940', *Economic Journal* (Vol. 50, Nos. 198–9, 1940).

Cole, Ken, John Cameron and Chris Edwards, *Why Economists Disagree* (Harlow: Longmans, 1983).

Collini, Stephan, 'Political Theory and the "Science of Society" in Victorian Britain', *The Historical Journal* (Vol. 23, No. 1, 1980).

Commons, John R., 'Hobson's 'Economics of Unemployment"', *American Economic Review* (Vol. 13, No. 4, Dec. 1923).

Connolly, William, *Appearance and Reality in Politics* (Cambridge: Cambridge University Press, 1981).

Copi, Irving M., *Introduction to Logic*, 5th edn (London: Collier Macmillan, 1978).

Crick, B., *In Defence of Politics* (Harmondsworth: Penguin, 1964).

Crowley, Brian Lee, *The Self, the Individual, and the Community: Liberalism in the Political Thought of F. A. Hayek and Sidney and Beatrice Webb* (Oxford: Clarendon, 1987).

Culbertson, W.P., Jr and R. B. Ekelund, Jr, 'John A. Hobson and the Theory of Discriminating Monopoly', *History of Political Economy* (Vol. 9, No. 2, 1977).

Dangerfield, George, *The Strange Death of Liberal England* (New York: Capricorn Books, 1961 [1935]).

Darby, Phillip, *Three Faces of Imperialism: British and American Approaches to Asia and Africa, 1870–1970* (New Haven: Yale University Press, 1987).

Davis, Horace B., 'Hobson and Human Welfare', *Science and Society* (Vol. 21, 1957).

Davis, Lance E., and Robert A. Huttenback, *Mammon and the Pursuit of Empire: The Political Economy of British Imperialism, 1860–1912* (Cambridge: Cambridge University Press, 1986).

de Jouvenel, Bertrand, *Sovereignty: An Inquiry into the Political Good* (Chicago: University of Chicago Press, 1957).

Der Derian, James, *On Diplomacy: A Genealogy of Western Estrangement* (Oxford: Basil Blackwell, 1987).

'Philosophical Traditions in International Relations', *Millennium: Journal of International Studies* (Vol. 17, No. 2, 1988).

Dougherty J. E., and R. L. Pfaltzgraff, Jr, *Contending Theories of International Relations* (New York: Harper, 1990).

Downs, Anthony, *An Economic Theory of Democracy* (New York: Harper and Row, 1957).

Doyle, Michael, *Empires* (Ithaca: Cornell University Press, 1986).

Dunn, John, *Rethinking Modern Political Theory: Essays, 1979–83* (Cambridge: Cambridge University Press, 1985).

Etherington, Norman, 'Reconsidering Theories of Imperialism', *History and Theory* (Vol. 21, No. 1, 1982).

'The Capitalist Theory of Capitalist Imperialism', *History of Political Economy* (Vol. 15, No. 1, 1983).

Theories of Imperialism: War, Conquest and Capital (London: Croom Helm, 1984).

Ferguson, John M., *Landmarks of Economic Thought*, 2nd edn (New York: Longmans, 1950).

Fieldhouse, D. K., *The Colonial Empires* (London: Weidenfeld and Nicolson, 1965).

Economics and Empire, 1830–1914 (London: Weidenfeld and Nicolson, 1973).

'"Imperialism": An Historiographical Revision', in Boulding and Mukherjee (eds.), *Economic Imperialism: A Book of Readings*.

(ed.), *The Theory of Capitalist Imperialism* (London: Longmans, 1967).

Fletcher, Ronald, (ed.), *The Science of Society and the Unity of Mankind: A Memorial Volume for Morris Ginsberg* (London: Heinemann, 1974).
Fox, William T. R., *The American Study of International Relations: Essays by William T. R. Fox* (Columbia: University of South Carolina Press, 1968).
Frank, Andre Gunder, *Capitalism and Underdevelopment in Latin America* (New York: Monthly Review Press, 1969).
Freeden, Michael, 'J. A. Hobson as a New Liberal Theorist: Some Aspects of his Social Thought Until 1914', *Journal of the History of Ideas* (Vol. 34, No. 3, 1973).
'Introduction' to Hobson's *Confessions of an Economic Heretic* (Brighton: Harvester, 1974).
New Liberalism: An Ideology of Social Reform (Oxford: Clarendon, 1986 [1978]).
Liberalism Divided: A Study in British Political Thought, 1914–1939 (Oxford: Clarendon, 1986).
'Human Rights and Welfare: A Communitarian View', *Ethics: An International Journal of Social, Political and Legal Philosophy* (Vol. 100, No. 3, 1990).
'J. A. Hobson as a Political Theorist', in Pheby (ed.), *J. A. Hobson After Fifty Years.*
(ed.), *J. A. Hobson: A Reader* (London: Unwin Hyman, 1988).
(ed.), *The Minutes of the Rainbow Circle, 1894–1924* (London: Royal Historical Society, 1989).
(ed.), *Reappraising J. A. Hobson: Humanism and Welfare* (London: Unwin Hyman, 1990).
Freeman, Robert, (ed.), *Marx on Economics* (Harmondsworth: Penguin, 1962).
Friedberg, Aaron L., *The Weary Titan: Britain and the Experience of Relative Decline, 1895–1905* (Princeton: Princeton University Press, 1988).
Gallagher, John, and Ronald Robinson, 'The Imperialism of Free Trade', *Economic History Review* (Vol. 6, No. 1, 1953).
Africa and the Victorians: The Official Mind of Imperialism (London: Macmillan, 1961).
Galtung, Johan, 'A Structural Theory of Imperialism', *Journal of Peace Research* (Vol. 8, No. 1, 1971).
Gill, Stephen, and David Law, *The Global Political Economy: Perspectives, Problems and Policies* (Hemel Hempstead: Harvester Wheatsheaf, 1988).
Gilpin, Robert, *War and Change in World Politics* (New York: Cambridge University Press, 1981).
The Political Economy of International Relations (Princeton: Princeton University Press, 1987).
Gourevitch, Peter, 'The Second Image Reversed', *International Organization* (Vol. 32, No. 4, 1978).
Politics in Hard Times: Comparative Responses to International Economic Crises (Ithaca: Cornell University Press, 1986).
Gray, John, *Liberalism* (Milton Keynes: Open University Press, 1986).
Liberalisms: Essays in Political Philosophy (London: Routledge, 1989).
Grieco, Joseph, 'Anarchy and the Limits of Cooperation: A Realist Critique

of the Newest Liberal Internationalism', *International Organization* (Vol. 42, No. 3, 1988).
Grunberg, Isabelle, 'Exploring the 'Myth' of Hegemonic Stability', *International Organization* (Vol. 44, No. 4, 1990).
Haas, Ernst, *The Uniting of Europe: Political, Social, and Economic Forces, 1950–1957* (Stanford: Stanford University Press, 1958).
Beyond the Nation-State: Functionalism and International Organization (Stanford: Stanford University Press, 1964).
Hall, John, *Liberalism: Politics, Ideology, and the Market* (London: Paladin, 1988).
Halliday, Fred, 'Vigilantism in International Relations', *Review of International Studies* (Vol. 13, No. 3, July 1987).
'State and Society in International Relations: A Second Agenda', *Millennium: Journal of International Studies* (Vol. 16, No. 2, 1987).
'Three Concepts of Internationalism', *International Affairs* (Vol. 64, No. 2, 1988).
Hamilton, D., 'Hobson with a Keynesian Twist', *American Journal of Economics and Sociology* (Vol. 13, No. 3, 1954).
Harrod, R. F., 'Epilogue' to Hobson's *The Science of Wealth*, 4th edn (Oxford: Oxford University Press, 1950).
Hayek, F. A., *The Road to Serfdom* (London: Ark Paperbacks, 1986).
Heilbroner, Robert, *The Worldly Philosophers* (Harmondsworth: Penguin, 1983).
Herz, J., *Political Realism and Political Idealism*, 2nd edn (Chicago: University of Chicago Press, 1959).
Hinsley, F. H., *Power and the Pursuit of Peace: Theory and Practice in the History of Relations Between States* (Cambridge: Cambridge University Press, 1963).
Hobbes, Thomas, *Leviathan*, ed. and intro. C.B. Macpherson (Harmondsworth: Penguin, 1968).
Hobhouse, L. T., *Democracy and Reaction* (London: T. Fisher Unwin, 1904).
Mind in Evolution, 2nd edn (London: Macmillan, 1915).
Liberalism (London: Williams and Norgate, 1911).
The Metaphysical Theory of the State (London: Allen, 1918).
Hodgart, Alan, *The Economics of European Imperialism* (London: Edward Arnold, 1977).
Hoffman, John, 'Three Approaches to the International System ...: A Reply to Dr. Little', *British Journal of International Studies* (Vol. 5, No. 1, 1979).
Holsti, K. J., *International Politics: A Framework for Analysis*, 3rd edn (Englewood Cliffs: Prentice-Hall, 1977).
The Dividing Discipline (Boston: Unwin Hyman, 1985).
Homan, Paul T., *Contemporary Economic Thought* (New York and London: Harper and Brothers, 1928).
Howard, M., *War and the Liberal Conscience*, paperback edn (Oxford: Oxford University Press, 1981).
Huntington, Samuel P., 'Transnational Organizations in World Politics', *World Politics* (Vol. 25, No. 3, April 1973).

Hurrell, Andrew, 'Kant and the Kantian Paradigm in International Relations', *Review of International Studies* (Vol. 16, No. 3, 1990).
Hutchinson, T. W., *A Review of Economic Doctrines, 1870–1929* (Oxford: Clarendon, 1953).
Independent Commission on International Development Issues, *North–South* (Cambridge, MA: MIT Press, 1980).
Inglis, Fred, *Radical Earnestness: English Social Theory, 1880–1980* (Oxford: Martin Robertson, 1982).
Jackson, Robert, 'Martin Wight, International Theory and the Good Life', *Millennium: Journal of International Studies* (Vol. 19, No. 2, 1990).
James, Alan, *Sovereign Statehood: The Basis of International Society* (London: Allen and Unwin, 1986).
Jones, Charles A., *International Business in the Nineteenth Century: The Rise and Fall of a Cosmopolitan Bourgeoisie* (Brighton: Wheatsheaf, 1987).
Jones, Greta, *Social Darwinism and English Thought: The Interaction Between Biological and Social Theory* (Brighton: Harvester, 1980).
Jones, Roy E., 'The English School of International Relations', *Review of International Studies* (Vol. 7, No. 1, 1981).
'The Myth of the Special Problem in International Relations', *Review of International Studies* (Vol. 14, No. 4, 1988).
Kadish, Alon, 'Rewriting the *Confessions*', in Freeden (ed.), *Reappraising J. A. Hobson*.
'The Non-canonical Context of *The Physiology of Industry*', in Pheby (ed.), *J. A. Hobson After Fifty Years*.
Kemp, Tom, *Theories of Imperialism* (London: Dobson, 1967).
Kennedy, Paul M., *The Rise and Fall of the Great Powers: Economic Change and Military Conflict from 1500 to 2000* (New York: Random House, 1987).
Keohane, Robert O., *After Hegemony: Cooperation and Discord in the World Political Economy* (Princeton: Princeton University Press, 1984).
'The Study of International Regimes and the Classical Tradition in International Relations', unpublished manuscript, June 1986.
International Institutions and State Power (Boulder, CO: Westview, 1989).
Keohane, Robert O., and Joseph S. Nye, *Power and Interdependence: World Politics in Transition* (Boston: Little, Brown, 1977).
(eds.), *Transnational Relations and World Politics* (Cambridge, MA: Harvard University Press, 1972).
Keynes, John Maynard, *The General Theory of Employment, Interest and Money* (London: Macmillan, 1967).
The Economic Consequences of the Peace (New York: Harcourt, Brace, and Howe, 1919).
Essays in Persuasion (London: Norton, 1963).
The Collected Writings of J.M. Keynes, Vol. v, *A Treatise on Money* (London: Macmillan, 1971).
The Collected Writings of J.M. Keynes, Vol. xi *Economic Articles and Correspondence: Academic*, (London: Macmillan, 1983).

The Collected Writings of J.M. Keynes, Vol. XIII, *The General Theory and After*, (London: Macmillan, 1973).

The Collected Writings of J.M. Keynes, Vol. XX, *Activities, 1929–31: Rethinking Employment and Unemployment*, (London: Macmillan, 1981).

The Collected Writings of J.M. Keynes, Vol. XXVIII, *Social, Political and Literary Writings*, (London: Macmillan, 1982).

The Collected Writings of J.M. Keynes, Vol. XXIX, *The General Theory and After*, (London: Macmillan, 1979).

Koebner, Richard, 'The Concept of Economic Imperialism', *Economic History Review* (Vol. 2, No. 1, 1949); and in Boulding and Mukherjee (eds.), *Economic Imperialism*.

Koebner, Richard, and Helmut Dan Schmidt, *Imperialism: The Story and Significance of a Political Word, 1840–1960* (Cambridge: Cambridge University Press, 1964).

Krasner, Stephen, (ed.), *International Regimes* (Ithaca: Cornell University Press, 1983).

Kruger, Daniel H., 'Hobson, Lenin, and Schumpeter on Imperialism', *Journal of the History of Ideas* (Vol. 16, No. 2, 1955).

Krugman, Paul, *Rethinking International Trade* (Cambridge, MA: MIT Press, 1982).

Krugman, Paul, and Maurice Obstfeld, *International Economics: Theory and Policy* (Glenview, IL: Scott, Foresman and Co., 1988).

Kuhn, Thomas, *The Structure of Scientific Revolutions* (Chicago: University of Chicago Press, 1970).

Langer, William, 'A Critique of Imperialism', *Foreign Affairs* (Vol. 14, No. 1, 1935).

Laski, Harold, *The Decline of Liberalism*, L. T. Hobhouse Memorial Lecture No. 10 (Oxford: Oxford University Press, 1940)

Lee, Alan J. F., 'The Social and Economic Thought of J. A. Hobson', unpublished Ph.D. thesis, University of London, 1970.

'Hobson, John Atkinson (1858–1940) Economist and Journalist', in J. M. Bellamy and J. Saville (eds.), *Dictionary of Labour Biography* (London: Macmillan, 1972).

Lenin, V. I., Review of Hobson's 'Evolution of Modern Capitalism', *Economica* (Vol. 5, No. 15, 1925) [alternative translation in *Lenin on Britain* (London: Martin Lawrence, 1934)].

Imperialism, The Highest Stage of Capitalism (Moscow: Progress, 1982 [1916]).

Linklater, Andrew, *Men and Citizens in the Theory of International Relations* (London: Macmillan, 1982)

Little, Richard, 'Three Approaches to the International System: Ontological and Epistemological Considerations', *British Journal of International Studies* (Vol. 3, No. 3, 1977).

Liu, William Tien-Chen, *A Study of Hobson's Welfare Economics* (Peiping: Kwang Yuen Press, 1934).

Lloyd, Trevor, 'Africa and Hobson's Imperialism', *Past and Present* (No. 55, 1972).

Long, David, '"Not At All Profound"? Reassessing Inter-War International Theory', paper presented at the Annual Meeting of the Canadian Political Science Association, Queen's University, Kingston, Ontario, Canada, 2–4 June 1991.

'Hobson and Idealism in International Relations', *Review of International Studies* (Vol. 17, No. 3, 1991).

Long, David, and Peter Wilson (eds.), *Thinkers of the Twenty Years Crisis* (Oxford: Clarendon, 1995).

Louis, William Roger, (ed.), *Imperialism: The Robinson–Gallagher Controversy* (London and New York: New Viewpoints, 1976).

McCloskey, Donald N., *The Rhetoric of Economics* (Madison: University of Wisconsin Press, 1985).

McKinlay, R. D., and R. Little, *Global Problems and World Order* (London: Pinter, 1986).

Manning, Charles, *The Nature of International Society* (London: LSE/Bell, 1962).

Markwell, D. J., 'Sir Alfred Zimmern Revisited: Fifty Years On', Review of *International Studies* (Vol. 12, No. 4, October 1986).

Marshall, Alfred, *Principles of Economics*, 8th edn (London: Macmillan, 1966).

Marx, Karl, *Capital*, (London: Lawrence and Wishart, 1954 [1887]), vol. I.

Theories of Surplus Value (London: Lawrence and Wishart, 1969).

Masterman, Neville, 'Introduction' to Hobson's *Richard Cobden* (London: Benn, 1968).

Merquior, J. G., *Liberalism, Old and New* (Boston: Twayne, 1991).

Meyer, Cord, *Peace or Anarchy* (Boston: Little, Brown, 1947).

Mill, J. S., *Utilitarianism, On Liberty and Considerations on Representative Government*, ed. H. B. Acton (London: Dent, 1984 [1972]).

Miller, J. D. B., *The World of States: Connected Essays* (London: Croom Helm, 1981).

Norman Angell and the Futility of War (London: Macmillan, 1986).

Mitchell, Harvey, 'Hobson Revisited', *Journal of the History of Ideas* (Vol. 26, No. 3, 1965).

Mitchell, Wesley C., *Lecture Notes on Types of Economic Theory* (New York: Augustus M. Kelley, 1969).

Types of Economic Theory: From Mercantilism to Institutionalism, ed. Joseph Dorfman (New York: Augustus M. Kelley, 1969), vol. II.

Mitrany, David, *A Working Peace System* (London: Royal Institute of International Affairs, 1943).

'A Functional Approach to World Organization', *International Affairs* (Vol. 24, No. 3, July 1948).

A Working Peace System, revised edn (Chicago: Quadrangle Books, 1966).

A Functional Theory of Politics (London: Martin Robertson/LSE, 1975).

Moon, Parker T., *Imperialism and World Politics* (New York: Macmillan, 1926).

Morgenthau, H., *Scientific Man vs. Power Politics* (Chicago: University of Chicago Press, 1943).

Politics Among Nations: The Struggle for Power and Peace, 3rd edn. (Chicago: University of Chicago Press, 1965).
'Introduction', to Mitrany, *A Working Peace System*, revised edn.
Navari, Cornelia, 'The Great Illusion Revisited: The International Theory of Norman Angell', *Review of International Studies* (Vol. 15, No. 4, October 1989).
Nelson, Keith L., and Spencer C. Ohlin, Jr, *Why War? Ideology, Theory, and History* (Berkeley: University of California Press, 1979).
Nemmers, E. E., *Hobson and Underconsumption* (Amsterdam: North-Holland, 1956).
Newman, Philip Charles, *The Development of Economic Thought* (New York: Prentice-Hall, 1952).
Niebuhr, R., *Moral Man and Immoral Society: A Study in Ethics and Politics* (New York: Charles Scribner's Sons, 1932).
Northedge, F. S., *The International Political System* (London: Faber, 1976).
Northedge, F. S., and M. D. Donelan, *International Disputes: The Political Aspects* (London: Europa, 1971).
Nozick, Robert, *Anarchy, State and Utopia* (New York: Basic Books, 1974).
Nye, Joseph, *Peace in Parts: Integration and Conflict in Regional Organization* (Boston: Little, Brown, 1971).
Oakeshott, M., *Rationalism in Politics and Other Essays* (New York: Basic Books, 1962).
Olson, William C., 'The Growth of a Discipline', in Porter (ed.), *The Aberystwyth Papers*.
Oneal, John R., and Frances H. Oneal, 'Hegemony, Imperialism and the Profitability of Foreign Investments', *International Organization* (Vol. 42, No. 2, Spring 1988).
Owen, Roger, and Bob Sutcliffe (eds.), *Studies in the Theory of Imperialism* (London: Longman, 1972).
Oye, Kenneth, (ed.), *Cooperation Under Anarchy* (Princeton: Princeton University Press, 1986).
Parekh, Bhikhu, and R. N. Berki, 'A History of Political Ideas: A Critique of Q. Skinner's Methodology', *Journal of the History of Ideas* (Vol. 34, No. 2, 1973).
Parkinson, Fred, *The Philosophy of International Relations: A Study in the History of Thought* (London: Sage, 1977).
Parsons, Talcott, *The Structure of Social Action*, 2nd edn (New York: Free Press, 1949).
On Institutions and Social Evolution, ed. and intro. Leon H. Mayhew (Chicago: University of Chicago Press, 1982).
Patnaik, Prabhat, (ed.), *Lenin and Imperialism: An Appraisal of Theories and Contemporary Reality* (London: Sangam, 1986).
Pheby, John, (ed.), *J. A. Hobson After Fifty Years: Free Thinker of the Social Sciences* (London: Macmillan, 1994).
Phillimore, Lord, *Schemes for Maintaining General Peace* (London: H.M. SO, 1920).

Porter, Bernard, *Critics of Empire* (London: Macmillan, 1968).
'Hobson and Internationalism', in Freeden (ed.), *Reappraising J. A. Hobson.*
Porter, Brian, *The Aberystwyth Papers* (London: Oxford University Press, 1972).
'David Davies: A Hunter After Peace', *Review of International Studies* (Vol. 15, No. 1, 1989).
Puchala, D. J., *International Politics Today* (New York: Harper and Row, 1971).
Quinton, Anthony, *Utilitarian Ethics* (London: Macmillan, 1973).
Radnitsky, Gerard, and Peter Bernholz (eds.), *Economic Imperialism: The Economic Approach Applied Outside the Field of Economics* (New York: Paragon House, 1987).
Rapoport, Anatol, *Conflict in Man-Made Environment* (Harmondsworth: Penguin, 1974).
Ratcliffe, S. K., *The Story of South Place* (London: Watts, 1955).
Rawls, John, *A Theory of Justice* (Cambridge, MA: Harvard University Press, 1971).
Reynolds, Charles, *Theory and Explanation in International Politics* (Oxford: Martin Robertson, 1973).
Modes of Imperialism (Oxford: Martin Robertson, 1981).
Robbins, Lionel, *Economic Planning and International Order* (London: Macmillan, 1937).
Rossman, Jim, 'Hobson's "Surplus Income" and Its Distribution', *Journal of Economic Issues* (Vol. 25, No. 1, 1991).
Ruggie, John Gerard, 'International Regimes, Transactions, and Change: Embedded Liberalism in the Post-War Economic Order', *International Organization* (Vol. 36, No. 2, Spring 1982).
(ed.), *The Antinomies of Interdependence: National Welfare and the International Division of Labour* (New York: Columbia University Press, 1983).
Schneider, Michael, 'Modelling Hobson's Underconsumption Theory', mimeo, 1990.
Schumpeter, Joseph A., *Imperialism and Social Classes*, ed. and intro. Paul M. Sweezy (New York: Augustus M. Kelley, 1951).
History of Economic Analysis (New York: Oxford University Press, 1954).
Seligman, Ben B., 'The Impact of Positivism on Economic Thought', *History of Political Economy* (Vol. 1, No. 2, 1969).
Semmel, Bernard, *Imperialism and Social Reform: English Social-Imperial Thought, 1895–1914* (Cambridge, MA: Harvard University Press, 1960).
The Rise of Free Trade Imperialism: Classical Political Economy, the Empire of Free Trade and Imperialism, 1750–1850 (Cambridge: Cambridge University Press, 1970).
Sen, A. K., and Bernard Williams (eds.), *Utilitarianism and Beyond* (Cambridge: Cambridge University Press, 1982).
Sen, Amartya, *On Ethics and Economics* (Oxford: Basil Blackwell, 1987).
Shaw, Martin, (ed.), *War, State and Society* (London: Macmillan, 1984).
Siegelman, Philip, 'Introduction' to Hobson's *Imperialism* (Ann Arbor: University of Michigan Press, 1965).

Singer, Peter, *The Expanding Circle: Ethics and Sociobiology* (New York: Farrar, 1981).
Skidelski, Robert, *Politicians and the Slump: The Labour Government of 1929–1931* (London: Macmillan, 1967).
Skinner, Quentin, 'Meaning and Understanding in the History of Ideas', *History and Theory* (Vol. 8, No. 1, 1969).
Smart, J. J. C., and Bernard Williams, *Utilitarianism: For and Against* (Cambridge: Cambridge University Press, 1973).
Smith, Adam, *The Wealth of Nations*, Books I–III (Harmondsworth: Penguin, 1982 [1776]).
Smith, S., 'International Relations as a Social Science', *Millennium: Journal of International Studies* (Vol. 16, No. 2, 1987).
Snidal, Duncan, 'The Game *Theory* of International Politics', in Oye (ed.), *Cooperation Under Anarchy*.
Stokes, Eric, 'Late Nineteenth-Century Colonial Expansion and the Attack on the Theory of Economic Imperialism: A Case of Mistaken Identity?', *The Historical Journal* (Vol. 12, No. 2, 1969).
Strachey, John, *The End of Empire* (London: Gollancz, 1959).
Strange, Susan, 'The Study of Transnational Relations', *International Affairs* (Vol. 52, No. 3, 1976).
'Protectionism and World Politics', *International Organization* (Vol. 39, No. 2, 1985).
States and Markets (London: Pinter, 1988).
Strange, Susan, and Roger Tooze (eds.), *The International Politics of Surplus Capacity: Competition for Market Shares in the World Recession* (London: Allen and Unwin, 1981).
Streit, Clarence K., *Union Now: A Proposal for a Federal Union of the Leading Democracies* (London: Jonathan Cape, 1939).
Suganami, Hidemi, 'A Note on the Origin of the Word International', *Review of International Studies* (Vol. 4, No. 3, 1978).
'The 'Peace Through Law' Approach: A Critical Examination of Its Ideas', in Trevor Taylor (ed.), *Approaches and Theory in International Relations*.
'Reflections on the Domestic Analogy: the Case of Bull, Beitz and Linklater', *Review of International Studies* (Vol. 12, No. 2, 1986).
Domestic Analogy and World Order Proposals (Cambridge: Cambridge University Press, 1989).
Swartz, Marvin, *The Union of Democratic Control in British Politics During the First World War* (Oxford: Oxford University Press, 1971).
Tawney, R. H., *The Acquisitive Society* (New York: Harcourt, Brace and Co., 1920).
'Hobson, John Atkinson', in L. G. Wickham Legg (ed.), *Dictionary of National Biography, 1931–40* (London: Oxford University Press, 1949).
Taylor, A. J. P., *The Trouble-Makers: Dissent Over Foreign Policy 1792–1939* (London: Penguin, 1985 [1957]).
Taylor, Paul, 'Functionalism: The Theory of David Mitrany', in Paul Taylor

and A. J. R. Groom (eds.), *International Organisation: A Conceptual Approach* (London: Pinter, 1978).
Taylor, Trevor, 'Utopianism', in Steve Smith (ed.), *International Relations: British and American Perspectives* (Oxford: Basil Blackwell, 1985).
(ed.), *Approaches and Theory in International Relations* (London: Longman, 1978).
Thorndike, Tony, 'The Revolutionary Approach: the Marxist Perspective' in Trevor Taylor (ed.), *Approaches and Theory in International Relations.*
Tooze, Roger, 'The Progress of International Functionalism', *British Journal of International Studies* (Vol. 3, No. 2, 1977).
'Liberal International Political Economy', in R. J. Barry Jones (ed.), *The Worlds of Political Economy: Alternative Approaches to the Study of Contemporary Political Economy* (London: Pinter, 1988).
Townshend, Julian, 'J. A. Hobson and the Crisis of Liberalism', unpublished Ph.D. thesis, University of Southampton, 1973.
'Introduction' to Hobson's *Imperialism* (London: Unwin Hyman, 1988).
J. A. Hobson (Manchester: Manchester University Press, 1990).
Veblen, Thorstein, Review of Hobson's *Imperialism, Journal of Political Economy* (Vol. 11, No. 2, 1903).
Vincent, R. J., 'The Functions of Functionalism in International Relations', *The Yearbook of World Affairs* (Vol. 26, 1973).
Nonintervention and International Order (Princeton: Princeton University Press, 1974).
'Edmund Burke and the Theory of International Relations', *Review of International Studies* (Vol. 10, No. 3, 1984).
Walker, R. B. J., 'History and Structure in the Theory of International Relations', *Millennium: Journal of International Studies* (Vol. 18, No. 2, 1989).
Waltz, Kenneth N., *Man, the State, and War: A Theoretical Analysis* (New York: Columbia University Press, 1959).
Theory of International Politics (Reading, MA: Addison-Wesley, 1979).
Warren, Bill, *Imperialism: Pioneer of Capitalism* (London: New Left Books, 1980).
Weiler, Peter, *The New Liberalism* (New York: Garland, 1982).
Wight, M., 'Why is There no International Theory?', in Butterfield and Wight (eds.), *Diplomatic Investigations.*
Williams, Michael, 'Rousseau, Realism and *Realpolitik*', *Millennium: Journal of International Studies* (Vol. 18, No. 2, 1989).
Winslow, E. M., *The Pattern of Imperialism: A Study in the Theories of Power* (New York: Columbia University Press, 1948).
Wolfers, Arnold, and Lawrence Martin (eds.), *The Anglo-American Tradition in Foreign Affairs* (New Haven: Yale University Press, 1986).
Woolf, Leonard, *International Government: Two Reports*, intro. Bernard Shaw (New York: Bretano's, 1916).
The Framework of a Lasting Peace (London: Allen and Unwin, 1917).
Zimmern, Alfred, 'Nationality and Government', in his *Nationality and Government* (London: Chatto and Windus, 1918).

Index

Note: Because the entire volume is about the work of J. A. Hobson, the use of his name as an index entry has been kept to a minimum.

aggregate demand, failure of, 44, 46
Allett, John, 39
Angell, Norman, 140, 173, 185–8, 238 n.41
'any/every' paradox, 39, 41–3, 99
arbitration, 158
  definition of, 149
arbitration and collective security, Hobson's proposals, 167–9
arbitration and conciliation, 145–8
  sanctions for non-compliance, 146, 148
arms industry, 105
Ashley, Richard, 70
atomism, *see* individualism
autocracy, *see* state autocracy
autonomy, 54–5

balance of power, 144, 181–2
  international system, 57–60, 68, 69
  laissez-faire, 60
barriers to trade, *see* tariffs
Barry, Brian, 39
Bentham, Jeremy, 17
Berki, R. N., 16
Boer War 88, 92–3, 189
  and First World War, 190–2
Bright, John, 58

Cain, Peter, 112–13
capital export, 85, 91–2, 93, 99–100
  economics of, 76–78
  in *Imperialism*, 112
capital mobility, 137
capitalism, 52
  maldistribution of income, 43–5, 86–8
  parasitism, 16, 65
  and war, 80, 96, 105, 184, 185, 190
Carr, E. H., 178
Case for Arbitration, The, 149
central control in the international system, 98
centralisation
  of government, 106
  of political power, 106
centralised force, *see under* collective security
Chamberlain, Joseph, 126
civilisation, *see* nationhood and civilisation
Clarke, Peter, 24, 46, 112–13
Clarke, William, 7
Cobden, Richard, 121, 173, 238 n.41
  balance of power, 58
  capitalism, 81
  free trade, 121
  international system, 60
  radical liberalism, 183–5
Cobdenism, 92, 196, 197
  free trade, 101, 123, 131, 142
  as an international system, 57, 60–2, 68, 69
  non-intervention, 61, 62
Cobdenism and Hobson, 95, 113, 140, 174
Cole, G. D. H., 174, 187, 188
collective military force, *see* collective security
collective security
  centralised force, 144–72 *passim*
  economic blockade, 150
  international air force, 161
  see also force
collective security and arbitration, Hobson's proposals, 167–9
colonialism (colonisation), 73
colonialism and imperialism, 74
combination
  political and economic, 87, 96
  trusts, 216–17 nn.15–16
combination in industry, 32–3, 65, 77–8, 87, 93–4
  growth of, 63, 64, 131, 229 n.34

competition, 77, 99
 decline of, 63
 imperial, 103–5, 133
 in the international system, 98
 international trade, 123
Comte, Auguste, 11
concentration, *see* combination in industry
Conciliation Commission, 146–8, 151
constructive internationalism, 167, 196; *see also* new liberal internationalism
consumption (*see also* underconsumption), 18, 20
 stimuli, 42
contradictions and dichotomies of Hobson, *see* Hobson, J. A., contradictions and dichotomies
co-operation, 28, 47, 165
 international, 65–66
 and organisation, 32, 65, 67–8; international, 49, 53, 65
 social, 29
 and surplus, 30
co-operative labour, 28
co-operative surplus, 35, 37
 centrality to human development, 31
 co-ordination and organisation of, 68
 definition of, 29
 and free trade, 64
 and imperialism, 64
 and international government, 163, 165, 170
 international relations, 62, 68, 70
 and *laissez-faire*, 64
 theory of, 1, 10, 28–48, 57, 135
 see also productive surplus; social surplus; surplus value; unproductive surplus
cosmopolitanism, 50, 51–2
 spiritual, 211 n.12
costs, 34–9, 208 n.31
 definition of, 35
costs of growth, *see* productive surplus

Davies, David, 161
Democracy After the War, 16
Democracy and a Changing Civilisation, 161
democratic organisation, social reform, 85
democracy, peace and internationalism, 162, 184
depression, 128; *see also* trade depression
determinism, in Hobson's theory of imperialism, 90; *see also* economic determinism
dichotomies of Hobson, *see* Hobson, J. A., contradictions and dichotomies
Dickinson, Lowes, 168–9
diplomacy, 179–81
disarmament, 158, 168
dispute settlement, 145–48; *see also* arbitration and conciliation
distribution
 of benefits of natural resources, 115–16
 capitalism, 43
 cause of underconsumption, 39, 43–4, 76, 130
 human law of, 36–7, 43–4, 136
 imperialism, 81, 86
 inequalities of, 59, 99
 maldistribution of income, 39, 43–6, 76, 77, 81, 100–1, 130
 theory of, 34, 37, 47
 and war, 81
 see also wage policy
domestic analogy, *see* international government, domestic analogy; international relations, domestic analogy
domestic economic intervention, 132
domestic reform, 161–2
Douglas, Maj. C. H., 45
Durkheim, Emile, 16

economic determinism, 2, 70
 in international relations, 86–90
 Marxism, 87
economic internationalism, 52, 115, 121–43; *see also* free trade; internationalism; liberal internationalism; new liberal internationalism
Economic Interpretation of Investment, 115
economic militarism, 102
economic nationalism, 107
 Hobson's critique of, 124–6
economic valuation, 19
economics and politics
 autonomy, 61, 87
 interdependence, 184
 see also political economy
economism, 215 n.92
 in Hobson's internationalism, 69–71
 Hobson's theory of imperialism, 86
 Waltz, Kenneth, 86–90
Edgar, Florence, 5
equality of opportunity, 135
ethics, individuals vs nations, 59
evolutionary development, 30–4
export of capital, *see* capital export

federalism, 154–5, 169
 global, 51, 55, 57
 principle of, 54–5
federation, international, *see under* international government
Fieldhouse, D. K., 94

finance
  Hobson's concept, 95, 114–15
  international, 112–15
First World War, 58, 100–1, 108, 182, 196
  and Boer War, 190–2
  impact on Hobson, 58, 67, 179, 189–93
force, use of, 181–2; *see also* collective security
foreign investment, 112–15
foreign policy, 180–1
  imperialistic, 80, 72–96
Freeden, Michael, 2, 8, 15, 174
free trade, 102, 121–43
  Cobden's principle of, 61, 62
  co-operative surplus, 64
  institutionalisation, 130–4
  and international co-operation, 123–4, 134
  and *laissez-faire*, 130–2
  new liberalism, 132
  through international government, 109–10, 133–6
  through national economic reform, 131–4
  unemployment, 128–30
functionalist integration theory, 197

Gladstone, William, 173
global federalism, 51, 55, 57
Great Depression, 100–1, 190, 194
Great War, *see* First World War

Hague Conference, 149
'have'/'have not' nations, 104–5
Hegelian dialectics, 175, 205 n.87
hegemonic stability theory, 222 n.85
Hobbes–Machiavellianism, 57
Hobhouse, Leonard T., 7, 187, 192
Hobson, J. A.
  and Angell, Cobden and Mitrany, 185–8
  anti-semitism, 92, 114
  biography, 4–7
  contradictions and dichotomies, 16, 90, 141, 155, 165–6, 167–8
  memberships, 6
  theories, *see individual theories*
  travels, 5–6; in South Africa, 5, 88, 92–3
  writings, 241–5
  see also Cobdenism and Hobson
Howard, Michael, 182
human law of distribution, *see* distribution, human law of
human valuation, 19
humanism, 21

Idealists, 24
'illth' and wealth, 18, 20, 203 n.56; *see also* wealth
imperial control, 78–80, 97, 104
imperial expansion, 97, 104
imperial necessity, 72, 85, 90
imperial protection, 101–3, 126; *see also* imperial control; protectionism
imperial rivalry, 130
imperialism, 57, 68, 69
  anti-democratic forces, 105
  and Christian civilising mission, 83–4, 94, 104
  and Cobdenism, 64, 92
  and colonialism, 74
  combination in industry, 76
  conspiracy theory, 92–3
  and co-operative surplus, 64
  critiques of Hobson's theory, 83, 86–96, 119–20
  determinism, 90
  domestic impact, 106–9, 224 n.34
  economic bases, 75–81
  economic determinism, 70, 86–90
  effects of, 108–9
  financial sector, 76–80, 87, 93, 217 n.26
  foreign investment and international finance, 92, 112–15
  foreign markets, 91–2
  good government, 83–4
  Hobson's concept of finance, 95
  Hobson's critiques of arguments for, 83–4
  Hobson's remedies, 84–6
  ideology and psychology, 81–4
  international relations, 97–120
  Lenin, V. I., 1, 89, 218 n.37
  maldistribution of income, 81, 85, 86
  Marxist, 72
  militarism, 104
  monopolisation of territory, 100
  nationalism, 52
  natural resources, 91–2, 115–19
  neo-Marxist, 72
  and organic analogy, 75, 82, 90
  perceptions and popular beliefs of the time, 91
  political economy of, 87, 88
  population pressure, 83–4
  rationality, 94
  reform 84–6, 89, 140
  scientific necessity, 83–4
  security, 94
  structural theory, 93–4
  supporters, 81–3
  territorial expansion, 99–100
  theory of, 2, 62–5, 72, 86–90, 131, 142, 184, 197
  underconsumption, 76–7, 85, 91

imperialism *(cont.)*
and unproductive surplus, 62, 64, 68, 90
and war, 75, 80, 104, 120
see also international relations; new imperialism
Imperialism, 15, 76, 81, 86, 88, 149, 170
capital export, 112
capitalism, 16, 52
critiques of arguments for imperialism, 83
exploitation, 115–16
finance, 95
international government, 3, 4
nationalism, 72–3
Say's Law, 113–14
imperialistic foreign policy
capitalism, 80
domestic determinants, 72–96
import taxes, *see* tariffs
improperty, 82
individual thrift, 42
individualism, 19, 21
individuals vs nations, ethics, 59
industrial combination, *see* combination in industry
industrialisation, 100, 101
industry
social control of, 32–3
state organisation of, 33
interdependence, 55, 68
inter-imperialism, 98, 110
basis for war, 112
Berlin Conference, 111
China, 111
conflict in capitalist system, 112
League of Nations, 111, 118
nationalism, 112
international federation, *see under* international government
international force, *see* collective security
international government, 53–5, 66–7, 121–43
alternative to balance-of-power system, 144
as arbitrator of Great Powers' claims, 109
collective military force, *see* collective security
co-operation and peace, 153–55
co-operative surplus theory, 163,165
domestic analogy, 168
economy-of-force argument for, 164
and free trade, 109–10, 133–6
international federation, 51, 55, 153, 154
labour mobility, 137–9
mandate policy, 110
membership and structure of, 150–3, 167
non-intervention policy, 109
organic analogy, 163, 165
proposals for, 56–7, 109–10
resource policy supervision, 11
see also centralised force; League of Nations
International Labour Organisation (ILO), 134, 136
international law, 177–8
international organisation, 51, 66–7
functionalist approach, 2, 186–7
see also social organisation
international political economy, Hobson's contribution, 142–3
international relations, 57
as a backward social realm, 166–7
competition, 98
co-operative surplus, 57, 70
critiques of Hobson's work, 69–71, 83, 86–90
domestic analogy, 55–7
evolutionary framework, 49–71
Hobson's pessimism, 165–7
Hobson's proposals for reform, 181
Imperialism, 3, 4
international systems, 57–67, 69–71, 98
militarism, 103
new liberal internationalism, 66
organic analogy, 49–57, 71
positive liberty as equality of opportunity, 135
sectionalism, 65
Towards International Government, 3
unproductive surplus, 57, 62
see also imperialism
international systems, 57–67, 69–71, 98, 104, 120
international theory, 1, 2, 173, 175; *see also* liberal international theory
international trade, 131, 141
internationalism, 50, 51–3
as a policy, 49
and cosmopolitanism, 51–2
democracy and peace, 162, 184
denial of, 73
economic, 52, 115, 121–43
economism, 69–71
free-trade, 122–4
Hobson's linear conception of international history, 171
Marxism, 215 n.91
nations, 51–3
spiritual, 162–3
theory of, 2, 57, 211 nn.3, 12
welfare, 197
see also economic internationalism; League of Nations; liberal internationalism; new liberal internationalism

isolationism, moral, 58, 59, 64; *see also* *Realpolitik*

Kant, Immanuel, 154
Keohane, Robert, 173, 193–4
Keynes, John Maynard, 121, 130, 168
  underconsumption, 42–3, 45–7

labour
  difference to work, 203 n.56
  mobility, 136–40, 320 n.69
laissez-faire, 3
  balance of power, 68
  Cobdenism, 60
  and co-operative surplus, 64
  economics, 35
  and free trade, 130–2
  liberalism, 21–3, 87, 96
  new liberalism, 131
Laski, Harold, 174
League of Nations, 189
  establishment of, 148, 192
  failure, 69, 142
  Hobson's critique, 155–9, 161–3, 172
  Hobson's defence, 159–60, 170
  Hobson's disillusionment, 161–3
  Hobson's proposals for reform, 160–1
  inter-imperialism, 111, 118
  and internationalism, 161–3
  mandate system, 117–19, 158–9
  see also international government
League of Nations, A, 144, 170
League of Peace, 150
Lenin, V. I., 30
  concept of uneven development, 119
  imperialism, 1, 89, 98, 218 n.37
  monopoly, 223 n.4
liberal international theory
  Hobson's contribution, 173–97
  see also international theory
liberal internationalism, 2, 176–82
  Cobden, 65
  continuity and change, 182–8
  transformation of, 121, 185–9
  see also economic internationalism; internationalism; new liberal internationalism
Liberal Party, 6, 189
  liberalism, transformation of, 21–5
  see also *laissez-faire*; new liberalism
life, 17
Lloyd George, David, 5

maldistribution of income, *see under* distribution
mandate system, 110, 117–19, 158–59

Manning, Charles 16
marginalism, 37, 208 n.42
Marx, Karl, 29–30
Marxism, 175–6
  economic determinism, 87
Massingham, H. W., 5
mechanical analogy, 23–4, 59; *see also under* organic analogy
mercantilism, 59
militarism, 97, 103–4, 107–8, 120
  economic, 102
Mill, James, 17
Mill, John Stuart, 30, 51, 73, 173, 183–5
Mitrany, David, 121, 190, 238 n.41
  functionalism, 185–8, 197
  liberal internationalism, 173, 174
monadism, *see* individualism
monopolisation, 98, 107, 119
Mummery, A. F., 5, 105
  The Physiology of Industry, 41–3, 209–10 n.61
Murray, Nicholas Butler, 192

national self-determination, principle of, 156
nationalism, 51–3, 73
nationhood and civilisation, 211 n.10
natural resources, development and allocation of, 115–19
needs, definition of, 36, 38
Nemmers, E. E., 45
neo-liberal institutionalism and new liberal internationalism compared, 193–4
new imperialism
  causes, 87, 97
  definition of, 62–5, 72–5
  growth in foreign investment, 92
  protectionism, 101–3
  see also imperialism
new liberal internationalism, 1, 49, 54, 68, 197
  criticisms of, 169–71
  definition of, 135
  development of theory, 3–4
  impact of First World War, 189–93
  international system of, 65–7, 69, 71
  see also economic internationalism; internationalism; liberal internationalism
new liberal internationalism and neo-liberal institutionalism compared, 193–4
new liberalism, 3, 21, 22, 25, 27, 195
  free trade, 132
  and *laissez-faire*, 131
  need for, 131
non-intervention, Cobden's principle of, 61, 62
Nozick, Robert, 39

Open Door, 110, 133

organic analogy, 8–27, 34, 49, 53, 197
antidote to mechanical analogy, 25–6
imperialism, 75, 82, 90
and international government, 163, 165, 170
and international relations, 49–51, 55–7
reactionary forces, 82–3
use of, 15–16
weaknesses of, 25–7
organisation, *see* international organisation; social organisation
organisation and co-operation, *see* co-operation and organisation
overproduction resulting from technological progress, 39
oversaving, 41–3, 46
caused by the 'any/every paradox', 39
see also saving
over-supply, cause of, 42
Oxford Idealists, 24

peace
centralised force, 144–72 *passim*
democracy and internationalism, 162, 184
democratic control of foreign policy, 170
first function of government, 163
through international co-operation, 144–72 *passim*
Permanent Court of Arbitration, 146–8
Physiology of Industry, The, 41–3, 47, 209–10 n.61
political economy
classical, 35
humanist, 19–21
international liberal approach, 2
see also economics and politics
political relations, secondary role to international economics, 141
population control, 230 n.69
Porter, Bernard, 93–4
price discrimination and separate markets, 92
private enterprise, 33
production, 18, 20
productive surplus, 35, 208 n.31; *see also* co-operative surplus; social surplus; surplus value; unproductive surplus
progress, quantitative conception, 34
protectionism, 101–3
Britain, 142–3
cartels, 106–7
free trade, 133, 134
Hobson's critique of, 124–30
international relations, 140
sectionalist policy, 126
see also imperial protection
Prussianism, 57

Radicals, 179
rational idealism, 65
rationality, 8–27, 32, 50, 65, 68
conscious control, 22
imperialism, 94
Rawls, John, 39
Realpolitik, 59, 60, 62, 63; *see also* isolationism, moral
reform
Hobson's proposals, 146–8, 181
international government, 56–7
international system, 98
see also social reform
retaliation, *see* tariffs
Ricardo, David, 122, 123
Ruskin, John, 17, 18, 19, 139

saving
levels of, 41–3
see also oversaving
Say's Law, 40, 41, 43, 44, 112–14 *passim*
science, 10–14
as a term, 11
sociology as a, 12–14
Scott, C. P., 5
Scott, Ted, 187
second image reductionism, 2, 87
'Second Image Reversed', 120
Second World War, 193
sectionalism, 105
imperialism, 65, 76, 81, 90, 97
inter-imperialism, 111–12
in international relations, 65
security, *see* collective security
self-determination, principle of, 54
separatism, national, 54
Smith, Adam, 128, 228 n.29
social determination of value, 29
social good, 24–5
social organisation, 30–4, 65; *see also* international organisation
social planning, 107
social progress
co-operative surplus as an element, 30
qualitative conception, 34
social reform, 13, 14, 84–6, 89, 90; *see also* reform
social surplus, 32, 47, 100–1
theory of, 2
see also co-operative surplus; productive surplus; surplus value; unproductive surplus
socialism, 33
socialist economics, Hobson's critique, 30
sovereignty, 177–8

criticism of, 53–4
state, 52, 53–5
Spencer, Herbert, 8, 11, 30, 81, 108, 123
state, role of, 22, 32, 38, 42, 54
state autocracy, 106, 107–8
Strange, Susan, 140
subsistence, *see* costs of maintenance
surplus value
critique of, 37–9, 46
distinctions, 208 n.31
distribution of, 36
guild socialism, 208 n.44
social co-operation, 30–1
theories of, 28–48, 49, 57–67, 197
see also co-operative surplus; productive surplus; social surplus; unproductive surplus

tariffs, 124–5, 128–9
reform policy, 126–7
unemployment, 129
Tawney, R. H., 174, 187, 188
Taylor, A. J. P., 195
territorial expansion, 98, 99, 103
Towards International Government, 149, 160, 164, 165, 169
trade, international, 131, 141
trade depression, 91
maldistribution of income, 44, 77
underconsumption, 45–6, 100, 101, 113, 129–30
see also depression
trade union organisation, social reform, 85

underconsumption, 85–6, 98
'any/every paradox', 99
combination in industry, 77
definition of, 39–40
and free trade, 131
global, 98–101
imperialism, 76–7
and international political rivalry, 119–20
maldistribution of income, 39, 43–5, 76, 77, 130
overproduction, 40–3
oversaving, 41–3
Say's Law, 112–13
theory of, 28, 39–48, 226 n.98
trade depression, 129–30
and unproductive surplus, 46, 47
and war, 105
see also consumption; distribution
unemployment, 126–30
and free trade, 128–30
and protection, 128–9
tariffs, 129
Union of Democratic Control (UDC), 6, 185
United States, 136, 162
unproductive surplus, 16, 85, 190, 208 n.31
capital export, 77
imperialism, 62, 64, 68, 90
international conflict, 68
international relations, 57, 62
maldistribution of income, 28
source of discord, 34–6
taxation of, 37
and underconsumption, 46, 47
see also co-operative surplus; productive surplus; social surplus; surplus value
utilitarianism, 17, 20, 21, 116

value, social determination of the total, 29
Versailles Treaty, 7, 127

wage policy, 85–6; *see also* distribution
Wallas, Graham, 187
Waltz, Kenneth, 180
critique of Hobson's imperialism, 86–90, 94, 97, 119–20, 162, 219 n.44, 231–2 n.17
war, 86, 100, 107
and capitalism, 80, 96, 105, 185, 190
costs of, 191
impact of, 107–8
imperialism, 75, 80, 83, 88, 104, 120
inter-imperialism, 112
maldistribution of income, 81, 88
replaced by arbitration and conciliation, 145–8
and underconsumption, 105
waste, *see* unproductive surplus
wealth, 17, 20
definition of, 18
and 'illth', 18, 20, 203 n.56
production and distribution, 99
Wealth and Life, 11
welfare
human, 17, 19, 28, 116, 139, 196
organic, 17
standard of, 204 n.62
theory of, 8, 17–19, 20
utilitarian, 17, 21
valuations of, 19–20
Woolf, Leonard, 168, 187
work, 17
difference to labour, 203 n.56
world economy, role of international government, 133–4
single, 122–3
world state, definition of, 150
World War I, *see* First World War
World War II, *see* Second World War

LSE MONOGRAPHS IN INTERNATIONAL STUDIES

Titles out of print

KIN WAH CHIN
The defence of Malaysia and Singapore
The transformation of a security system 1957–1971

RICHARD TAYLOR
The politics of the Soviet cinema 1917–1929

ANN TROTTER
Britain and East Asia 1933–1937

J. H. KALICKI
The pattern of Sino-American crises
Political military interactions in the 1950s

ARYEH L. UNGER
The totalitarian party
Party and people in Nazi Germany

ALABA OPUNSANWO
China's policy in Africa 1958–1971

MARTIN L. VAN CREVELD
Hitler's strategy 1940–1941
The Balkan clue

EUGEN STEINER
The Slovak dilemma

LUCJAN BLIT
The origins of Polish socialism
The history and ideas of the first Polish socialist party 1878–1886

www.ingramcontent.com/pod-product-compliance
Ingram Content Group UK Ltd.
Pitfield, Milton Keynes, MK11 3LW, UK
UKHW041905250926
475916UK00008B/395
9780521058049